BRING ON THE DANCING GIRLS

A Showgirl's life in World War II

Mary Logan

First published in Great Britain in 1998 by The Book Guild
Ltd
This edition 2012 published by Bonobo TV
www.bonobo.tv

ISBN 978-1-907729-05-8

Printed and bound in Great Britain by
Lightning Source (UK) Ltd, London

Mary had superb showbiz credentials. Born in 1921, she was the great niece of Alec Hurley, a fine music hall singer in his own right and the second husband of the legendary Marie Lloyd. Both her parents were entertainers, so Mary was destined for the stage. Her career began as a dancer in touring revues in the 30's – lodging with theatrical landladies, doing 'panto' in the winter and dreaming of London's West End. These dreams came true when Mary was made head-girl of the chorus in a show at the London Coliseum.

During the Second World War duty called and Mary was conscripted to ENSA (Entertainments National Service Association) and with her partner Maggie entertained troops in camps from The Orkneys to Land's End and later in France, Belgium and Holland. They were one of the first acts to entertain behind front lines on D-Day.

As the war came to an end, Mary was sent out to Egypt and this period will be covered in her follow-up book, 'Sand In My Shoes'.

In 1949, Logan married Bernard Spear, a comedian who had learnt his craft in variety theatres around Britain and who went on to host his own radio programme, 'The Midday Floor Show'. Logan and Spear joined forces as a double-act billed as 'Bernard Spear and Mary to say nothing of the dog', a reference to their pet dog who shared the stage with them. Bernard went on to become a successful and versatile character actor - he appeared in many films, including 'Chitty Chitty Bang Bang' (playing one of the comedy spies) and Barbra Streisand's 'Yentl' (Bernard played the tailor), theatrical shows (including 'The Music Man', 'Little Me', 'Hello Dolly' and 'Man of La Mancha'), TV series (including 'Never Mind The Quality Feel The Width' and 'My Son Reuben') and TV plays (including playing the father in Jack Rosenthal's moving television play, 'Bar Mitzvah Boy').

In 1998 Mary produced this autobiography – it sold out its first hardcover edition and has not been available in paperback until now. It's packed with hilarious stories, populated with larger-than-life artistes, extraordinary characters bursting with the camaraderie of both theatre and war. The book is fascinating proof that, whatever the odds, the show must go on.

Mary also wrote several nostalgic articles for The Stage newspaper, recalling some of the 'turns' she had appeared with in the days of Variety Theatre, including Sylvia, billed as 'Sylvia, Music from Glasses', one of variety's more bizarre speciality routines (Sylvia played tunes on glasses filled with differing amounts of water so as to produce different notes). In another article, Logan described in exquisite detail the act of the supreme and much-loved eccentric sand dancers, Wilson, Keppel and Betty.

Bernard Spear died in 2003 at the age of 83 in Sutton. Logan, who was born Mary Newton, died in 2009 in Twickenham at the age of 87 & is survived by a son, Julian Spear, who is married to the actress Carol Royle, and two grandchildren, Taran and Talitha.

To the memory of dearest
Maggie

INTRODUCTION

To pick up a copy of *The Stage* and read all the adverts from
unknowns seeking work in show business is to recognise the
eternal optimism that lurks within us all.

With most of the suburban theatres in the country catering
for bingo or pulled down to make way for office blocks and
supermarkets, it must be exceedingly difficult for a young
performer to get a foot on the first rung of the ladder these days.
It can't be an easy life and it gets tougher all the time, but it was
all very different when I was a child.

The years before the war were an era of prosperity in the
theatre. It was a time when the variety halls in the provinces
played to two packed houses a night, while in London the long
queues which stretched outside every theatre were such an
integral part of the West End scene that groups of buskers made
a good living by rushing from one queue to another to entertain
those who patiently waited for the doors to open for the gallery
or the pit.

It wasn't just the big stars who flourished either, performers in
all branches of the business enjoyed a bonanza and none more than
the touring 'pros'. Every Sunday the railway stations up and down
the country were alive with the bustle and clamour of travelling
road shows as they prepared to move from one town to another
with all their luggage, scenery and props.

Apart from the large extravagant productions that played at
the Grand, the Hippodrome and the Theatre Royal, there were
hundreds of unpretentious little revues and variety bills that did
the rounds of the smaller halls which clustered in and around
every town.

There was work for everybody. In the summer months even

the smallest seaside resort boasted one concert party. This type of show was a perfect training ground for performers to learn their craft, and as the end of the season approached they could relax in the knowledge that there was every likelihood of their being engaged for a Christmas pantomime.

It was in these smaller shows amongst the rank and file, or 'wines and spirits' as they're known in the business, that the true characters were to be found. The best stories originated from these touring pros who were always on the road, some never owning a home of their own but living their lives at the mercy of the legendary landladies.

Every performer had one thing in common, an intense loyalty to the theatre. The theatre's basic commandment was 'The Show Must Go On' and it did, even when the scenery fell down, the lights failed or the leading lady lost her voice.

Many climbed the ladder of success to become stars and reaped the rich rewards that were there for the taking, but on the bottom rung were the chorus dancers in touring revue ... and I was one of them.

The height of my ambition was to get into the chorus line of a West End musical and when I eventually attained this lofty position I really thought I'd got it made. I confidently imagined that I'd reached the pinnacle of my career, unless by some miracle the wheel of fortune came up with my lucky number to make me a star.

Sometimes I dreamed of how it would be to be plucked from the shadows of obscurity and thrust into the spotlight of fame and fortune, but although changes were in store this particular fantasy was not to be, because it was the war that altered my life. Instead of rolling along the Charing Cross Road in a red London bus for the first performance of the day at the London Coliseum, I found myself rattling about in an open truck over the cobble-stoned roads of northern France with minefields and battle-grounds providing the local scenery. Life was far from easy, it was a harrowing time full of insecurity and danger, but in spite of the circumstances youth is resilient.

I enjoyed being young and I still found plenty of things to make me laugh.

1

The minute that I stepped out of the Underground station at Kentish Town I knew it was the rubber factory that had copped it.

Clouds of dense black smoke hid the building which was burning so fiercely on the other side of the High Street, but the nauseating smell left no doubt at all which local landmark was the latest victim of the German Luftwaffe. Firemen were milling around everywhere, pumping water into the blazing building as fast as they could, but they had no chance of saving it, the fire had got too strong a hold. Great tongues of flame licked through the gaping window frames and no sooner had I left the safety of the station and put my foot on the pavement than the roof fell in with a whoosh and a roar, sending showers of sparks soaring into the pitch darkness like Roman candles on Guy Fawkes night. Picking a way over the hoses, I tiptoed through the water which was pouring out of every door and window of the factory and swirling across the road to choke the gutters.

It was an all too familiar sight in the streets of wartime London, one we had all got used to, and I didn't stop to watch but turned the corner and started to walk the rest of my way home. It was a journey that I made every night at about half past nine when I'd finished my day's work dancing in the chorus line at the London Coliseum.

I could save the precious battery of my torch that evening; the flames lit up the whole neighbourhood and for once I had plenty of company because as well as the firemen there were air raid wardens and ambulancemen all over the place. Usually at that time of night I was the only one walking up the dark streets,

1

groping my way along trying to pick out the kerb by the light of a small torch so that I wouldn't miss the turning.

All the houses that I passed looked derelict and unlived in, no lights shone from the carefully blacked-out windows and the panes of glass were criss-crossed with strips of sticky paper which was Britain's optimistic answer to the danger of flying glass if they were shattered during an air raid.

On the corner of my road was a depressing pile of rubble and bricks, all that remained of three houses which had been bombed in a previous raid and I couldn't help thinking that it would have taken more than a few strips of sticky paper to have done them any good.

I felt worn out. I got up tired in the morning, worked long hours at the theatre and crawled home at night even more exhausted. The show at the Coliseum was one of those lavish musical revues, the kind of glossy entertainment that afforded a welcome light relief from the harsh realities of war. Nervo and Knox, two of the original Crazy Gang, were the stars of this revue, which boasted a large cast and a chorus of 30 girls, and the show with its emphasis on comedy and spectacle provided a much needed escapism for those dark days.

We played the show twice daily and the theatre was always packed. The first performance was at two o'clock and the second at half past five. The new policy in the West End was to start the performance early so that the audience got home at a reasonable hour in case of an air raid.

However, I wouldn't be going back and forth to the Coliseum for much longer. The first thing that had caught my eye when I went through the stage door that day was a notice pinned to the board informing the cast that in two weeks' time we should all be out of work. It was like a low punch to the body. The dreadful spectre of unemployment was about to materialise again.

It was easy to tell from the raised voices tinged with panic which issued from the dressing rooms that the news had caught everyone on the hop and when I reached the room that I shared with six other girls and opened the door, a deafening scream and hysterical babble of voices greeted me. Generally in these

2

circumstances there is at least one girl who's heard through the grapevine of a new production about to be cast, but this time there wasn't even a rumour of an audition, so the immediate prospect facing us all was to take *The Stage* and frantically search the adverts hoping and praying for some sort of miracle.

As if that wasn't bad enough, I had another worry lurking at the back of my mind because I was liable to be called up. I forget which year it was that conscription was brought in for girls, but I had already had several deferments of my calling-up papers. My boss, Sherman Fisher, who ran the troupe of dancers, had managed to wangle this concession for me because I was the head girl in charge of the rehearsing and discipline of the other dancers, but with the show folding there would be no one with authority I could turn to for help. During the run of the revue I had got so used to my deferments being granted with the minimum of fuss that I was lulled into a false sense of security, but now that unemployment hovered over me I felt the first twinges of anxiety gnawing at the pit of my stomach.

It seemed as if I'd only just put my head on the pillow when I awoke to the cheerful whistling that heralded the postman as he clumped up the steps in his hobnailed boots. What's he got to be so blasted happy about? I thought as the letter box clattered open and the mail plopped down on the mat.

Even before I picked it up I had a funny feeling about the buff-coloured envelope. I could see the letters OHMS stamped on it and in my limited experience I'd learned that envelopes which carry this insignia generally bode no good for anyone. Inside was a typewritten slip of paper which baldly stated that the day after my services were no longer required at the theatre I was to report to the local Labour Exchange, where I would be directed into a munitions factory somewhere in the British Isles.

'What a way to start the day,' I said to myself. 'They obviously aren't going to waste much time, so now what are you going to do, Mary?'

I indulged in a little wallow of self-pity and thought how unfair life could be. After years of touring around the country in

3

tatty little shows constantly on the move, living out of a suitcase and staying in grotty digs, I had finally achieved my goal of working in the West End. Not only was I in a successful revue but I'd been made head girl, and just when I began to think that everything in the garden was lovely, this disaster had to strike to send me hurtling back to square one.

This was the second kick in the pants that had come my way since my age group had made me liable for conscription. The first incident occurred at the theatre following a matinee when a woman agent came backstage and asked for me. She told me that she'd noticed me in the line and was convinced that I had a photogenic face and could foresee a future for me in films. I knew this scene well, I'd rehearsed it a hundred times – although in my particular fantasy the agent was always a prosperous-looking man with a fur collar on his coat and smoking a fat cigar – so I should have been word-perfect. As it was, I stood transfixed and dumb-struck. It felt as if all the breath had left my body.

It can't be for real, I remember thinking. It must be some sort of dream. This sort of nonsense is all right for Cinderella but it just doesn't happen to girls like me.

It was the classic situation you firmly believe in when you first start in the business. You fully expect managers, film directors and agents to recognise your outstanding talent and whisk you away to a life of stardom and glamour, but after a few years of harsh reality and a glut of disappointments you come down to earth and are only too glad to settle for a job anywhere. But now standing before me was my own fairy godmother in the guise of this agent telling me she was about to wave her magic wand and transform my whole life.

She arranged to meet me the following day to discuss her plans for me over a business lunch, and I floated downstairs to the dressing room on a fluffy pink cloud. Fanciful pipe dreams wafted through my head and, egged on by my friends, I began to believe that the legendary miracle worker of show business was about to single me out for her favours. My imagination, which doesn't need a lot of encouragement, took over. I could practically see the banner headlines blazoned across the newspapers:

By the time I got home I was so excited that I hardly slept a wink all night.

The next day I met the agent as arranged at The Ivy restaurant. It was like a select club for the most famous stars of the day and to look around the room at all the well-known faces crowded together was like seeing an illustrated edition of *Who's Who in the Theatre*. There was a sweet smell of success mingling with the appetising aromas of haute cuisine and an exquisite air of casual confidence circulating among these demigods, a quality that singularly eluded the confines of the chorus girls' dressing room. How would it be, I wondered, to become an accepted member of this exclusive society, to know these idols personally and to be able to eat in expensive restaurants like this every day?

I tried not to stare too hard at the ravishingly beautiful Vivien Leigh sitting at the next table, since scooping the part of Scarlett in *Gone With the Wind*, she'd emerged as an international star of some magnitude, and here she was by my side looking fragile and delicate as she tucked into her meal with gusto.

Every time the door swung open another familiar face wafted in. It was like the finale of a star-studded show with all the current favourites following on one another's heels. Laurence Olivier strode in waving to all his friends before he joined Vivien Leigh. I spotted Ivor Novello at a table and then Jessie Matthews breezed in with a smile for everyone and after her came Bebe Daniels and Ben Lyon. I tried to remember them all so that I could tell the girls when I got back to the theatre.

The Ivy was obviously *the* restaurant to dine and be seen in and it made a refreshing change from Charlie's Café next to the stage door at the Coliseum, which was the only place I could normally afford to eat. At Charlie's I came out with clothes reeking of fried food.

While I enjoyed the best meal I'd had for years, I listened happily as the agent unfolded her plans for me. The first thing she wanted me to do was to get some really good professional

5

photographs and on the strength of these she'd arrange for me to be given walk-on parts in films, and if all went well, as she confidently anticipated, she was going to pull out all the stops and go to town on my career. Copies of the photographs, together with publicity stories, would be circulated to newspapers and magazines and in the meantime I would be groomed and polished and given the full starlet treatment.

I sat there completely mesmerised as she elaborated on all the details of how the film industry was on the lookout for new faces and she thought I was an ideal choice. I was more than ready to take it all in and do what she advised. I had nothing to lose, and who knew what might happen?

It was only after I'd gone to the considerable expense of having the studio photographs taken by one of the leading theatrical photographers of the day that I remembered to tell the agent that I was liable for conscription and that even now my boss had to apply at regular intervals for deferment papers.

She was really very charming about the whole thing as she handed me back my expensive photographs, but she explained that she couldn't put me under contract until she had something tangible to offer me and that would only come about after I'd made the trial appearance on film. So that was another rosy prospect nipped in the bud before it had a chance to bloom!

To make up for the disappointment the girls at the theatre clubbed together and treated me to a meal in Charlie's Café and a couple of light ales in the Lemon Tree pub next to the stage door. When they commiserated with me, I said 'Not to worry, it's all a part of life's rich pageant and it was a nice dream while it lasted.'

I tried to concentrate on my job and if I got a bit depressed I reminded myself how lucky I was to be in the West End instead of on tour, and just when I'd got over the letdown and was working on an even keel again ... wham, bang, this bombshell dropped through the letter box.

Another letter had arrived for me by the same post and when I picked it up I recognised my mother's handwriting. In the summer of 1939 my mother had been in a seaside concert party in Broadstairs, Kent. When the war broke out, the resort, which had been jam-packed with holidaymakers, emptied overnight and the concert party was forced to close down.

Within a few weeks Basil Dean had organised ENSA (Entertainments National Service Association) to provide entertainment for all the armed services wherever they were stationed in the British Isles. The Theatre Royal in Drury Lane was requisitioned as the headquarters for the new organisation and because the concert parties were already in working groups, produced and available, he called on them to start right away.

My mother was in one of these early shows that ENSA sent out and she was still at it. She had travelled to France in the initial stages of the war and had been evacuated just before Dunkirk and she was still touring around the military camps in Britain. I never knew where the next letter would come from. Every now and again without any prior warning she'd arrive home for a few days, then she was off once more.

It seemed a hell of a life to me, but her letter gave me an idea. I'd heard that dancers were always needed on ENSA and that the job was classed as warwork. I didn't have much choice, it was either ENSA or the munitions factory, but I knew if they took me on I would have to stay put until the end of the war.

I made up my mind there and then. After slapping on a bit of make-up, I rummaged around for my practice outfit and tap shoes and ran out of the house to get on a bus for Drury Lane to see if I could join ENSA.

2

I was born into a theatrical family. Both my parents earned their living from the stage, or as they always put it 'The Business', just as if there was no other business worth mentioning.

My mother's uncles had been stars of the Music Hall during its heyday when fortunes could be made by anyone who showed talent and had some initiative. The theatrical tradition started when their mother, who was a Miss Maria Turpin, married an Irish sea captain named John Hurley. For a time Mrs Hurley went to sea with her husband and travelled the world, but when her children were born she settled down ashore and ran a boarding house for sailors at an address in Wellclose Square near the docks in East London.

Wellclose Square lies close to the Tower of London, just to the rear of St Katherine's Dock, and if only the architects who transformed the dock into such a gem of charm and beauty had been given the contract to preserve Wellclose Square, it could have been equally delightful. The square escaped the devastation of the war only to succumb to the vandalism of modern architects who couldn't wait to jump on the bandwagon and tear down the houses to replace them with high-rise concrete monstrosities. When I think of the charming houses that stood in the square mellowing for hundreds of years and then see the dross which replaced them, which in less than a decade has turned into slums and embarrassingly large white elephants, I only hope that the former occupants will return to haunt the perpetrators of the crime and not give them another moment's peace.

Long after the war I took my husband along to show him my great-grandmother's house and the school where my grandmother, and my mother after her, took their first lessons. We crossed the main road and turned into a covered archway that led into the square and as we emerged the noise of the traffic speeding along The Highway receded and it wasn't difficult to imagine that we were back in the last century. The houses lining the square had Georgian windows and the doors were carved and panelled with Corinthian columns on either side with fanlights over the top.

The nucleus of the square was the school, which squatted sedately in the centre like a fat broody hen ruffling her feathers to protect and mother successive generations who came through the iron gates for guidance and learning. 'St Paul's School for the children of seamen' still stands with its clock tower and Gothic windows, looking incongruously beautiful and out of place against the background of faceless buildings.

The only other original feature to survive this architectural holocaust is Wilton's Music Hall, which a dedicated group of theatre-lovers is doing its best to preserve. You could easily walk by its plain frontage without realising what lies behind the wooden doors. The last time I went there the bar still gave off a smell of beer, the stage was virtually intact and in the auditorium the circle stands securely on its barley sugar supports waiting to be resurrected by the sound of music and laughter.

My great-grandmother lived at number 18. She had four sons and one daughter who was destined to be my grandmother. The four boys grew up to be handsome, tall, virile young men. Mrs Hurley was fiercely proud and ambitious for them and was determined that they would get on in the world.

The boarding house prospered and before long she required some domestic help in the running of the establishment. There was no labour shortage then; however, she foresaw that the necessity of employing young girls and having to house them might prove a temptation to her sons, who were at a vulnerable age. She realised that if the boys should lust after these domestics and perhaps be forced into shotgun weddings, it would effectively ruin her high-flying plans for them.

9

To prevent this catastrophe, she worked out an infallible system. She let it be known that the only girls she would consider employing in the boarding house were those unfortunate enough to have some minor disability. Not the kind of crippling disability which would impede their working capacity, but just enough to disfigure them and hopefully impair their chance of having a romantic involvement with one of her sons.

From that moment on, my grandmother told me, the house became full of girls with boss eyes or harelips and there was one poor creature who was completely unintelligible because of a cleft palate. The deterrent succeeded, and in the process of protecting her sons, Mrs Hurley inadvertently acquired a reputation in the neighbourhood as a generous benefactress to the maimed and afflicted.

In spite of having this domestic help, she was still a very busy lady with five robust children to bring up and a houseful of sailor lodgers to cater for, so to ensure a bit of peace and quiet for a couple of hours she made it her practice to eat the main meal of the day alone in her room. It was my grandmother's job as the only daughter to carry up her dinner on a tray, together with a silver tankard of ale.

Although living in this rough-and-ready area of dockland, Mrs Hurley had a strong sense of the dramatic. She obviously cherished this short respite from the turmoil of the day, because while closing the door on the gruelling demands of the household she invariably commanded her daughter, 'Let no one disturb me, Nellie, and if the Prince of Wales should call while I'm eating, tell him I am not at home!'

When the four boys grew older, their father apprenticed them to the circus. I've always thought it was pretty smart of him. In an age when the rich people were very rich and the poor couldn't do much about it, show business was one door that provided an escape from poverty and a way to beat the system.

It was the era of the Music Hall. There wasn't much money about for the ordinary man in the street at the time, but poor and rich alike crowded into the theatres to see their favourite stars singing the pop songs of the day. There was no radio or television constantly pounding out the tunes night and day, and the only way to hear them was to go to the local music hall and see the artistes performing them.

Every performer had his or her individual songs which gradually became known as errand boys whistled them and people pounded them out on the piano in the parlour and sang them in pubs. The melodies linger on. Wherever there's a sing-song today audiences still turn to these old favourites which have been handed down from generation to generation. They've become the folk songs of the Victorian and Edwardian age, such was the popularity of the Music Hall.

Any reasonably sized town had its fair share of theatres and not only in the busy centre; there were smaller halls in the suburbs too, so with all these outlets there was a good chance for anyone with a modicum of talent to earn a living and for the lucky few who made a hit, the glittering prospect of scooping the jackpot and becoming a star. 'Top of the bill' performers were treated like royalty and they could earn hundreds of pounds a week if they took a carriage and tore from hall to hall, playing several performances a night.

Even with the leisurely transport of the day, the stars travelled the world, working in America, Australia and South Africa. For the successful ones the rewards were great. The rate of income tax was so low that top performers were able to enjoy a luxurious lifestyle only comparable to someone winning the lottery today.

Three of Mrs Hurley's sons went from their circus apprenticeship into the glamour and excitement of the Music Hall and they all made a success. Each of them made a small fortune and went through it at a rate of knots and they all finished up penniless.

The boys were Alec, Johnny and Ted, and of the three it was Alec who made the biggest name. He became a headliner as a coster comedian and developed a unique style of his own. It was the days before microphones and the audiences were rough and noisy, consequently the comics belted out their songs in loud raucous voices to make themselves heard over the din. Alec had a sweet voice and specialised in singing numbers with a pretty melody and a subtle line of humour rather than the more blatant songs that the crowds were accustomed to hear. Gradually the audiences began to listen and appreciate his quieter style and eventually he became a big star and was able to headline and take out his own companies.

In his autobiography *My Crazy Life*, Bud Flanagan tells the story of how he modelled his own voice on Alec Hurley, who was his boyhood idol. Night after night Bud climbed the long winding stone steps to sit in the gallery and watch his hero and then went home to his bedroom to try and capture for himself Alec's style and tuneful way of singing.

Alec married Marie Lloyd, who was the uncrowned queen of the Music Hall. It was an idyllic love match that went sadly wrong.

Before they were able to marry, Marie and Alec lived together for several years in supreme happiness. They arranged it so that they could work on the same bills and my mother travelled with them because she was a soubrette in her uncle's company. Eventually Marie was divorced from her first husband and she and Alec were free to marry, but no sooner were they husband and wife than they began to tour separately. Alec would top one bill and Marie another because it was more profitable that way.

Marie Lloyd was a superstar; she was fêted wherever she went and the temptations must have been enormous. One day when Alec returned from his tour to their home in Golders Green with my mother, who lived with them as a daughter, he found that Marie had left him. She had run off with a young jockey named Bernard Dillon, who had just become the sporting personality of the moment by winning the Derby. He was half Marie's age and I suppose she must have felt flattered, but it was an action she lived to regret.

Alec died of pneumonia at the age of 42, although my grandmother always maintained that he just lost the will to live when Marie deserted him, I don't know if that's true but I do know that he and Marie both died vowing their love for one another.

When Alec's brother Ted went on the boards he changed his name to Hanley to avoid any confusion on the theatre bills. He never reached the heights as a performer but he became a legend within the intimate ranks of his fellow professionals because of his unintentional humour. His words were joyfully repeated over and over again within the close confines of show business circles, rather like the stories of Sam Goldwyn a few decades later.

To a friend who was regretting the sad decline of the British Empire by complaining, 'Ah Ted, the old Empire's not what it was. It grieves me to see the way it's going downhill', he replied quite seriously, 'You're absolutely right, and from what I hear they're not playing to any business at the Hippodrome either.'

His classic and much quoted remedy to a fellow pro, who suffered from a weak chest was 'I tell you what you want to do. Nip along to the chemist and buy yourself some Friar's Balsam, pour a few drops into a jug of hot water and then throw a towel over your head and ignore it.'

Johnny was a partner in a very successful double act called Fine and Hurley. His partner was Alec Fine and their act was a very funny version in the 'Cohen and Kelly' style.

There was another brother, Alfred, who never tried his luck on the stage. He packed his bags and went to Australia to make his fortune and after ten years he came back a rich man.

An uncle of mine was still a small boy living at home when Alfred returned. No one in the family had expected him but he stopped the cab on the corner of the street to speak to an old friend. As soon as he was recognised the news spread like wildfire, the women shouted the glad tidings from door to door and when he eventually arrived at the house he was accompanied by a triumphant procession of neighbours and scruffy children cheering him along and hanging on the back of the cab.

Like his brothers, he had no difficulty in learning how to spend his money. He had left England from his home in the East End but he returned to take a suite at the Hotel Cecil, which was where visiting royalty stayed, on a par with Claridges today.

The money trickled through his fingers like water and the first two things he found he couldn't live without were a racehorse and one of the new-fangled motor cars.

My mother told me of the excitement that the car caused. Alfred decided to give all the kids in the family a treat and he drove down to the East End. I suppose he wanted to show off as well – there weren't too many cars about in those days and I bet most of the folk down there had never seen one in their lives.

An enormous crowd of curious neighbours and envious passers-by congregated around the reckless band of intrepid travellers as they prepared themselves for the maiden journey. The children had all been dressed in their Sunday best and Alfred had got himself up in a special outfit with a long dust coat, flat cap and goggles. He had stopped at Fortnums to buy some hampers of food and they were strapped on the back together with rugs and umbrellas in case it rained.

One of the local boys surveying all these elaborate preparations called out, 'Hey! Come and look, I think the Hurleys at number eighty-three are doing a flit.'

'Nah!' another replied. 'Any fool can see they're setting off for America!'

At last they were off, amid cheers and plenty of free advice as well as warnings to 'be careful for Gawd's sake'. They got as far as the corner of the road before this wonderful new invention broke down and they had the humiliating experience of having to get out and struggle back with the hampers, rugs and umbrellas under the derisive eyes of their former admirers.

Those were the golden rumbustious days of show business, the days when they banged the big drum on entering a town. When my mother worked in Alec Hurley's company and they played Dublin, the people were so proud of Alec's Irish parentage that as the boat arrived a band would be waiting on the quay to escort and play him into town. And when he and Marie Lloyd were at the Tivoli Theatre in the Strand, they hired an open-topped bus to promote business. After emblazoning it with showbills they crammed it with performers in costume and with a band of musicians playing all the latest tunes rode it up and down the streets of London.

When my mother started her stage career she was little more than a toddler. One Christmas she was engaged to dance in a children's troupe in a pantomime at a rather tatty suburban hall near her home in the East End.

Alec Hurley heard about this momentous occasion in the annals of the theatre and decided it would be a bit of a lark if he and Marie Lloyd went along to witness his niece's debut. Their entrance caused something of a furore at the theatre because the manager had never entertained two such stars in his sleazy fleapit before and he got himself in a flurry of excitement as he bowed them into the stage box and hurried backstage to tell the cast.

My mother, who up till then had been ignored, found herself suddenly promoted from the most insignificant member of the company to the centre of attraction and she revelled in all this unexpected attention and basked ecstatically in the reflected glory.

The pantomime was *Babes in the Wood* and in the scene where the babes are lost in the forest, the children's troupe made their entrance dressed as little birds to cover the sleeping babes with leaves. As part of their costume they all wore brown close-fitting caps with yellow beaks attached and when the little girls skipped on carrying wands, because of course they were fairy robins, my mother was the smallest child on the end of the line. Instead of concentrating on what she was doing she couldn't resist showing off in front of her famous uncle and aunt. She was so busy looking at them in the stage box that she was blissfully unaware that she had yanked off the cap from the girl in front of her and was dancing around the stage with a bright yellow beak dangling from the end of her wand.

Marie and Alec were in hysterics to see their niece scoring a comedy sensation in the pantomime and in spite of her highly unprofessional performance, when she was 13 Alec Hurley engaged her to appear in his company. She was featured with him in sketches as his sweetheart and sang and danced in the musical numbers.

It was a marvellous experience for her because instead of

playing 'the dumps', as most performers are forced to do at the beginning of their careers, she did the rounds of all the 'number one' theatres in the large provincial towns.

When she was 19, Alec and Marie were booked to appear together at the Palace Theatre, New York, and she was thrilled when she knew that she would be included in the company and going with them. There weren't too many people tripping backwards and forwards across the Atlantic in those days and for a youngster coming from the East End it was a great experience.

Marie Lloyd was always a generous woman and she indulged in a gigantic shopping spree. As it was winter, she bought all the members of her company fur-lined coats for the trip, and for my mother a pair of white buckskin boots as well, which were her pride and joy.

Living as she did with her aunt and uncle, my mother enjoyed the comfort of first-class travel and stayed in the best hotels, as well as being included in all the invitations which were showered on them from the American stars and big businessmen all anxious to entertain Marie Lloyd.

While playing at the Palace, she met some other British performers who were also making their first appearance in America. Some of them were destined to become big stars themselves, although no one could foretell this rosy future at the time. Certainly not for the juggler on the programme who was inclined to hit the bottle and had the rather dull name of W. C. Fields.

Another British act on the bill was Fred Karno's Company. Fred Karno specialised in presenting a knockabout act using new young comedians. One of these comedians sat in the stage box as though he was a drunken member of the audience heckling the other performers. At the band call he came to my mother and several of the lesser artistes on the bill and asked if they would help him out by sitting in the box with him to make it look more authentic, and they were all pleased to do this.

After playing the Palace, Marie Lloyd and her company went on a tour of several other theatres and my mother bought herself an autograph book and asked various acts to sign it. I have that book to this day, but it's a great pity she didn't get the autograph of the young comedian in Fred Karno's Company – his name was Charlie Chaplin.

When her uncle Alec died, my mother tried her luck in musical comedy. She was touring in *Our Miss Gibbs* with Leslie Henson and he advised her to join a concert party if she wanted to get good all-round experience. She took his advice and found a niche that she liked, or perhaps she lacked the push and ambition to get any further because she stayed put and her working life settled into a comfortable and pleasant rut.

The concert parties opened with a short tour at Easter before going on to a seaside resort for the resident season and remaining there until the end of September. After the summer there was plenty of concert work at Masonic ladies' nights and similar functions before the start of the pantomime season, which rounded off the year and carried her over very conveniently to the beginning of the next concert party year.

It was when she answered an advertisement for a soubrette to join one of these summer shows that my mother first met my father.

My father had no theatrical background. He was born in the county town of Cheltenham and his mother was widowed when she was still a young woman with a small baby to bring up. She must have been a remarkable woman in those pre-suffragette days of unliberated ladies, because with little or no experience she took over a general store and branch post office and became an efficient and astute business lady.

My father was educated at the local grammar school and as he grew older developed a talent for music. He took up the mandolin and banjo and became so proficient in both instruments that he gave lessons. Gradually he acquired a passion for the stage and while still a young man formed his own concert party, calling it 'The Mad Hatters'.

It was an advertisement for this show that my mother answered and she was engaged on the spot and stayed with the company for several seasons.

The advent of the First World War created a tremendous boom in the field of entertainment and business was so good that my mother took over the management of a second company, a sort of 'Mad Hatters Mark 2'. My father got more and more involved with the administration of these shows and gave up performing to set himself up as a theatrical agent in his home town of Cheltenham. He held the lease of the Montpelier Gardens and not only booked the shows in there but also in numerous other pitches which had sprung up to cater for the need.

However, the romance between my parents was not the sort of love affair idealised by the writers of popular fiction. There was to be no happy sound of wedding bells because my father was already married. Hidden away somewhere he had a wife and daughter, although exactly where they lived remained one of life's mysteries.

Meanwhile, back in her little shop in Cheltenham, I'm quite sure that his Victorian mother knew nothing of the situation, and when my arrival was imminent it must have come as a nasty shock because my parents had no intention of having children. In conversation they always referred to my father's mother as Mrs Newton and to the day she died I'm sure that she was completely unaware that I existed.

When I grew old enough to realise that the mysterious Mrs Newton was my grandmother, I couldn't understand why we never paid her a visit. All manner of excuses were handed out to me. Mrs Newton wasn't well or Mrs Newton was too busy with the post office, sometimes Mrs Newton was on holiday herself, until I began to accept that I was never going to meet the elusive Mrs Newton.

So Mrs Newton she became to me and Mrs Newton she has stayed to this day. When she died my mother inherited some beautiful antique furniture from her which has now passed down to me. When friends admire it, I find myself saying, 'Yes, isn't it lovely? It once belonged to Mrs Newton.'

When I was born my father was the lessee of the Pier Pavilion at Penarth in South Wales and the business must have been pretty good at the time because my mother went to a private nursing home in Ealing for the confinement. As soon as he saw me, my father put a golden sovereign in each of my hands to bring me luck, but as a true portent of the ups and downs to come I was brought back from the nursing home to start life in theatrical digs in Acre Lane, Brixton, and I never saw or got my hands on the two sovereigns again.

My father was the least domesticated man in the world; he had no inclination to rent, much less buy a house of his own and had no desire to put down any roots. He often said that given a choice his ideal would be to live in the heart of London at a hotel in Piccadilly Circus with all the traffic swirling round him and within a stone's throw of every theatre in the West End; but as a hotel in Piccadilly was beyond his means he had to settle for living in furnished rooms and theatrical digs in Brixton.

However, we saw very little of my father because all his business interests were centred in and around Penarth and Cheltenham, and as my mother was constantly working, the problem arose as to who would look after me. Nursemaids were cheap then and my mother managed to engage a girl for ten shillings a week (50p in today's money) and her keep, but this didn't prove satisfactory and she was dismissed after a few months. My father who was a trifle eccentric, came home, took one look at the girl and said, 'Get rid of her. I don't trust her, she's got a funny-shaped head.'

This was the one and only occasion that I remember hearing of him showing any fatherly concern or asserting his parental responsibility in any way.

My mother made enquiries and scouting around among her friends she heard of a woman in Barnet called Mrs Powell who boarded performers' children. There was obviously a ready market for her services because she had a very good business running her house as a sort of children's kennels.

Mrs Powell was a hatchet-faced woman with an evil temper who kept the children under her protection cowed and frightened. The parents were all away working on tour and only too relieved that they'd managed to find someone to look after their offspring to ask too many questions or pay any heed to the complaints they might make.

19

I came out of it better than most, because I was still a baby in a cot when I went there. Some latent maternal feelings must have been aroused in Mrs Powell's bosom for she took a fancy to me and I was spared the miseries which she meted out to the older children.

I still know one who was there. She's getting on a bit now but she remembers with fear the harrowing treatment that Mrs Powell administered to them. She struck them about the ears and head for the smallest offence and as a result the children developed nervous tics and stammers and began to wet the bed. When they did she beat them again and sent them upstairs without supper and they were left to cry themselves to sleep.

It was while I was safely tucked away at Mrs Powell's that my mother decided to up and leave the digs in Acre Lane. She found rooms in an establishment owned by a retired circus performer called Mrs Foster. The digs were in a large detached house set well back from the road in a more salubrious area of Brixton so things were on the up and up.

No sooner had my mother unpacked the cases and slid them under the bed than my father arrived from Penarth on one of his short spasmodic visits and they decided to bring me back to the new digs to spend the weekend with them. Two days later when they returned me to the house in Barnet, the door was opened by a flustered housemaid who told them that Mrs Powell had been rushed to hospital during the weekend suffering from peritonitis and had received her just deserts by dying during the operation. This unexpected news sent my parents into a panic because my father had to return to Penarth and my mother was due to go to Llandudno for the summer season and they had no time to find a suitable place for me.

To the surprise of Mrs Foster, my parents returned to Brixton still holding the baby, and when they told her of their predicament, she and her daughter held a conference. The outcome was that they offered to look after me until my mother returned at the end of the season and was able to make other arrangements.

Mrs Foster was the widow of a ringmaster and her daughter Rose was the only one who showed no inclination to follow the family tradition of working in a circus. She was a plain, frumpish, middle-aged spinster who thoroughly enjoyed domestic life and the comfort of sleeping under the same roof each night, quite unlike her sister Amy. Amy was travelling with a circus and whenever it pitched tents in or around London, she came to see her mother and sister. When you saw them together it was hard to believe that she and Rose were even remotely related to one another.

Amy was as pretty as a china doll, all pink and white and golden curls. She was as slender and graceful as thistledown so it always came as a surprise to touch her hands which were as hard and strong as a bricklayer's. Her arms were as firm and taut as tempered steel, which wasn't to be wondered at when you remembered that twice a day she was thrown about from one trapeze to another by her brawny Italian husband and his three brothers. Sometimes he came with Amy to visit the family, and to my great delight he'd toss me high in the air and swing me around until I got too excited. Then Mrs Foster would shout to him to stop 'or there will be tears before the night is out'.

I was three years old at the time but I have vivid impressions of the life in that house in Brixton, a life that revolved around the basement kitchen and the matriarchal figure of Mrs Foster as she stood in her spotless white apron stirring the soup, looking rather like a hard-working peasant woman. Her face was lined and free of make-up and she always dressed severely in black with her hair pulled tightly away from her face and screwed into a small flat knot on top of her head. Although she was short, slim and wiry, she was a formidable lady and it was a brave person who had the courage to cross her.

Mrs Foster made no concessions to me as a child; she treated me in exactly the same manner as she did her 40-year-old daughter Rose and we all had our individual chores to do around the house. She ran the house with the precision of a well-oiled machine. It was she who gave the orders and presided over the kitchen, Rose was in charge of the shopping and cleaning the bedrooms and it was my job to tidy up and do the dusting.

Sometimes when she had a quiet moment Mrs Foster would talk to me about her days in the circus. I never tired of hearing her describe her act and begged her to tell me over and over

21

again. She painted a colourful picture for me of her husband standing in the centre of the ring tall and handsome in a red-tailed coat and shiny black top hat. 'Ladies and gentlemen', he would thunder (this was the best part of the story, I knew it by heart and mouthed it silently with her), 'now for your delight, we have the Queen of the Circus on her white Arab stallion ... Miss Belle Foster.'

Then the lights would dim and a large white spotlight focus on the curtains where she made her entrance dressed in a pink and white tutu, riding bareback on a magnificent white horse. The horse settled into a slow steady jog as she jumped to her feet to perform her tricks, adjusting herself all the time to the horse's rhythm. One of her tricks was to untie her silk sash and, using it as a rope, dance and skip on his broad back as he plodded carefully round the ring never altering his footing or pace.

She always paused at this point to tell me that at my age, she was already hard at work, being trained by her father, who strapped her into a leather harness so there was no danger of her tumbling off. She peered steadily at me through her steel-rimmed spectacles as if to emphasise what an idle life I led by comparison, but I would have gladly swapped the dusting and tidying up for a life of magical excitement in the Big Top.

The highspot of her act was when the clowns came tumbling on and positioned themselves around the ring, holding up paper hoops which she triumphantly burst through to the heady applause of the captivated audience.

'Now that's enough of that,' she'd say as she finished the story and started to spoon the coffee into a large blue enamel pot which always stood at the ready on the gleaming range that was the focal point of the kitchen. The range had a comforting coal fire which was lovingly tended by Rose, who never allowed it to go out. It was the first job she did in the morning and she banked it up last thing at night before she went to bed.

When I'd finished my morning duties around the house, Mrs Foster allowed me to sit on a little wooden footstool by the range to wait for the daily event we all looked forward to with keen anticipation. I sat quietly, straining my ears to listen for the moment when the wrought-iron gate in the front garden creaked open. As soon as I heard the first squeak I ran to the basement window and waited until a little procession of feet came into view. They were old ladies' feet and most of them were encased in black side-buttoned boots. They came steadily towards the house and then slowly and ponderously lowered themselves down the stone steps of the area until they reached my level.

It was the time of the morning when all the retired circus folk in the district congregated in the kitchen, which was warm and homely and fragrant with the delicious aroma percolating from the coffee pot and an appetising smell of home-made biscuits escaping from the side oven of the range.

Most of the women, for it was only the women who observed this daily ritual, came from families that had been in the circus for generations. They had worked all over the world and this was their chance to talk and reminisce about the old tenting days and the countless countries they had played and travelled to.

We all sat together around the big square kitchen table, which was covered with a red chenille cloth edged with some fascinating bobbles.

'Stop fiddling with that fringe, child!' Mrs Foster would say absent-mindedly every day as she laid out the cups and saucers.

It was lovely sitting there listening to all their nostalgic stories. I couldn't understand everything because sometimes they lapsed into German or French, but I laughed when they laughed and sighed when they sighed for the good old days 'the like of which we'll never see again'. I remember liking the feeling of being a member of the club and when Mrs Foster served the coffee and biscuits I copied them by dipping my biscuit into the coffee, The coffee was strong, bitter and black, and although I didn't like it at first, very soon the flavour grew on me and I acquired a craving for it.

The kitchen walls were almost covered with a collection of framed shiny photographs of these old friends taken when they were in the prime of their professional lives. My favourite picture was the one of Lockhart's elephants; it showed them all standing in a row with one foot raised, looking rather like an outsized corps de ballet on a comical postcard that you see at the

23

seaside. Mrs Lockhart was posed with them. She was a pretty young woman with an hourglass figure encased in a velvet leotard and she smiled bravely for the camera as she balanced fearlessly on the raised legs of the two central elephants.

Looking at the same Mrs Lockhart sitting beneath her picture munching away contentedly, it was hard to believe it was the same person. She was now old and grey, with rolls of fat spilling over the top of her corsets, and she looked completely unconcerned about her former glory as she dunked her biscuits in her coffee and got fatter and fatter by the minute.

When some of the older ladies reached for their handbags I was fascinated to discover that they kept them under their long skirts. It was a traditional custom for the women to take charge of the money this way and I don't suppose it inconvenienced them because they wore layers of petticoats under their skirts. It looked very odd to me, but at least they were spared having to search for their handbags when they left and a mugger would have been hard put to get his hands on the cash.

It gave me a secure and comfortable feeling to be a part of that household and for years afterwards I looked back on that period of my life with a warm glow of nostalgia, rather like the old circus ladies remembering the happy days of their youth under the Big Top.

3

When my mother returned to London after the summer season at Llandudno she was horrified to find me completely hooked on strong black coffee. So, partly because she wanted to remove me from this unorthodox atmosphere and also because she had begun to develop a nesting instinct and craved for a home of her own, she decided against all my father's nomadic wishes to look for an unfurnished flat.

Without bothering to ask his advice and taking advantage of the fact that he was well out of the way in Penarth, she toured the district and found a three-roomed flat in the next road. So once again we dragged out the suitcases and packed all our belongings to move away from the circus environment into our very own home.

I can't imagine what my father thought when he heard of our new way of life, but he put a brave face on it and co-operated as best as he could by recruiting a Welsh girl from a large family who was anxious to leave her overcrowded home and come to London. It was arranged that Glynis would come to the new flat to help with the housework and look after me when my mother was away working.

But my father wasn't so happy when he came back to London and had to climb several flights of stairs to reach our top floor flat.

'It's just like living in a lighthouse!' he complained, and another time as he was halfway up the stairs, he had to hang on to the bannisters to catch his breath. 'What in God's name made you choose this place?' he gasped 'It's only fit for a mountain goat to bring up its young.' He moaned about anything and everything.

Times were hard then and the streets abounded with pedlars and out-of-work musicians trying to make a few bob. Every morning soon after nine o'clock a cornet player shuffled into the crescent. He wasn't very good and the sound of him straining to reach the note drove my father up the wall. Like most theatre folk, he didn't relish getting up early in the morning and as soon as he heard the first reedy tuneless notes being squeezed out of the cornet he would scream 'Shut all the windows!', sending my mother, Glynis and me rushing about in a frenzy of activity trying to hermetically seal every crack and crevice in a vain effort to shut out the noise.

'What sort of a neighbourhood is this,' he grumbled, 'where an honest man can't get a wink of sleep after nine o'clock in the morning?' He completely disregarded the fact that he'd been quite happy to live a stone's throw away in Mrs Foster's digs, from the fuss that he made you'd have thought he'd been made to move to an alien country.

He was 16 years older than my mother and had been brought up by Mrs Newton in strict Victorian fashion. When he was at home he used the same methods on me. It was he who named me Mary 'because if it's good enough for the Queen of England and the mother of God I'm bloody sure it's good enough for my child'.

I never felt at home with him. He was rarely in London and so I didn't get to know him well enough to feel at ease with him.

One day my mother encouraged him to take me for a walk while she cleaned the flat – she had become quite house-proud since achieving her ambition of having her own home and she and Glynis were always making curtains and putting up pictures. As we walked down the long flights of stairs, she leaned over the bannisters shouting instructions at my father, 'Whatever you do, don't be late for dinner, Bill!'

My father didn't attempt to answer or even glance back.

'And keep your eyes on that child and make sure she doesn't leave your side!'

He continued down the stairs, humming a little tune under his breath as the voice above rose to a screech.

26

'And be especially careful that you look after her when you cross the road!'

'A bachelor gay was I,' sang my father as he slammed the front door loudly behind him.

No sooner had we left the house than he stopped for a moment on the pavement to light a cigar and the two of us sized each other up through the haze of smoke. I don't know what he made of his daughter but to my eyes he looked elderly; he was well over 50 and much older than any other child's father that I knew. Even so, in my opinion he cut a dashing figure, from his bowler hat tipped at a jaunty angle right down to his shoes and dove-grey spats. A monocle dangled from a silk cord round his neck and a pearl on a gold pin secured the knot in his tie. I felt quite proud to be with such a dapper man of the world.

Our first stop was to buy him a rose to pin on the lapel of his velvet-collared overcoat, and just when I thought we must be on our way he paused again to get a shoeshine from the bootblack on the corner of the crescent. He totally ignored me, never once glancing down to speak to me or hold my hand. From time to time he raised his hat to greet a friend and sometimes he stopped to chat to a fellow pro about the state of 'The Business', leaving me to stand and wait until they tired of talking shop. Then he strode off, forcing me to break into a trot to keep up with his long strides until we came to the main thoroughfare.

He stopped on the kerb and I wondered if he would do as my mother said and look after me when we crossed the road, but after checking the traffic his hand descended from the heights, grasped me firmly by the nape of the neck and propelled me over so fast that I went red in the face and nearly choked.

We ended up in Robsart Street. This was our nearest shopping centre and I liked going that way because there was a public house on the corner which intrigued me. I had often heard my father refer to it as 'an absolute gold mine' and I was dying to see the gold.

As we came up to it that day, the cellar flaps opened and two

27

brawny men trundled several barrels from a horse-drawn cart and carefully lowered them down on a rope. I rushed to stare down into the cavernous depths, expecting to see an Aladdin's cave of glittering treasure, but it was terribly disappointing. The cellar was dank and dark with a nasty sour smell and I could only suppose that the precious gold was stashed out of sight in the large round barrels.

Then we stopped at a hardware shop. The doorway was festooned with zinc baths, watering cans, carpet beaters and all the other necessary household paraphernalia, and I couldn't imagine what they had to sell in this shop that would appeal to my undomesticated father.

The shop was full of customers, but my father wasn't the man to stand and wait patiently. His voice rang out loud and authoritatively. 'I want a good strong cane for this young lady!'

The shock struck me like a smack in the face and after the first few mortifying moments I kept my eyes firmly fixed on the floor, trying to avoid the stares of the other customers who were all straining their necks to get a good look at this wild monster of a child who warranted such heavy chastisement.

Worse was to come. When the shopkeeper searched through his stock and produced a cane, my father pushed me forward to take it from him, and if that was not bad enough, I had to carry it all the way home.

My father was completely unaware of the misery he was causing me. He hummed a merry tune as we made our way back and stopped once more at the flower stall to buy my mother some violets.

When she saw the cane she was horrified, but my father couldn't see what all the fuss was about.

'But it's the way I was brought up,' he said, 'and there's nothing wrong with me.'

He had his lighter side, though, and a sly sense of humour that often infuriated my mother. One day when we were shopping in Oxford Street and he'd irritated her more than usual, she started nagging him and, once started, found it impossible to stop.

'You made up your mind that you wouldn't like the flat

before you even saw it,' she said to him, quite justifiably, 'and although I've done my best to turn it into a comfortable home that any other normal man would be proud of, you're too pig-headed to admit that I was right to rent us a place of our own.'

She kept on and on and my father didn't say a word, he just let her carry on until a bus cruised slowly past, then he jumped on to the conductor's platform and leaned over the back rail to tip his hat and smile sweetly at my frustrated mother.

'I'll see you both later in the eagle's nest,' we heard him say as the bus gained speed and he disappeared into the traffic.

It was about this time that the business at the Pier Penarth took a turn for the worse and started to go downhill, and although my father tried his best to unload the lease, no one could be found to take it over. When he did come home, his chief occupation was in wandering around the flat praying loudly for a fire to destroy the pier, lock, stock and barrel, so that he could collect on the insurance.

'Dear Lord,' I heard him groaning as I passed the sitting room door, 'you sent fire down on the people of Sodom and Gomorrah, you demolished the walls of Jericho. Couldn't you find it in your heart to send a few measly flames down to destroy the Pier Penarth?'

Fires were a very real hazard for the wooden piers; it was only too easy for cigarette stubs to get wedged between the slats and for the wind to fan them into a blaze. Every summer brought its list of casualties but my father didn't have the luck for this to happen to him and he was forced to work out his lease and watch all the former profits trickle away.

In spite of this worry, he didn't attempt to economise on staff. I have some pictures taken at the time which show him posing with his employees outside the pavilion, and the number of them wouldn't disgrace a theatre the size of the London Palladium.

All that winter after my father had gone back to Wales, Glynis was a tower of strength, helping in the flat and looking after me. My mother sent me to a nursery school in the crescent and for a time everything went along swimmingly.

Brixton was home to most of the performers when they were in London. It was easy to rent accommodation in those days and even if they didn't want to set up a permanent home there were scores of furnished flats, rooms and theatrical digs.

We lived in a tight, insular society; friends who often worked and toured together lived near one another and kept open house when they were at home. Their children all played together and if one couple had to go up to town on business, the kids went to the family next door.

The rooms that my parents had occupied in Mrs Foster's had been taken over by a circus family of wire-walkers. Sometimes when we kids went round to the house to see if their children could come out to play, they'd be rehearsing on a wire that their father had rigged up in the garden. We watched open-mouthed as over and over again they took it in turns to stagger along the wire while their parents shouted instructions and stood underneath to break their fall if they slipped. As soon as they had mastered one trick they had to learn another; there seemed no end to it, and the rest of us felt pretty sorry for them. We voted it a rotten way to earn a living – it all looked too much like hard work. As the comedian said as he watched an acrobat tying himself in knots on a trapeze 60 feet above the stage, 'The trouble with that fellow is he's just too lazy to learn a comic song!'

We kids decided to stick to the comic song business and thanked the Lord we weren't born into the circus.

But changes were on the way for me. For some time I'd been aware that when my mother was out at night working in cabaret and Glynis thought I was safely asleep, she had been slipping out of the flat. Soon we all knew that one of the Robsart Street shopkeepers was courting her and it became obvious that we were going to lose her to the charms of the local greengrocer.

My mother's next summer contract was at Sandown on the Isle of Wight and when Glynis married her shopkeeper we were on our own again. We shared a furnished house on the island with another member of the company who also had a child and the arrangement worked well because Denise and I were company for one another when our parents were working. But as the end of the season approached my mother started to panic about me again; the knotty question of how to cope with looking after me was a recurring problem that she never solved until I was older.

Denise's parents had rented a house in Hastings for the winter months and they enrolled her in a small private school that also catered for a few boarders. My mother was always a prey to impulse. If an opportunity like this came her way which appeared to offer a solution to her immediate problem, she seized upon it as the right answer, without further investigation. So at four years of age, without any warning or explanation, I was packed off to Hastings.

I still remember the terror I felt at finding myself in a strange house in an unknown town. I thought it must be a punishment for something I'd done, or else what reason could there be for banishing me from home?

I'd enjoyed going to the nursery school in the crescent; it was only a few doors away from the flat and I could walk there on my own without having to cross the road. I missed my friends, the other performers' children whose mothers welcomed me into their houses and who in turn were welcome in mine.

I cried in desperation and fright every time someone spoke to me, and then they lost their patience and put me to bed for punishment. Looking back, I recall the whole miserable time in Hastings as being bundled off to bed for one misdemeanour or another. I stayed there until the end of the summer term and when I came home my mother was horrified to find that I'd been badly neglected.

My hair hadn't been washed or trimmed and I was still wearing winter underclothes in the heat of a hot summer and my school trunk was full of dirty clothes. My father was most indignant. He wrote them a furious letter, refusing to pay the fees, and the proprietors never answered or pursued the matter so he felt he'd scored a victory over them, but the whole experience changed me from a bright, talkative little girl into a shy, withdrawn child.

The following summer my mother was in Ramsgate for the season. The pianist of the company was a kindly middle-aged man and she confided in him about the problems of caring for me and her worry over my schooling. His only daughter was grown up, but she'd attended a convent school in Muswell Hill when she was a child and he told my mother that it was a well-known fact that convents were renowned for the standard of their education and the nuns were ideal for looking after children.

It was the same story all over again, and guess what? That winter I found myself a boarder in the convent at Muswell Hill. No matter that we lived in South London and the school was miles away north of the Thames, or that it was Roman Catholic while my parents were of indeterminate faith. When pressed, my mother always said she was Church of England, and although my father professed to be of stauncher Protestant convictions and didn't like the idea of my being indoctrinated 'with all that blasted Popery', he wasn't at home often or long enough to make much of a stand.

The only time in his life that he took me into a place of worship was to hear Vespers one evening in Westminster Abbey. Once there, he spent the whole service sitting with his back to the altar ignoring the proceedings while he noisily admired the performance of the choir singing in the balcony.

'What a marvellous sound,' he enthused, completely oblivious to the annoyance he was causing the more fervent members of the congregation. 'Listen to their harmonies. What couldn't I do with them in the show at the Pier Penarth!'

My father's visits were so infrequent, and when he did come home he only stayed a couple of days, that my chief memory of him was arriving with a Gladstone bag as his only piece of luggage, just big enough to hold a change of underwear and some shirts. He had not the slightest aptitude or natural inclination for any household task and my mother often said that he was totally incapable of making a cup of tea or even boiling a kettle.

Once, when she was entertaining at one of her concerts, my father was home on one of his rare visits and we were left alone together. I think we both dreaded these occasions; he had no idea how to occupy himself in the flat, much less talk to a child.

I could see that he was champing at the bit. He had a nervous habit of drumming his fingers under the table and there was a look of desperation on his face. It wasn't a pub that beckoned him, because in a profession not renowned for its sobriety, he was teetotal, but he just couldn't bear the 'ball and chain' bit and felt himself trapped within the four walls. He sat staring at me for a long time without saying a word, then, 'I fancy a cup of cocoa,' he said suddenly. 'Go in the kitchen like a good girl and make me one.'

Now I was about as domesticated as he was, considering I was only seven years old at the time and hardly ever at home to learn any cooking skills, but I was so nervous of him that I didn't like to confess my ignorance. I think he imagined that every girl was born with a built-in knowledge of all the domestic arts and an ability to look after men.

I opened the larder door, found a tin of cocoa and slowly and painstakingly read the instructions on the tin, trying to ignore my father getting more and more irritated at the delay.

'Where is it? For God's sake, what are you doing?' he kept shouting, while I was trying to blend the powder into a smooth paste and boil the water.

When I eventually presented it to him, terrified that I had failed the test, he was all smiles. 'Clever girl,' he said to me. 'It's lovely, just the way I like it.' I didn't think it looked too great myself, but I suppose not having a home life had its disadvantages, although he never realised it. All he was used to in Penarth was his landlady's cooking, which wasn't the best of yardsticks.

My father's main reason for coming to London was business. No sooner did he arrive and put down the Gladstone bag than he was up to town to spend the whole day arranging for a summer show to play the pier pavilion the following year or discussing some other venture. On each night of his stay he'd be off to a theatre to catch up on the new productions that had opened since his last visit.

One evening he came back from the West End in a hurry, 'Put your coat on,' he said to my mother, 'and get the kid washed and dressed. We're all going to the play tonight.' It was no use my mother protesting that we had no time to get ready or that I was far too young to sit through a straight play.

'Nonsense!' my father said. 'No one's ever too young to enjoy and appreciate a well-acted play. She can't start a moment too soon.'

When we arrived at the theatre we passed by the well-lit foyer and turned the corner into a narrow alley at the side, where a crowd of people sat on wooden stools lined up by a plain door. These stools were hired out for sixpence each to ensure a place in the queue for the gallery. My father had reserved three earlier in the day and we claimed ours just in time because the door opened as soon as we got there and the queue surged forward to buy their tickets and clamber up the steps to get a good seat. I was breathless after all the rushing and glad to sit down on the red plush bench. The theatre was much grander than the seaside pavilions I was accustomed to; there were two other circles besides the gallery and the whole auditorium was decorated with ornate gilt plasterwork depicting Cupids at play, and on either side of the proscenium arch were the two conflicting masks of comedy and tragedy.

The familiar excitement gripped me as the house lights dimmed and I leant forward to peer down at the stage from under the brass rail that ran around the balcony. The curtain went up on a stage set that was just like a sitting room in an ordinary house and the actors were all dressed in everyday clothes; it seemed very strange after the concert parties, where girls came on singing and dancing and the comedian wore a funny hat and told jokes. The play was *The Late Christopher Bean* and I think the actors were Cedric Hardwicke and Edith Evans, so my father had picked a good play and he was right, I did enjoy it.

Coming home on the bus, I sat quietly in my seat not wanting to speak to anyone because I was reliving the whole wonderful evening and didn't want to break the spell. I can remember the plot to this day and it would have made a nice ending to the story if I could say that the emotional experience triggered my ambition to be an actress, but alas it was not the case.

From this time on my father came home less and less, and when I questioned my mother she put me off by explaining that since he'd taken the cinema it was harder for him to get away.

When the lease at Penarth finally expired, he had decided against all his natural instincts to pack in presenting shows for the live theatre and go into the motion picture business. There had been a lot of talk in the papers that the government was to develop Milford Haven into a gigantic oil refinery. It appeared to be the ideal choice of location because of the perfect natural harbour and my father figured that if he could get in at the beginning he would stand to make a fortune when the workers arrived to build and maintain the plant.

Of course, in his enthusiasm for the new venture, he didn't make allowances for the tantalising delays that all government plans are prone to. It wasn't until World War Two that prosperity came to Milford Haven, only it came too late for my father. By that time he was dead and somebody else made whatever fortune that was going.

I was about 12 when I found out the truth about my parents. I'd always had a feeling there was something odd about the family set-up, but it was only as I got older and was boarding in the convent that I began to compare my home life with the other girls and found it wanting.

My mother kept an ottoman trunk in her bedroom, which over the years had become a glory-hole. All her press cuttings, old photographs and programmes from the various shows were chucked in, with the firm conviction that they'd all be sorted out 'one day when I've got the time'. And if anything was mislaid in the flat she was always confident that it would turn up in the ottoman. Sometimes I came home from the convent for the weekend and the ottoman was always a source of fascination for me; no matter how many times I delved into it, I always came across something I hadn't seen before.

One day, sifting through all the junk and cuttings, I found a newspaper. Its pages were yellowed and torn and I was turning them, idly wondering why it had been kept, when I saw a picture of my father leading a young bride into a fashionable church, and under the photograph was the caption 'Impresario gives away his beautiful actress daughter'. I remember thinking that the reporter was coming on a bit strong to call my father an impresario, and then immediately everything fell into place.

35

In a flash I understood the reasons for my father's brief and rare visits and the hesitant and fumbling answers my mother gave when I asked her when she was married and where were the pictures of her as a bride. I caught on to why I was never taken to see the mysterious Mrs Newton and a host of other things which had always worried me. It took that one moment when I picked up the newspaper for it all to make sense, and when I tackled my mother with my discovery, although she was embarrassed, she confirmed what I already knew.

After the first initial shock I became intrigued to think that somewhere I had a sister, and I wondered if I'd passed her in the street without knowing. Although in those days it was considered a definite social handicap to be illegitimate, I didn't see it that way. I blew the whole thing up in my imagination and seized on the romantic possibilities of posing as a tragic heroine in one of those 'purple passion' novels.

At the same time, I didn't go splashing it around the convent. I realised it wouldn't go down too well with the nuns, and in fact I didn't tell anyone, not even my closest friends.

I remained a boarder at the convent until I was nearly 15, and although I didn't like it, in time I got used to it.

4

Life at the convent settled down into a humdrum routine of school terms and holidays. It was a reasonable education and the nuns were strict disciplinarians, but I think on the whole they were fair. Although the food was awful, somehow we seemed to thrive on it, and I liked and got on well with the other girls.

There were only about 30 boarders in a school of 200 day pupils, so we were very much an insular group and because we were a minority we developed a fierce loyalty to one another. We stood as one in any conflict between a boarder and a day pupil as a matter of principle, totally disregarding any question of whether 'our girl' was in the right or not.

I attended all the Catholic church services. My mother gave her permission because otherwise I would have had no religious upbringing at all and, like many parents who have little or no devout convictions themselves, she felt a twinge of conscience at my growing up in the same way.

I may have been short of some fundamentals in the convent but the one thing I had a superfluity of was religion. There was a private chapel in the school building which we attended night and morning, special masses were celebrated there for saints' days and festivals and the priest came along every Wednesday for Benediction. On Sundays we all walked in a crocodile round to the local church for morning mass and then trooped back in the evening for the late service.

My father's fears that I would be contaminated by 'all that blasted Popery' were nearly justified when at an impressionable age I contracted a bad dose of religion. Any free time that I had was spent on my knees in the school chapel praying for the sinners of this wicked world, so much so that I was in serious danger of developing housemaid's knee.

I was quite convinced that it was my destiny to be a saint; however, the mania only lasted as long as most other childish crazes and I turned straight from all hopes of canonisation to a passion for collecting film stars' photographs.

I think it was being chosen to play the Madonna in the Christmas nativity play that brought on the bout of piety. For one thing, I'd always fancied myself in blue, but in retrospect I can see that the main reason for my delight was that for a short period of time, being the star of the play I was the centre of attention.

My big moment came in the final scene when the cast posed to make an exact replica of the Christmas crib on display in the chapel. It was very effective. I sat downstage with the beautiful blue dress draped attractively round me as I cradled the infant Jesus (one of the girls' dolls) in my arms, surrounded by adoring shepherds and their sheep, three kings of assorted colours and Joseph tucked well behind me, out of the way so that he didn't intrude. I was enraptured!

In the following school term, instead of a religious play there were plans to stage an elaborate pageant. The linking theme was to be the history of Calais, which just happened to be the home town of the French nun in charge of production. The pageant was to span the years and depict many events which had involved Calais, one of them featuring the gallant stand of the burghers who defied the English under Edward the Third. I thought it sounded about as exciting as a long drink of cold water until I heard that the climax of the entertainment was to be a dramatic tableau centred around the character of Mary Tudor.

This was the plum role in the pageant and it represented an acting challenge, and after my recent success in the nativity play there was no doubt in my mind that I would be chosen to play the part of the tragic queen. It was the melodramatic quality of the piece that appealed to me so much and I visualised myself choking with emotion as I said the memorable lines, 'When I die you will find Calais written on my heart.' I rehearsed the line over and over again and found that if I gave my arm a sharp pinch as I said it, it was possible to spurt genuine tears, which brought an authentic touch of realism to my characterisation. By the time it came to the first rehearsal, I attended ready to give the performance of a lifetime.

The first setback occurred when the parts were given out and the other boarders discovered that they were not in line for a principal role, and as if that wasn't bad enough I was told that far from being the star of the production as I confidently expected, I was destined for the least demanding part of the whole pageant. I was to be the last miserable burgher on the end of the line!

To add insult to injury, it was one of the despised day pupils who landed the prize part of Mary Tudor. I looked at her with undisguised loathing; it was hard to keep my hands off her. I knew she wasn't going to be any good in the role because she hadn't put her heart and soul into it like me ... or got an arm black with bruises to show for it.

Every time we rehearsed, the injustice of it rankled within my breast, and by the time it came to the performance, when the entire school, nuns and parents were assembled in the hall, I had worked myself up into a state. The last straw, as far as I was concerned, came when the nun in charge handed out the costumes and Mary Tudor was given a flowing blue dress with long full sleeves and a flattering white headdress. I coveted that blue frock and knew that, given the chance to wear it, I would have delivered a bravura performance of some magnitude.

In terrible contrast, the costumes allocated to the six burghers were rough, shapeless shifts made of coarse sackcloth, and the bitterest humiliation of all was that we had to make an entrance shackled together in a chain with a rope around our necks. It was too much to bear. How could I endure the ridicule of the whole school?

Wild excuses raced through my head. Could I say that I'd suddenly been taken ill? Or perhaps I should swoon to the floor in a faint? I was in an agony of indecision. But before I could make up my mind, our cue came and the wretched line of burghers, with me bringing up the rear, shuffled on stage linked together around the neck by the damned rope.

The fortunate girls who'd had the luck not to be chosen to take part in this epic production were sitting in the audience, and it was the muffled sound of their suppressed laughter and the contented manner in which they were settling down to enjoy this fiasco that made up my mind for me.

As we stood strung out in a line across the stage, linked together like sausages, I glanced scornfully at the others. They were all day pupils and I felt no loyalty to them, so I gave a sharp tug on the rope around our necks. It had the stunning impact of a surprise attack and sent the unfortunate burghers reeling. I waited patiently until they'd got themselves sorted out, and when they appeared to be off guard I did it again.

This time one of the girls stumbled and lost her footing, and before she could regain her balance I gave another jerk on the rope and sent her sprawling, bringing the rest of us down with her. I hadn't meant to go so far, but the first titter from the audience went to my head and brought out the ham in me, and the ultimate pleasure was that by the time it got to Mary Tudor's famous line, the school hall was so convulsed with laughter that nobody heard it. Even the starched white bonnets of the nuns were quivering, while the Catholic priest who sat in pride of place in the middle of the front row had his handkerchief to his face, wiping the tears from his eyes.

I had to write 500 lines as punishment for that incident, but it was worth every single word!

Several of the girls were boarding at the convent while their parents were away in India, working for the railways or in some other government position. Although most of the children had been born in India, it was the custom to send them to England for their education because the climate was considered to be better for a growing child. Those who had no relatives in this country were forced to spend the holidays in school, and because my mother was generally away touring at Easter and Christmas, I was another one who had to remain behind convent walls for these two periods.

The nuns did try their best to unbend and be a bit more lenient with the few girls left in their charge at this time. They arranged visits to museums and art galleries and their idea of a special

40

treat was to take us to Westminster Cathedral or the Brompton Oratory, but as I had got the religious bug out of my system by then, the outings left much to be desired.

It was hard for the nuns to relax their strict daily routine; their lives were run on such rigid lines and the school itself was spartanly functional and very short on creature comforts, so it was hardly a home from home.

The high spot of my year, which I looked forward to with mounting excitement as the time grew near, was the long summer holiday. It was the one time that I scored over the other girls, because where they considered themselves lucky to spend a fortnight of their vacation at the seaside, I went to join my mother for the entire eight weeks at whichever resort she happened to be playing in concert party.

It was then that I was most aware of the contrast between the rigorous discipline and religious environment of the convent and the slap-happy attitude of my other world.

As day followed day and the holiday crept nearer, I worked myself up into a fever pitch of nervous tension. I was terrified that something would happen to prevent my going. My one big fear was that I would fall victim to measles or chickenpox, or whatever the latest affliction was that currently scourged the school.

When the time finally arrived, I was carefully chaperoned by Sister St Teresa to the railway station. By then I was white-faced and weak-kneed from not being able to keep a mouthful of food down all day. The further we travelled from the convent, the more flustered Sister St Teresa got and she lost all her usual intimidating authority. She became thoroughly inept and awkward even doing an everyday thing like buying tickets on the bus, and by the time we arrived at the station she was totally out of her depth.

In the few miles that we'd travelled from the school our positions had been completely reversed and she was so bewildered that I had to take her hand and practically lead her to the booking office to buy the ticket and find out which platform the train departed from. Once there, she was determined to do her duty and wouldn't leave until she'd put me in a Ladies Only compartment and humiliated me further by asking my fellow passengers to keep an eye on me and make sure that 'no strange man' spoke to me.

She was quite right, of course, but it was a different story when the train at last puffed into the seaside station. Far from being chaperoned, no one met me at all and I came out into the town and found my own way to the concert party pavilion. Once there, I tore through the stage door, savouring the nostalgic scent of greasepaint, size, dust and smoke.

'I'm here, I'm here!' I shouted, rushing into the dressing room. It was lovely to be welcomed by my 'aunts' and 'uncles', which was how I addressed the other members of the company, and after my mother had greeted me – 'My, how you've grown. We look almost like sisters!' – I was hugged and kissed and cried over by everyone in turn. Julie, the soprano, produced a bottle of port that she always kept on the dressing table. 'It's so good for the voice, dear, especially in the seaside air!' and a large glass was poured for me to celebrate my release from captivity, and the hated uniform was discarded and temporarily forgotten.

Every daylight hour of my holiday I spent like any other child, playing on the beach and running in and out of the sea all day long, but at night I was expected to help out in the pavilion by selling programmes and ice cream, dressing the performers and doing any odd job that needed to be done. I got to know the show by heart, but it was always the dancing that attracted me, and by attending rehearsals I soon picked up the basic steps and progressed from there until I'd mastered all the routines. It acted as a therapy for my shyness when I was recovering from my traumatic experience in Hastings, and with every step I learned I got more self-assured and cockier by the minute.

My mother knew I was cured when one year, to her surprise, I shot up on to the stage during a children's matinee and won a contest with a spirited performance of the Charleston, which was the latest dance craze at the time. There was no stopping me after that and I did the rounds of all the other shows, winning all the competitions and walking off with all the prizes, until they found out I was connected with the rival company and barred me from entering.

I think it was at that time I made up my mind to be a professional dancer when the happy day dawned and I was old enough to leave school.

It seems a lifetime ago now, but in those halcyon days of show business, the concert party was resident in the town for four months in the year, whereas today most shows think themselves lucky to get a few weeks in July and August, and the smaller resorts don't attempt to stage one at all.

The season was planned with the precision of a well-organised campaign. As soon as the concert party came into town it was vitally important to establish good relationships with the local hoteliers, boarding-house keepers and tradesmen. The proprietor of the company, who was generally the comedian, made himself known to all these extremely important people who after the long quiet winter were only too glad to see a new face in town, especially someone who cracked a joke or two and was just as anxious to have a successful season as they were. After a convivial drink and lunch with the members of the Rotary Club, the shopkeepers would agree to help with publicity and hang posters in their windows to advertise the show.

The landladies were wooed with complimentary tickets and flattery because the comedian always included the names of their boarding houses in the sketches and jokes, even playing one against the other to foster a spirit of rivalry. When the crowd from Seaview were in, he'd put a gag into a domestic sketch by saying, 'What do you call this food? I've tasted better at the Langham', which was the boarding house next door.

Names were changed according to which landlady was in front on a particular night and quite a bit of crafty research was done to ensure he'd got it right, because, apart from hanging up the posters in her hall (next to the hatstand and the place where the children kept their buckets and spades), if the landlady took a fancy to the show she'd organise her guests into parties and book two or three rows of seats for each week of the season.

Nothing delighted these parties more than when the comedian came on stage at the opening of the show and said, 'Good evening to you all and a special good evening to the group of people from the Lansdowne Guest House.' It was a case of one hand washing another because the landlady got a good advertisement, the pavilion played to a full house and the holidaymakers felt that they'd been singled out for special attention. It's called 'getting them on your side' and it's still done today in the 'warm-ups' before a television transmission.

The posters around the town boasted 'Four Complete Changes of Programme', which alternated every three days, the idea being that the holidaymakers could see all four programmes during their fortnight's stay. It's a different world today, gone with the lifestyle of a more simple age, but before the war the performers became local celebrities and the public *did* go to see the four performances; not only that, but they hero-worshipped individual artistes and bought bouquets to present to their favourites.

There was a family atmosphere about the set-up and it does seem strange at the present time, when so many never go to see a live show, to remember that these unpretentious entertainments were packed the entire summer whatever the weather. It was part and parcel of their summer holiday for everyone to go to see the seaside show.

Lower down on the social ladder were the pierrots and blackfaced minstrels who performed in open-air pitches on the sands. Not only did they have to contend with all the noise from the beach and also the martial sounds of the military band as it oompa-pahed away in the bandstand on the promenade, but the pros in these shows had to take their turn in 'bottling' – collecting pennies by shaking a leather bag under the noses of the crowd.

Concert parties, playing in the comparative luxury of pavilions, considered themselves a cut above these alfresco entertainments, but whatever the size and standard of show, they all followed one basic rule and that was to put on a children's matinee with talent contests, competitions and games. The lucky winners were rewarded with balloons, sticks of seaside rock and any other prize that was cheap and cheerful.

The matinee was just another special programme to bring in a houseful of people, and there were several other events to keep the public interested. Friday night was carnival night. In the morning there was always a call at the pavilion for everyone to help with the task of filling paper bags with novelties. Any children connected with the company were dragged unwillingly off the beach to help with the job of putting a squeaker, some streamers and a paper hat into the bags which were handed to the audience so they could let themselves go and join in the carnival finale.

Another chore of mine was to give a helping hand as unofficial dresser. Concert parties didn't run to the luxury of hiring professional dressers, and as there was a fair amount of changing and only two rooms, one for the 'boys' and one for the 'girls', a bit of free assistance didn't come amiss.

The soprano Julie always seemed to be turning up in shows with my mother. I was never surprised to see her name on the posters when I arrived in town and over the years I came to know her very well.

Julie was buxom and pretty, rather like an overblown rose, but for some reason she thought herself superior to the others and always gave the impression that she'd strayed through the pavilion stage door in mistake for the Royal Opera House. While the rest of the company spent their free time sunbathing on the beach, she could be seen strolling leisurely along the promenade wearing what was commonly called a tea gown, with long white gloves and carrying a parasol to protect her complexion from the sun. She was never seen without these gloves and wore a clean pair every day, but her big piece of one-upmanship was that she refused to sleep on any pillow but her own. At a train call she could be seen a mile off as she stood on the platform clutching it to her ample bosom as if it contained all her worldly goods.

She had an extensive wardrobe of rather cluttered-up evening frocks. I always wanted to tear off the diamanté trimming and take a pair of scissors to the frills and bows – it would have improved them no end – but any criticism on my part wouldn't have gone down at all well. I knew that she thoroughly enjoyed me fastening her frocks and dressing her hair, although no one could have guessed by her officious manner.

45

Julie never called me by my name, she always addressed me as 'child', only she pronounced the word with two syllables as 'chee-ild'.

'Come over here, chee-ild,' she would bellow across the room, intoning the words with all the airs and graces of a *grande dame* in a Victorian melodrama. 'Come and help me arrange my re-cal-ci-trant hair. It looks like a spider's retreat. And woe betide you if you jog my hand while I'm doing my eyes,' she warned me, staring fixedly at me through the mirror while I stood behind at the ready with the comb.

Her eyes, as she well knew, were her best feature. They were large and dark and it took ages for her to make them up. She approached this task with all the concentration of a Japanese geisha girl about to perform an elaborate tea ceremony, laying out each piece of equipment in its chosen place on a clean white cloth.

First she put a lump of black greasepaint in the bowl of a spoon and held it over a candle until it melted into a sticky black goo, then, dipping in a matchstick, she meticulously coated each and every eyelash until they all stood up stiff and spiky like a row of park railings. The finishing touch was a red spot applied to the corners 'to make my eyes sparkle from the front'. The result of all these preparations gave her an expression of acute astonishment as though she'd just received a sudden and severe shock. However, she preened at her reflection and I could see she was delighted at the effect, and when I'd arranged her hair to her satisfaction and crammed her into her frock, she sat back with a satisfied sigh.

'You've done very well, chee-ild. Now how can I reward you?' She knew and I knew what she was going to give me but she enjoyed the pretence. She hummed and hawed until her eye fell on the bottle of port 'Ah!' she said with an air of triumph, 'the very thing, a nice glass of port to bring the roses to your cheeks.'

I was seven years old when I first met Julie, and looked very delicate with pale waxy skin and the sort of blonde hair that's almost white. In earlier times I would have been a tremendous asset in a melodrama because I was a dead ringer for the part of

46

Little Willie in *East Lynne*. People always felt vaguely worried about me; I could see a look of concern come over their faces when we met and once I heard a woman talking about me to her friend. 'I know the signs,' she whispered dramatically. 'A case of pernicious anaemia if ever I saw one.'

I hadn't the faintest idea what she was talking about, but I knew what was expected of me and tried to arrange my features into an expression of patient and noble suffering, just like the pictures of the martyrs I'd seen in the Catholic books in school.

I don't know if Julie thought this too, but whatever job I did for her during the evening was always rewarded with a glass of port. I thoroughly enjoyed it; my only worry was that I'd end up with a figure like hers.

To help fill the programme, the soprano and the baritone were required to join forces and sing duets besides doing their solo acts, and this always promoted speculative gossip amongst their fans. The local residents, especially the landladies, gradually became involved with the personal lives of the performers as the season progressed. Half their enjoyment was finding out who was married to who, how many children they had and, best of all, if there was a romance going on in the company. 'Oh yes,' I heard one landlady say knowingly, 'when those two are singing I can tell by the look in her eyes that she's madly in love with him. There'll be wedding bells for those two at the end of the season, you mark my words!'

Little did she know that Julie was keeping a wary eye on the baritone to make sure he didn't belt out his last note before she got in with her own top C. As for the baritone, he was surreptitiously doing his own number with the pretty little soubrette from the opposition show and most nights he would have willingly strangled Julie for waving her arms about and masking his face.

However, any bad feelings were forgotten in the general spirit of magnanimity which prevailed on the last night of the season. On this night a special gala show was organised, consisting of all the most popular and often-requested items from the four programmes. The pavilion was always overbooked on this most popular evening and we kids were sent scurrying around to the

47

furnished flats our parents had rented for the season, to raid them for chairs to seat more people and saucers and spoons for the ice cream.

At the finale, when the whole company stood on stage to acknowledge the applause, the bouquets and gifts mounted up until they were stacked high at their feet. With tears of emotion running down their faces and ruining their make-up, the performers linked arms with the audience to sing 'Auld Lang Syne' and vowed that they'd never had such a happy season and would all return without fail the following year.

One Easter holiday I persuaded my mother to let me join her on the pre-season tour in Cardiff, where the company were playing a week. I sat in front one night to watch the comedian, who was a mate of mine. He had a pleasant voice and always finished his act with a popular song. But this particular evening he was having a rough time; he hadn't gone down too well and he knew that if he didn't pull something out of the bag he'd walk off to his own footsteps. He looked down at me. 'Little girl,' he said, 'you don't know me, do you? How would you like to come up here and help me sing this song?'

'Who me, mister?' I answered, and although I was bursting to jump up, I allowed him to persuade me and pretended to be unwilling.

We worked the number together in true vaudeville style with his hand on my small shoulder, and when we crossed the stage and turned, I nipped back in front of him to maintain the star position.

The audience loved it and we kept the routine in at every town the show played, but we could only get away with a stunt like that on tour. For one thing, in a resident season, the locals would have known who I was, and for another, there were all sorts of restrictions concerning child performers. The authorities were liable to turn up at any theatre to check that children working on stage had the necessary permits and were abiding by the rules and regulations, but it was difficult for these welfare workers to keep an eye on shows that were always on the move; some small companies played only two or three nights in a place and many others only did fit-ups or one-night stands.

There was a family act called The Piccolinos who specialised in these one-night stands, we were always meeting them on our travels and they lived and went everywhere in a bus that the father had fitted up like a caravan. They were never short of work and the whole family joined in the act, playing instruments, singing, tumbling and juggling. The youngest child in this versatile group, although only a boy of seven, was already a talented acrobat. His father had been training him since he was an infant and he couldn't bear to wait until the boy was of the proper age, so he made him up like a clown and he worked in the act with the others.

If by some unlucky chance an official from the local council came backstage to make enquiries, the boy knew well enough to keep his mouth shut while his father went into a well-rehearsed routine. He lit up a cigar for the child to smoke, poured him a double Scotch and blatantly introduced him to the welfare officer as a Hungarian dwarf.

5

My maternal grandmother was the most stable influence in my childhood. She was the only one of my immediate family who lived in a permanent home and could be relied upon to stay put. When I wrote to her from the convent. I knew that my letter would be answered and not sent around the country from theatre to theatre in a frantic attempt to catch up, which was what happened so many times with my mother and aunt. My grandmother lived in a very ordinary bay-windowed villa in East Ham with nothing to distinguish it from any of the others in a long uniform row of terraced houses, but for me it was the one place that represented a secure haven in an insecure world.

I've been told that my grandma looked like a gypsy when she was young, with blue-black hair and dark eyes, but I only remember her as a cuddly lovable lady with crisp white hair curling about her head. Her eyes were brown and full of laughter and she had rosy apple cheeks just as though she'd lived all her life on a farm. In fact she hated the country; she was a true Londoner and was quite oblivious to the noise, smoke and sometimes stifling proximity of the neighbours. She was once persuaded to take a holiday in the countryside but to everyone's surprise she was back in East Ham the following day.

'I never slept a wink,' she complained loud and long to anyone who would listen. 'First it was the terrible silence that kept me awake, and then when I did drop off it only seemed like minutes before the cocks started to crow, and what with the terrible racket from the birds, to say nothing of the cows and sheep, I couldn't wait to get back to London for a good night's sleep.'

My mother's younger sister Joan ran her own dancing act with two other girls, week in and week out they were constantly on the move, touring in musical revue. If it was at all possible, my aunt Joan and the two girls Wadie and Billie tried to get back to my grandmother's house for Sunday dinner, and because these family occasions were few and far between, my mother took me along too. My grandmother usually bought an enormous joint of beef for the get-together and every time she opened the oven door to baste the meat and potatoes, an appetising smell wafted out from the scullery to fill the house and make my mouth water.

While she waited impatiently for the latecomers, she kept one eye on the clock. The clock hung on the wall in a handsome mahogany case and was wound up by brass weights which my grandmother carefully polished each week. It was impossible to ignore because it had a slow, deliberate tick that appeared to get louder and louder until it intruded into the conversation. An ominous whirring sound was an indication that the clock was summoning all its resources to strike the hour and this was always an anxious moment because nobody knew how many chimes to expect.

It had been known to strike 36; this was the house record. It was quite famous among the neighbours, who spoke of it with a quiet pride as if it was an eccentric member of the community, and on at least two occasions I know for a fact that betting men had laid odds on it.

The clock was in the most important room in the house, the over-furnished kitchen, which we all used as a living room. Pride of place on opposite walls was given to two large pictures of my grandmother's favourite brother Alec Hurley, the one who married Marie Lloyd and who died so tragically young. These photographs hung on the wall over two horsehair sofas which were the bane of my young life. It was impossible to sit still on them; the coarse hair poked through the cover to irritate and itch and I was forever fidgeting and wriggling about on them. A large square dining table covered with a chenille cloth almost filled the entire room and when we sat down to eat dinner there was hardly an inch of space to spare, with the sofas

51

crowding in from two walls and an upright piano on the third. Anyone unlucky enough to be sitting on the remaining side of the table ran the risk of having their back scorched from the fire in the kitchen range.

One room in the house was crammed full with the props and costumes that my aunt used in her dancing act and as my grandmother's house had no telephone, Joan always communicated by telegram when she was on tour. A constant stream came to the door bearing messages such as 'Send three pairs of pink sequinned costumes to the Theatre Royal Hanley by the next post'. It was the one and only house in the East End where telegrams were not feared as harbingers of bad tidings; in fact, the telegram boy became such a regular visitor that my grandma made him bring his bicycle into the front garden and stop for a cup of tea and a bite to eat whenever he called.

My grandmother had a bit of a name in the district as a character herself. For as long as anyone could remember she had celebrated her birthday in May, when quite by chance she had to check the family documents for an insurance and to everyone's surprise, including hers, she discovered that in fact her true birthday was in August.

When she was in her sixties, we were all distressed to learn that my grandmother for the first time in her life was seriously ill. She visited her family doctor, who promptly gave her a letter of introduction to a specialist at the hospital, and he instructed her to take along a specimen of her urine for examination.

She was quite terrified at the thought of having to set foot in a hospital and it took the combined efforts of all the family and her neighbours before she reluctantly agreed to go. When the day arrived she put a specimen of her urine in an old medicine bottle and, carrying it in her straw market bag, went to catch the bus for the hospital. She was sitting worrying about the appointment with the specialist when the woman in the next seat drew her attention to the trickle of liquid running from her bag in a steady stream down the whole length of the bus... So, having arrived at the hospital without a specimen, my grandmother kept her appointment with the consultant, who examined her and diagnosed severe heart trouble. He warned her that she was

52

seriously ill and advised her to go home and stay in bed until further notice, and just in case she wasn't panic-stricken enough by then, he added in his opinion she was in such bad shape that he doubted if she would ever be able to get up and walk about again.

She told me afterwards that the first thought that went through her mind was that she didn't have a decent pair of sheets to be laid out in. They went a bundle on funerals in the East End. There was always quite a bit of rivalry about putting on a good show for a death in the family and she didn't want to let the side down, so she stopped off at the market on the way home and bought a new pair of sheets. When she got home she put the new sheets in the chest of drawers, had a nice hot bath and then got into bed quite prepared to die.

'I lay there for best part of the day,' she said.' I looked up at the cracks in the ceiling until it nearly drove me mad and then I got up, tipped the medicine down the sink, did the washing up and got on with the ironing as usual.'

She did die of heart trouble, so the specialist was right. The only thing was that she died on her feet and it was 20 years later!

Sometimes my grandma made the long trip across London to the convent in Muswell Hill and took me back with her for the weekend. It was a treat to look forward to and savour.

I slept in my aunt Joan's room at the back of the house; she was always on tour and seldom at home for more than a day or two. It was only a slip of a room on the half-landing but if it was the winter my grandma spoilt me by lighting a fire in the tiny black iron grate. After the austerity of the convent, that bedroom represented the highest form of luxury. The fire burned brightly and gradually hollowed out to become a mysterious magic grotto sparkling with diamonds, and as it burned the scene changed to eerie tunnels and ghostly caves. At the time, I felt that life had nothing better to offer than to lie in bed snug and warm, watching the glowing fire in its prettily decorated grate and the shadows flickering on the ceiling while occasional homely sounds drifted up from the kitchen below.

I'm reminded of that room when passing by the windows of the exclusive antique shops in the Kings Road today. They often have identical fireplaces for sale and I wonder what my grandma would say if she could see the price tickets.

Before being allowed out to play with the neighbours' children in East Ham, I had to pass a rigorous inspection of my neck, hands and fingernails.

'Let's have a look behind your ears,' my grandma would say, 'I don't expect you to come back clean from playing, but you don't set foot outside the house until you're spotless.' She was a great woman for cleanliness. The steam was always billowing out in great clouds from the stone copper in the corner of the scullery, which was the nearest approach to a washing machine at the time. The water had to be put in manually with buckets and it was heated with a coal fire in a small grate under the boiler.

My mother told me that when the family were children, my grandma couldn't bear to waste the hot soapy water after the weekly wash, so she popped the children one by one into the copper, and although the fire was out by then sometimes it was still pretty hot and all the kids would have to hop up and down trying to keep their feet off the bottom.

Although there were the usual squabbles, there was a great feeling of camaraderie among the neighbours. They all knew they were in the same boat with very little money, and without wishing to glamorise the bad times, I'm sure that the hard life made them more helpful to one another. Women would pass the children over the fence for a friend to mind while they went shopping and the older people had some standing and respect in the community. If my grandma wanted an errand run, she went out of the front door and called the nearest child. She never had to call twice and the reward she gave was a ha'penny, which bought a bar of chocolate or a piece of liquorice and it was considered the going rate for the job.

One woman in the street, called Mrs Blyth, was unofficial mother to dozens of children. She had no family of her own but she fostered the children from a nearby orphanage. There were always three or four living with her and if a mother was ill or having another baby, Mrs Blyth was the one who looked after the other children in the family during the emergency. Every child in the street knew her house as well as his own and I stayed there once myself when my mother was away and my grandma couldn't manage to have me. I've since found out that every street in the East End had its own 'Mrs Blyth', and she was generally a woman with no children of her own.

Sometimes when I was at East Ham for the weekend, Great-Aunt Polly came to tea. Unlike the rest of the family, she had never been on the stage herself, but it could only have been the theatre's loss because she was a flamboyant character with the aristocratic manner of a dowager duchess.

When she was expected I got my grandma's permission to go into the front parlour so that I could see her arrive. The parlour was a cold, uncomfortable room that was only opened for weddings and funerals and it smelt musty from disuse and never having a fire lit in it, but from the corner of the bay window there was a good view of the street and as soon as she turned the corner there was no mistaking her. Aunt Polly strode purposefully along, scattering the groups of children playing hopscotch on the pavement. She didn't look to the right or left but swept up to the front door and rang the bell with the tip of her furled umbrella.

When I opened the door, she raised her arms in a dramatic gesture and took a step back as if she couldn't believe her eyes.

'God in Heaven, Nellie!' she said in a loud stage whisper. 'This poor child looks like a wax doll; those Catholic nuns must be starving her. If you don't want her to go into a decline, feed her up with beef tea and a spoonful of brandy.'

Aunt Polly sat down and put her two feet firmly on the fender in front of the range and prepared herself for a good gossip. According to her, there were no common or garden children in the family, each one was either 'a living prince' or 'a fairy princess'.

'Drink up your milk,' she said to me, stirring in a nip of her brandy when my grandma wasn't looking, 'or you'll never have rosy cheeks and meet your Prince Charming.'

We soon heard the reason for her visit, 'Nellie! My daughter has met her prince,' she told us, 'and he's just gorgeous!'

She began to describe her first meeting with this paragon of

55

manhood, pronouncing every word syllable by syllable in a voice reminiscent of Edith Evans in her prime.

'His name, would you believe, is Clarence. He's got black patent-leather hair, he wears butter-coloured gloves and violet spats *and* he carries a rug over his arm. He is in every way ... a perfect gentleman!'

To this day if I hear someone described as a perfect gentleman, I get a mental picture of a man dressed in this bizarre and colourful manner.

At one time of her life she was called to give evidence on a friend's behalf in a court case. It was an opportunity she couldn't resist and she made a meal of it. The local newspaper reported that Mrs Hurley gave her evidence in a highly dramatic fashion. I can well believe it.

To see the way Cockneys are portrayed in television plays, one would imagine that everyone from the East End was a brawling drunk with a coarse accent and constantly swearing. My grandmother would have been horrified at this misrepresentation. Although she was born and bred in the East End of London, she had a soft voice and when she went out for the evening one bottle of Guinness was a treat for her.

By today's standards she was a prude. For instance, she could never bring herself to mention the word 'bust' to describe a woman's bosom, much less any other more basic jargon. If she admired a well-endowed figure she'd say, 'Now that's what I call a fine neck on a woman,' and it was ages before I cottoned on to what she really meant.

My aunt Joan had a Jewish girlfriend whose name was Millie Lipshitz. She was a constant visitor to the house when my aunt was home but no matter how many times she came through the door, my grandma couldn't bring herself to say her surname.

'Your friend's here, Joan,' she'd call up the stairs.

'Who is it, Mum?' Joan would ask, knowing full well who it was.

'It's Millie.'

'Millie who?'

But nothing would get her to pronounce the embarrassing name and she'd laugh and blush and say, 'You know who it is.'

She was always busy and anyone in the house was press-ganged into helping with the chores. When some woman called to see my aunt one day on business and Joan was out, my grandma asked her to wait, but the sight of her sitting idly on the sofa became too much for my active grandma. Reaching for a tea towel she said to the woman, 'While you're sitting there doing nothing, dear, just give these drinking glasses a rub over.'

Her mother's maiden name had been Maria Turpin, and my grandma always insisted that we were related to Dick Turpin the notorious highwayman, although Heaven knows it was nothing to boast about. All my childish misdemeanours were attributed to his evil influence. 'That's the Dick Turpin coming out in you!' she scolded me, but secretly I think she was rather proud to be associated with such a romantic villain.

She often said that she'd rather rear a bunch of rogues than a band of fools, and as actors were once classed as rogues and vagabonds, I suppose you could say that she got her wish.

Sometimes I woke up in the morning to find my aunt Joan sharing the bed with me. It happened when she'd travelled overnight to take advantage of a week out.

With Joan at home there was no relaxation; on the contrary, a period of manic activity started immediately. The copper in the scullery worked overtime belching out steam as it strained to cope with the suitcases of laundry which had accumulated over the weeks of living in digs.

Bang went the front door as Joan rushed up to town for an interview with an agent, and *crash* it went again as she struggled in with yards and yards of sequinned material she'd bought on the way back.

Soon the doorbell would ring to herald Wadie and Billie, who'd sit down for a cup of tea and discuss future plans for a new act, and they'd only be in the house about half an hour before the door slammed again as they tore off to the dress-maker to be measured and fitted for the new costumes.

'Gypsies!' my grandmother said. 'That's what they are, always on the move.'

I helped Joan to pack up one set of costumes and unpack another in the props room. The floor was stacked high with trunks and tea chests all bearing labels to identify the contents. One said LEOTARDS and another contained TAP SHOES and there were PANTO OUTFITS and SAILOR COSTUMES etc., but apart from the clothes the room was a treasure trove of knick-knacks. There were piles of boxes which held a fascinating mixed bag of tambourines, castanets, swords, ribbons and artificial flowers.

We sorted through everything and when we came upon the top hats and black canes they were irresistible. 'Come on,' said Joan, 'I'll teach you some new steps.'

There was no place in the crowded little house, so we went out of doors to practise on the concrete garden path at the back. The two of us tapped up and down wearing the hats and holding the canes and as we danced, we passed and repassed the kitchen window where my grandma was preparing the meal. I could see her shaking her head as she foresaw another one of the family getting bitten by the show business bug, and when the neighbours came out in their gardens to watch, she complained to them.

'Will you take a look at my grand-daughter,' she said. 'There'll soon be another one off to join the gypsies.'

My aunt Joan had begun her dancing career in a children's troupe. It was here she had met Wadie and Billie. The three of them struck up an enduring friendship and when they grew up and were more experienced they launched out and started their own act.

Children's troupes were a popular and regular item on many variety bills. They all followed a similar pattern and it was hard to tell one from another because they not only worked alike but they all wore the same type of costume. The children had big butterfly bows on their tap shoes and another one tied on their hair and they dressed in short gingham smocks like those made fashionable by Shirley Temple, the juvenile darling of the cinema. This style had two advantages. First of all, it emphasised the youth of the performers and secondly it helped to camouflage the developing breasts of the older girls in the back row.

Not only did they look alike but these acts were all produced in the same way. The golden rule was 'Come flood, fire or hostile audience, keep on the move and smile at all times.'

The format was for the children to rush on stage full of bounce and energy and sing an opening chorus in excruciatingly shrill voices, followed by a lively tap routine. Then individuals would come out of the line to do their specialities, cartwheels, flip-flaps, jumping splits and so on, while the remaining girls kept up a relentless jigging at the back. I think the basic idea was to impress on the audience how young and full of beans they were.

At some time during the act they'd stage an acrobatic number, and as my aunt Joan was a big strong girl she always came off worst in this part because she was picked to be the bearer. The bearer is the one who lifts and takes the strain of the others and it's she who supports the entire troupe in a 'living pyramid' for The Big Finish. Joan told me that by the time it came to propping up the pyramid, she was perspiring so much from all her previous efforts that often the girls started to slither down, and instead of a spectacular human tower they ended up a crumpled heap on the stage.

Now that they'd progressed to having their own act, the three girls generally worked in touring revues and pantomime. The advantage of working in a revue was that the management paid for the railway tickets and fixed the run of the tour, so it was much better than playing on individual variety bills where each week the performer had to make his own way to a different town and pay his own fare.

There were hundreds of touring dates scattered around the country, especially up in the north, and it was in this type of show that one met the larger-than-life characters that the business was famous for. Every time Joan came back to the house in East Ham she had a fund of stories to tell and I never tired of hearing them.

After a pantomime season with *Dick Whittington*, she kept us laughing with the story of the old 'actor laddie' who had been booked to play King Rat. This old boy had seen better days, but in spite of being down on his luck, no sooner had he been paid at the end of the week than he was off to the local pub, or 'hostelry' as he called it, for his tipple.

When the management finally refused to advance him any more 'subs' on his salary, he turned his attention to the other pros in the pantomime. He confronted each of them in a long black coat with a moth-eaten astrakhan collar and swept off his Homburg.

'Could you possibly see your way clear to spare a groat for a poor Thespian whose throat is parched for the want of a flagon,' he begged in his deep resonant voice, and then he continued in a confidential aside, 'I shall of course repay the loan when the ghost walks on Friday.' For those who don't know the expression, pay day in the theatre is always referred to as the ghost walking.

The time came when he owed the other pros more than he could ever hope to repay, so they decided to teach him a lesson and put a stop to his mumping for once and all. The first half of the programme in *Dick Whittington* always ends with a dramatic shipwreck. This is the King Rat's scene because as the masts and sails come crashing down and thunderflashes explode, he stands alone in a green spotlight hurling a string of curses at Dick Whittington.

The 'actor laddie' took full advantage of this great chance to ham it up and delivered his lines as if he was playing King Lear instead of King Rat, and it was in this scene that the other pros decided to put their plan into action. Taking one of the thunderflashes, they surreptitiously hid it in a bucket which they put under the ship's rail just where the King Rat placed his feet.

His big moment arrived and King Rat bounded up and stood astride on the rail. 'Curses on you...' his rich Shakespearian voice rang out as he pointed an accusing finger at Dick Whittington. The flash exploded between his legs with an almighty bang.

'Jesus Christ!' he screamed, frantically clutching himself by the crotch of his wrinkled tights, then he caught sight of the cast giggling amongst themselves and realised he'd been set up.

All his carefully rehearsed lines went out of his head. 'Bugger

60

you, Dick Whittington,' he yelled. 'And that goes for your sodding cat as well!'

The stage manager hastily brought the curtain down at least two minutes early for the interval, while the mothers in the audience rushed their bewildered children out to console them with ice cream and orange juice.

Once Joan and the two girls played a resident season with a small fit-up show in an out-of-the-way town in Lancashire. The comedian in the company was, to put it mildly, the unsubtle type known in the business as a red-nose comic, but nevertheless in this particular town he was the right man for the job. The local people took him to their hearts and lapped him up. He only had to put his face round the curtain wearing an oversized check cap or a revolving bow tie for the audience to fall about.

It was the custom in a resident show for the company to put on several changes of programme, and when it came to the last production, it was generally the case of scraping the bottom of the barrel for material. This show was no exception and the company all offered suggestions until the comedian's wife, who was the soprano, suggested that a scena of British heroes and historical figures would make a strong finish on which to bring the curtain down for the interval. This type of number was always called a 'Give us your kind applause number' because it was a certain winner as the audience were bound to applaud if only out of patriotism.

Being a very small cast, everyone in the company had to take part in this stirring extravaganza and the comedian was brought in to play 'The death of Nelson.'

Came the performance, the piano struck up a rousing march and on walked the soprano as Florence Nightingale, closely followed by the Duke of Wellington, Grace Darling and the rest of the cast to delighted 'Oohs' and 'Ahs' from the dutifully impressed audience. The climax approached, the lights dimmed and a curtain rose upstage to reveal the comic lying on a rostrum doing his level best to impersonate the pitiful figure of Horatio Nelson on the point of death.

Much to the fury of his wife, as soon as the crowd recognised their favourite they went off into gales of laughter. She was

61

incensed that her carefully rehearsed drama was not being appreciated and, leaning forward with her lamp, she hissed reprovingly at the hilarious audience, 'Shush! Serious!'

Compared to the rest of the family, who had all got off the mark when small children, I was an idle layabout, but it was my Aunt Joan who altered all that. The years had passed. I was 15 and the time had come for me to leave the convent. My grandmother had arranged for me to stay with her and when I arrived at the house in East Ham Joan was at home.

As soon as I walked through the door she said, 'Don't put your case down. You're not stopping. I've fixed you up with a job – you start next week at the Palace Theatre Burnley.

6

So I began my life as a dancer in touring revue. There was a steady demand for this type of entertainment at the time; the industrial towns in the north of England had so many theatres that when you had worked the entire circuit with one show and it eventually folded, another would be speedily thrown together and put on the road to take its place.

It was before the age of the nude shows which gradually took over and swamped the music halls, and the revues were all very innocuous, although the managements gave them titillating names such as *Naughty Parisian Nights* or *Bedroom Scandals* to try and persuade the hard-working mill and factory workers that we were about to bring a little salacious excitement into their mundane lives. Our audiences were easily pleased and not over-critical of this undemanding style of entertainment which was doled out to them week after week. They packed the halls twice nightly and life settled down into some sort of routine.

After a while all the towns began to look alike and merge into one. Although life revolved around the 12 performances a week at the local theatre, a great part of the time was spent on trains, taxis and living in theatrical digs. In a touring revue, two, three or even four girls shared digs to keep down the expenses. The only rooms that the dancers could afford were in the working-class area of the town and every morning we awoke to the clatter of metal-toed clogs as the workers clip-clopped along the cobblestoned streets for the mills.

Sometimes we were disturbed even earlier by the 'knocker-upper' (a slightly different meaning to the word these days) but at that time he was a reliable man whose job it was to go around the district armed with a long pole rat-a-tatting on bedroom windows to ensure that folk wouldn't be late for work.

Sunday was the one morning that we never had a lie-in. While the mill workers turned over and snuggled under the bedclothes secure in the knowledge that on this day they were free from the deafening racket of the looms, we were stirring ourselves to pack up and travel on to the next town.

All hell broke loose as we rushed about, getting in each other's way, cramming the last bits and pieces into protesting suitcases. We yanked open drawers, peered into cupboards and grovelled under the beds to make sure that nothing was left behind, until the landlady got impatient and yelled upstairs that breakfast was ready and she wasn't going to make a fresh pot of tea for anybody, even if it was stone cold.

I remember Sunday morning as one frantic panic-stricken rush, of bolting down a slice of toast and a cup of tea while keeping an eagle eye on the clock and taking it in turns to dash to the front door to see if there was any sign of the taxi we'd ordered. This was one of the worst moments of a harrowing day, it was very much an 'if it' situation and every week we lived in dread that the taxi wouldn't turn up. The taxi firm knew we were leaving town so they didn't have to rely on local goodwill, and more than likely if they got a better fare and couldn't be bothered to show up, we'd be left high and dry.

Meanwhile, the landlady was as anxious to be rid of us as we were to leave her because she had to get the rooms cleaned and ready for the next group of girls that were due to arrive with the new show in town. In an emergency she would scurry about to wake up a little man that she knew, who might be persuaded 'for a small consideration' to take us to the station in his van, and it was then and only then that we paid the landlady for the week's lodging.

One of the golden rules I learned from my mother was never to pay the landlady on a Saturday night in case she went to the pub and took on a 'skinful' and was incapable of getting up early on Sunday to make breakfast and see us off.

Over the years my mother had formulated a special routine that she meticulously observed when going into new digs. Before agreeing to stay she inspected the bed to make sure it had clean sheets, and she wasn't content just to pull back the coverlet, because an unscrupulous woman had been known to iron the fold-back in an effort to deceive the innocent and unwary. When she was quite satisfied that the sheets were clean, she opened her handbag, took out a mirror and inserted it in the bed to make sure it was thoroughly aired. Only when the mirror came out clear and unmisted did she start to take off her coat, and then I knew the digs had come up to standard and we could stay. I never had the courage to go through this embarrassing ritual myself though, and I don't think the landladies would have stood for it in my day.

When the taxi eventually arrived we scrambled in with a mountain of suitcases, parcels and the inevitable carrier bags, while the driver bitterly complained about the number of passengers. He assured us that he hadn't expected so many and furthermore he was convinced that the amount of luggage would put paid to the springs of his ramshackle vehicle.

Any upsets we'd suffered at the hands of the landlady during the preceding week were instantly forgotten with the tremendous relief of being away at last, and we'd all shout 'Bye bye, Ma. See you next time we're in Barnsley!' ... or Bolton or Huddersfield or whichever town it was that we couldn't wait to leave.

All the noise and commotion would generally succeed in waking the neighbours and bring them to the windows, and so to the accompaniment of curses, shaking fists and cries of 'Why can't you let honest working people have a lie-in of a Sunday?' we'd be off at last for the train call.

The company arrived at the station in twos and threes, looking wan and pale, not having fully recovered from the violent shock of having to get up early, and proceeded to bring chaos and confusion by completely taking over the buffet and newspaper stall and littering up the platform with untidy piles of suitcases, hat boxes, golf bags, children and pet dogs. There was a saying at the time that 'only actors and fish travel on a

Sunday', although this altered with the outbreak of war and you had to fight for a seat on any day of the week with all the servicemen and women on the move.

When the train puffed into the station we all piled in and noisily sorted ourselves out into groups of travelling companions and the usual card schools. The main topic of conversation was in holding post-mortems on what the digs had been like in the town we were leaving and, more important still, where we were going to stay the following week.

Many a time we arrived at the next town with no digs fixed and then the chilling prospect that faced us was to tramp around the streets looking for any sort of accommodation. Tantalising smells of Sunday dinners wafted out of doors and windows to torment us and as time went by we knew that even if we did get in somewhere we probably wouldn't be lucky enough to get anything to eat that day.

The ideal way to fix digs was to write off weeks ahead of arrival, in fact as soon as the tour list was given out, so that the landlady expected you and had a meal waiting, but if you were with a large company the supply sometimes didn't meet the demand and then it was any port in a storm. In desperation many girls went to the vicar for assistance. The clergy were generally a good bet because they knew everyone in the parish, and another tip worth trying was the local police station. Women who might be a little wary of letting to 'those theatricals' were less likely to refuse if they opened their door to find the vicar or a policeman on their doorstep to endow us with an air of respectability. Sometimes these weeks turned out better than living in the run-of-the-mill digs because women unused to letting were more anxious to please.

I knew a girl called Wendy who cottoned on to this. At heart she was a real hard cookie, but she had a face like Little Orphan Annie and she perfected a method of finding digs that was all her own. She never attempted to book in advance, and when the train arrived at the station, she said goodbye to the other girls and trotted off alone to the most prosperous area of the town. Wendy carefully chose the best-looking house, knocked on the door and proceeded to tell the owners the hard luck story of how

66

she was touring for the first time in her life, and could they help at all because she had no idea of how to set about finding accommodation. She pouted prettily as she shyly confessed with wide-eyed innocence that she didn't fancy sharing with the other girls in case they led her into wicked ways. It worked like a charm. Wendy got the comfort of living in a luxury house for the week and sometimes the people wouldn't take a penny from her.

This gave the rest of us the needle and we gave her a rough time, until she explained that really she was doing everyone a good turn. She wasn't taking a bed away from any of us, and as for her benefactors, she was sure they were better people for the experience. When she left at the end of the week and tearfully clutched their hands in thanks, they assumed the self-righteous air of salvationists and were quite convinced that they'd protected a lily-white virgin from being violated in the squalid part of town where the rest of us were hanging out.

Luckily Wendy's stay only lasted a week, otherwise her generous hosts might have begun to wonder why such a naïve blue-eyed babe was in show business in the first place.

Some landladies were marvellous women. The better ones fussed over us like mother hens and tried to feed us up with good food while we lived with them. Many got a vicarious thrill from mixing with show people, it made them feel a cut above their neighbours and the one thing they loved better than anything was to hear the gossip going round the theatre, especially if it concerned a well-known star.

The rooms they let generally had an air of cluttered seediness, with the mantelpiece hidden under a sea of photographs from former lodgers. All the pictures were signed with flowery messages, such as 'To darling Ma, I can't wait to come back. A real home from home.' Once I saw a message that struck me as being slightly ambiguous. A girl had written 'To Ma, I'll never forget your steak and kidney pie! Love and kisses Sylvia', and I wondered if the pie had been a gastronomic delight or if it had given poor Sylvia 'the trots' for the week.

The landladies were just as vague. Ten to one if I recognised a face in the collection of postcards and remarked casually, 'I see you've had Maud Taylor staying here,' she'd be inclined to sigh heavily and murmur, 'Yes, and what a week I had with her,' making me nervous of pursuing the subject in case Maud had blotted her copy book and the landlady held it against me for the week.

The chorus had to put up with superior affectations from some of them. 'Of course, I don't usually let to the chorus,' we often heard, 'I generally have the big Tops and Bottoms here.' Top and Bottom of the bill were the two best positions on the advertising posters, reserved for the star performers, and we knew perfectly well that no star would cross the threshold of her sleazy little house and she was just trying to impress us, but we were in no position to retaliate when we relied on her optimistically for a decent week's food and accommodation.

Those touring days have gone for ever and a whole breed of landladies with them. Legends grew up around some of the digs and every pro kept a book of favourite addresses, rather like a personal *Good Digs Guide*, which he would recommend to his fellow pros. I've heard that tramps and door-to-door salesmen put marks on house gates to indicate to each other if it's a good touch or not. In the same way, if a performer saw the words 'Quoth the raven' in a landlady's guest book, he knew he was in for a rough week. The quotation from Edgar Allan Poe continues 'Quoth the raven, nevermore'.

Many landladies had been pros themselves before they married, and letting digs was a way for them to keep in touch with the business as well as earning some money after they'd retired from the stage.

My aunt Joan had done several summer seasons in Morecambe and she always stayed at the same house with a lady called Florrie, and when I started touring she passed the address on to me.

In her youth Florrie had been a high diver in a circus, one of those intrepid ladies who climb a tall ladder and then hurtle down into a small tank of water. There were several pictures on the walls depicting her at the peak of her career, wearing an Edwardian costume which showed off her sturdy legs, hourglass waist and unyielding bolster of a bosom.

If we were there in the summertime, sometimes she'd suggest that we all go down to the beach for a swim. It was at this point that a desperate look came into the eyes of those in the know as they cast around frantically for an excuse to get out of going, but Florrie wouldn't take no for an answer; she insisted that everyone must join in. She'd make up a picnic and we'd all have the time of our lives, but what really made her day was if she discovered that there were some non-swimmers in the party.

'Don't tell me you can't swim!' she'd say. 'Luckily you've come to the right person. I'll teach you in no time at all – it'll be a piece of cake.'

The first time I went with her she'd managed to muster two non-swimmers in the group and we made quite a crowd as we walked down to the beach carrying the picnic baskets and bathing gear.

Florrie had been leading the way but when we all ran down to the sea I missed her and looked around to see where she'd got to. The sight of her in a swimsuit came as something of a shock. She was knocking on a bit by this time and she presented a formidable figure, with her large bust and hips rapidly turning to fat, reminding me somewhat of a Japanese wrestler.

The reason that she hadn't rushed down to the sea with the rest of us was that she was quite unashamedly whipping up a crowd. Florrie bounded along the beach, slapping her arms across her mighty bosom. Every now and again she stopped to execute a spectacular cartwheel and then she'd touch her toes and do a knees-bend, and the whole time she kept up a running commentary in a voice to waken the dead.

'What's it like in the water today?' she hollered. 'I don't know whether to come in or not.'

This didn't go down too well with some of the more reluctant bathers who hadn't wanted to go swimming in the first place until Florrie had persuaded them, but they needn't have worried, I'd been told she'd rather be hanged, drawn and quartered than not take the plunge. The passers-by on the promenade stood riveted by all this commotion and more and more stopped to stand and stare until gradually a sizeable crowd collected. It was the best free show they'd seen for years.

Florrie kept an eye on their ever increasing numbers and when she judged the time was right, 'Watch out, here I come!' she bellowed, making a sudden dash and charging into the waves, for all the world as if she was about to swim the Channel. She struck out with a strenuous crawl, swimming strongly out to sea until she was about a quarter of a mile from the shore and the onlookers began to fear for her safety, then she turned back, churning up the water with all the power and strength of a paddle steamer.

Once satisfied that all eyes were on her, Florrie happily got into her stride and showed off with every trick she knew. Whooping joyfully, she bounced up and down, turned somersault after somersault and ducked anyone who had the temerity to get in her way. Then she swam underwater, surfacing unexpectedly several yards away, only to submerge again and pull some poor unsuspecting holiday-maker down by the legs.

'Pity there's not a high diving board,' she grumbled, heaving her ungainly body out of the water on to the jetty, only to plunge in again and cause such a terrific wash you would have thought that someone had flung a ton of coals into the sea.

All of a sudden she remembered the two non-swimmers, who already felt the first twinges of alarm and had a fearful premonition of what was in store for them. Their suspicions were fully justified.

'Come on, its easy!' she shouted. Then, hardly giving them a glance because she was so busy playing to the gallery, she seized hold of them by the arm, leg, neck or any other part that came to hand while the poor devils threshed about gasping for air and begging for mercy.

Of course Florrie didn't really want to teach them how to swim, she just wanted to perform again in front of an audience, but in the process she damned near drowned those two unfortunate souls and probably gave them a complex about water for the rest of their lives.

Although Florrie had been happily married for donkey's years to a railwayman, and in spite of the fact that she was hovering dangerously on the brink of old age, she held on strongly to the illusion that she could always return to 'The

Business'. She kept her old theatrical skip upstairs in the attic and whenever she and her old man had a row, she'd tear up the stairs, drag out the basket and start to pack for her big comeback.

But it was gorgeous staying with Florrie. She was a good cook and she had no fussy rules and regulations.

Good digs were a joy, and many a star preferred to live in them rather than a hotel because the landlady catered to the special needs of a performer, providing the luxury of a private sitting room to relax in during the day, the pleasure of coming back to a hot meal after the show and breakfast at any hour of the morning.

Unfortunately, they were few and far between, and there were a lot of duff ones where the meals were badly cooked and in the winter you huddled over a meagre fire and shivered in bed because there weren't enough blankets. In most of the digs, the price you paid for the rooms included the landlady cooking your meals, although you had to buy and bring in the food. A rotten landlady would pinch some of your meat, protesting that it had shrunk when she cooked it, and she'd put many hidden extras on the bill, including charging you for every scuttle of coal used.

Once when I was in pantomime, the actor who was playing the Emperor in *Dick Whittington* swore that his landlady was overcharging him for his coal and then pinching it back again when he was at the theatre. I told him the story of my aunt Joan and the King Rat and it gave him an idea. He took some of the explosive powder used in the thunderflashes backstage and carefully concealed it in the largest lumps of coal in his scuttle before leaving for the matinee at the theatre. When he went back to the digs between houses, the place was in pandemonium and the landlady was in hysterics.

'Oh sir,' she gasped, 'while you were at the theatre I had the most terrifying experience. God alone knows what they're putting in the coal these days, because I made up the fire in my kitchen range when without a word of warning there was an almighty bang and half the grate flew out. It burned a big hole in the rug and half-frightened the cat to death, and if I hadn't had the presence of mind to put my hand in front of my mouth, I'd have lost my new set of teeth as well!'

I was never very keen on working pantomime; to me it was just a stopgap to tide me over until the new productions started in the spring. There were always twice as many costume changes in pantomime and a lot of dance routines to learn without much job satisfaction.

To master an intricate routine could be an exciting experience if you had an imaginative choreographer, but there wasn't much chance of this happening in panto. It was all go! There was never a chance to sit down in the dressing room and put our legs up on the dressing table, which was our favourite form of relaxation. We followed ourselves on, first as village maidens, then jolly Jack Tars and then gossamer fairies in the inevitable transformation scene. We were forever clattering up and down the steps, flinging off one costume and dragging on another, and when we'd done one performance we had to start all over again. In fact many times I've worked a matinee followed by two evening performances and it was easy to lose count of which show was which. What a relief it was to hear the last call of 'All down for the Palace scene!', which signalled the end of another day.

As soon as I signed the contract and knew the subject of the pantomime, I knew what I'd let myself in for. If it was *Dick Whittington*, there were always mops and buckets for the sailor number, it was an even bet that the opening village scene had a maypole and in *Robin Hood* there were bows and arrows. When I had advanced up the ladder to the position of head girl, as far as I was concerned the whole ghastly conglomeration of props came under the heading of 'hazards', just waiting for one accident-prone girl to drop or trip over and make a complete shambles of the routine. The most perilous of these traps were tambourines and we always had them in the gypsy scene. If one girl fumbled and dropped hers, it seemed to be contagious and bring about an avalanche.

I grew to hate the whole predictable set-up. The curtains would open to reveal a rural set with a caravan centre stage while the girls whirled about in gay abandon to the music of a

Hungarian czardas. The dance got more and more frenetic as we pirouetted round with skirts and ribbons flying and the music played faster and faster, only to stop abruptly with a last wild crash on the tambourines, whereupon we draped ourselves into picturesque groups to dress the stage, with bosoms heaving after all the exertion.

At this point the leading singer burst out of the caravan dressed as the gypsy king with a red handkerchief on his head and brass curtain rings in his ears (held on by elastic bands). This was his one big chance to shine in the pantomime – and it was also the moment when a slight hubbub broke out in the audience as mothers seized the opportunity while the comics were off-stage and nothing much was happening to take their children out for a quick pee. I envied them because we were forced to stand listening as the singer belted out a couple of choruses of 'A Gypsy am I' and then went on to tell the audience that he couldn't live without 'A Life on the Open Road', when we all knew perfectly well that he lived in a stifling bedsitter in Brixton.

If a management had a particular set of costumes in the store, they didn't wait for an appropriate subject to make use of them. A routine would be worked into any pantomime to take advantage of the costumes, which were brought out of mothballs year after year. Once when I was in *Robinson Crusoe*, for no apparent reason the chorus marched on for an archer routine in a woodland glade, which had absolutely nothing to do with the plot. The sole reason was that the management had the costumes. I thought I detected a look of surprise on the faces of the audience when we made our appearance but nothing was ever said. I loathed those costumes. In a quick change it was a struggle pulling on thick black tights and a velvet tunic topped with a cape and feathered hat and of course there was the dreaded hazard ... long bows and arrows.

One day I met an older lady who had been a dancer herself. She had long since retired but she'd been a fellow sufferer in pantomime and she was sympathising with me while I belly-ached to her about this archer routine, When I told her which management I was working for, it turned out that she'd been

73

signed with the same company and worn the very same costumes 20 years previously. It brought it home to me that the props and costumes had a much longer working life than the poor dancers!

Nevertheless, like it or not, it was through the medium of pantomime that most girls started in the business. All the theatres dotted around the country put on a pantomime at Christmas. Chorus girls were at a premium at this time of year and very often in the provinces (or providences, as my great-uncle Ted called them), local troupes were brought in to meet the demand.

Any girl who didn't have two left feet could get a job in panto when the need was greatest, and once in a professional company, she had the chance to learn the ropes from the more experienced dancers. Those with a genuine talent improved their standards and went on from there, while the ones who didn't make the grade dropped out. But I do think, and this is one of my pet theories, that these touring productions provided a means of escape for girls with a bit of spirit who felt trapped living in some one-horse town where the only available work was the mill or the factory. The stage gave them an outlet that the girls today haven't got. Of course many of them found that it wasn't as glamorous as they'd expected and were happy enough to return home, but by then they'd got the rebellious bit out of their systems and probably settled down all the better for it. Others took to it like a duck to water.

It wasn't a case of roses all the way, because although outside the theatre your life was your own, once through the stage door a very strict discipline was enforced. The head girl had a position of power; some were martinets and the other girls called them 'dragons' but they were obeyed.

It was the responsibility of the head girl to call rehearsals if the work got slack and fell below standard, and she had to check behaviour onstage and in the wings. The rules were strict; girls weren't allowed to sit around in their stage costumes or hang around the wings if they weren't making an entrance, they weren't allowed to bring fish and chips into the theatre in case the smell permeated into the auditorium and woe betide a new

74

girl who wasn't over-particular about personal hygiene or wore grubby undies. No one bothered to use the subtle approach – the culprit was told the brutal facts in basic English. One head girl that I worked with had a habit of pouncing on an offending article of grimy clothing. 'And who's the owner of this pretty frilly?' she'd chant, waving it about for all to see and comment on, and it was remarkable how quickly the unfortunate girl got the message.

One of the perks of the business which helped to lessen the miseries of a week in grotty digs was the unwritten law that we were able to pass in free to the other theatres and cinemas in town. This was knows as 'getting in on the Wilkie', 'Wilkie' being Cockney rhyming slang for visiting card, taken from Wilkie Bard, the old Music Hall star.

Most chorus girls didn't go to the expense of having their own cards printed but we were always on the lookout for the other acts' cards and kept a selection in our handbags for this purpose. I've passed myself into the local theatre in every capacity from a juggler to a trapeze artist and seen some damn good shows in the process.

This was strictly a winter or bad weather pastime and as soon as summer came along we girls would get out and about to try and get a tan. But many of the old variety pros wouldn't stir themselves. All they knew of life was the digs, the local cinema, the theatre and, of course, the pub.

Once in Bolton I went into the stage door and bumped into the lady who did a contortionist act while juggling at the same time. (There must be easier ways of making a living.)

'Hello,' I said. 'Have you been to the park? It's lovely at this time of the year.'

'Park? Is there a park round here?' She looked dumbfounded, just as if I was talking about the mysteries of outer space.

'Yes, the park,' I answered. 'It's only a little way up the road.'

'Now tell me,' she asked, turning towards me with an air of total bewilderment, 'which town are we in?'

She genuinely had no idea where she was. After arriving in the town and going to the digs, she rehearsed every morning, went to the cinema in the afternoon, worked at the theatre at night and that was it. She neither knew nor cared about the place she was in, and they say that travel broadens the mind!

To have my Sundays free seemed like a vision of the Promised Land; it was the dream I clung to when I spent the best part of the day travelling from one set of crummy digs to another. I made up my mind to try and break away from the treadmill and make an all-out effort to realise what had become a burning ambition.

I was determined to get into the chorus of a West End musical.

7

At the outbreak of war no one in show business circles knew what to expect, but after the first panic things had settled down more or less as usual.

In some provincial towns, there wasn't a lot of difference to be seen except for the men being called up and the streets gradually filling up with uniforms. Apart from the military targets, it was the large city centres and industrial towns which bore the brunt of the heavy bombing and many of the smaller places never heard an enemy aircraft overhead.

Little by little the young men in show business disappeared from the scene as they were conscripted, and some of the older performers who thought they'd never get another date were brought out of reluctant retirement to fill the gaps.

During the Battle of Britain and the intensive Blitzkrieg on London, every West End theatre had closed, with the exception of the famous Windmill. However, when so many Londoners refused to leave the capital and all the servicemen came home on leave, there was such a need for entertainment that permission was given, and the managements agreed to reopen the theatres. It was decided that the times of the performances should be much earlier than usual, to lessen the chances of so many people crowded together under one roof late at night being killed in an air raid.

One Thursday when I bought our trade paper *The Stage*, I saw that a reputable firm was advertising for dancers for a number one tour, adding the magic words, 'With West End run to follow', and I determined to get the job. I found out later that this was a regular 'catch-me' advert to entice girls to sign for a tour and that the attractive bait of a West End contract hardly ever materialised, but in my case ignorance was bliss and I decided to audition.

It wasn't going to be easy, though, because the advert stipulated 'ballet essential' and I'd never put a ballet shoe on in my life. But determination teamed with inexperience is a very strong combination and I prevailed upon a friend who was a trained ballet dancer to come to my rescue and give me a crash course in the basic skills. I wasn't so far out of my tiny mind to imagine that I'd ever be able to actually dance in a ballet, but I hoped to assimilate enough to get by at the audition and worry about the rest later.

Put like that, it sounds simple, but it nearly killed me. Sweat poured out of me as I struggled with the exercises at the barre and strained to turn my feet out in the correct manner. I found myself walking about like a sea lion, but gradually I progressed to the fundamental steps and was able to recognise the French terms for them.

I kept at it between lessons until my muscles nearly gave out, and I massaged my toes with surgical spirit to toughen them up before I attempted to get up on pointe, but it didn't seem to help because they bled every time. However, I persevered; pain or no pain, I was determined to land that job.

London auditions were generally held on-stage at one of the West End theatres, and as there was always a production on at the time, no dressing rooms could be allocated for the dancers. Just the same, we were expected to appear in full stage make-up wearing practice dress. We had to achieve this in the cramped space at the side of the stage and it wasn't easy with so many girls, but we were all so eager to pass the audition that no one thought of complaining.

I passed the first part of the test for tap and modern dance and was told to return to the theatre in a week's time for the ballet section. Andree Howard, who was a well-known ballet choreographer, was to take the crucial audition, but luckily in my supreme ignorance I hadn't heard of her. I found out later that she had a daunting reputation.

My friend from the ballet lent me a tutu which had seen better

78

days, so I washed, starched and ironed it and presented myself at the theatre, looking a cross between the Sugar Plum Fairy and an advertisement for Persil. But just to prove that miracles can happen and faith is able to move mountains, I made it!

I floated home on wings. Anyone would have thought that I'd nailed the prize part of leading lady instead of being an insignificant member of the chorus.

Having safely signed the contract, I think that Andree Howard rumbled me because, fortunately for me and the show, I wasn't picked to dance in the full-scale ballet which was a feature of the programme, but I never for a moment begrudged the pain and effort involved. This show was to be my stepping stone to the dizzy heights of the West End theatre.

We rehearsed in London at the old Scala Theatre behind Tottenham Court Road and I was delighted to learn that my salary for the tour of this number one production was to be £4 10s a week (£4.50), a whole pound more than I'd earned in touring revue.

I managed very well on this munificent wage and saved money in my Post Office account. I had to, there was no mum and dad waiting at home to look after me when I was out of work.

I shared digs with three other girls and we always tried to book two bedrooms and a sitting room, but more often than not had to settle for a bedroom and a bedsitter, and then we took turn and turn about for the luxury of having the separate bedroom. The landlady charged the four of us about £1.50 for this accommodation, and that included her cooking the meals. We each put a pound in the kitty for our food, and if that didn't cover it we had another whip-round towards the end of the week.

The only other basic expense was sharing the taxi fare on Sunday morning, so sometimes I saved a pound a week and still had some spare cash to spend on riotous living!

We opened this epic tour in Leicester, and the dress rehearsal started early on Sunday morning just as soon as we'd dumped our cases in the digs and arrived at the theatre. I'm sure that nowadays Actors Equity has restrictions on how many hours a dancer can work, but there was no such rule then. If a new girl asked the others how long the rehearsal would be, the answer she got was 'Nine a.m. until unconscious, darling!'

Dress rehearsals are always nightmares. Over and over again we raced up the stairs from the dressing room to the wardrobe on the top floor for costume alterations and then down to the stage to work the numbers with the orchestra. It all looked a hideous mess; there seemed no way at all that the show could be staged the following night. Hour after hour went by, no one left the theatre and we all existed on a diet of coffee and sandwiches sent in by a nearby transport café.

At three in the morning we stumbled out exhausted, to find there were no taxis and we had to find our way back to the digs in the impenetrable darkness of the wartime blackout.

When the show opened the next night it all went smoothly, so when it received an enthusiastic reception everyone felt justified in relaxing with a sigh of relief and settled back for what we hoped would be an enjoyable tour. The only remaining worry was to fix comfortable digs each week.

After Leicester, the next date was at the Hippodrome Coventry and it was a marvel that the theatre was still standing after the devastating Blitz which had flattened most of the city. So many houses had been demolished that it was a great problem finding digs, and although the first impression on arriving was that the people of Coventry must have evacuated the town, they were all there somewhere – and what's more, they turned up in their thousands to patronise the theatre.

My room-mate was a girl called Babs. She was a seasoned campaigner and it was she who eventually came up with an address, and although she had no idea what the digs were like, it was no time to be fussy, we were grateful to get in anywhere.

When the four of us arrived, it was to find that we were booked into a poky little terraced house in a seedy run-down neighbourhood.

'I'm sorry, girls,' Babs apologised. 'I'm afraid I've let you all in for a miserable week.'

The town was depressing enough, with acres of ruined houses and piles of rubble which was all that was left of the shopping

80

centre, but Babs was wrong, the week brought us all the unexpected pleasure of a surprise party. It was one of those tiny houses where the front door opened directly into the living room and the whole place was so small that not only were you pitched into the front room but almost catapulted out of the back as well.

The landlady kept such an enormous fire going in this rabbit hutch of a room that we were forced to keep the front door open to avoid suffocation. As the neighbours walked by on the pavement outside they all looked in and called out, 'How's things then?' and 'Everything all right at the Hippodrome then?' It wasn't the sort of place to hang out if you were keen on a bit of privacy.

The lavatory was in the back yard and at first sight the house looked as if it had been built without a staircase, but the landlady opened a cupboard in the sitting room to reveal a steep flight of steps like a ship's ladder which led up to the box-like bedrooms.

She turned out to be an absolute love and she was just like a mum to us all that week. Every night we came back from the theatre to demolish a huge, indigestible supper washed down with pints of scalding tea. We ate this with no ill effects whatsoever. Luckily, we all had stomachs which could absorb the food range of an ostrich – our only trouble was in keeping them topped up. The landlady always joined us at the supper table for a cosy chat and then she told our fortunes in the tea leaves, predicting a rosy future in show business for us all with a happy marriage to follow.

So much for the giddy life of a showgirl! I thought as we all left the Hippodrome, because the four of us couldn't wait to get back to the warm little house after the performance. Our surrogate mum had the pyjamas airing in front of the roaring fire and after the meal we sat scorching our 'million dollar legs', contentedly dreaming as the landlady foretold success, health and wealth and everything else we were anxious to hear.

The week was all the nicer because it was unexpected and when we left on the Sunday morning all the neighbours sacrificed their usual lie-in to see us off to Liverpool, where we were due to play at the Royal Court Theatre.

We'd fixed rooms in Islington, the digs area of Liverpool, and when we arrived there were five of us to share the taxi because Sonnie had booked a room in the same digs. Sonnie was one of the few dancing boys in the show. He was slightly 'over the hill' but he'd been recalled because of the man shortage. He had a wicked 'camp' sense of humour and we were grateful for him that week, because as it turned out we were sorely in need of a laugh.

The landlady was a sour-faced woman who hardly opened her mouth to speak. She gave the impression that she had a permanent grudge against life and gradually it got us down.

'Look at that hatchet face,' Sonnie said as she brought the dinner in without a word. 'I'm sure she's got the evil eye.'

I don't think she cracked her face once.

'Here comes Lot's wife,' Sonnie whispered *sotto voce* as she snatched the empty plates from the table.

Her taciturn behaviour became contagious. When she came in we found that our own lively conversation faltered and then petered out altogether.

'This place is doing me no good at all,' Sonnie grumbled. 'I tell you, duckie, I'm no longer the life and soul of the party. This woman has succeeded where no one else has in giving me a pain where I ought to have pleasure!'

Time hung heavily on our hands and when Saturday crawled round we couldn't wait to be on the move again. We came back unusually early from the theatre to get packed and ready for the train call the following morning.

Walking up to the front door of the grey, depressing house, I thought at first that we'd made a mistake and gone to the wrong address. Instead of the funereal quiet, a woman's voice was raucously belting out the chorus of 'Nellie Dean'. Whoever it was finished with an ear-splitting crescendo and then without drawing breath launched headlong into 'Don't Dilly Dally on the Way'. It sounded just like turning-out time at the pub.

When Sonnie opened the door, the first thing we saw was the landlady, she of the woeful countenance, doing a knees-up with skirts held high and flashing her pink celanese bloomers for all the world to see.

82

'Oh my Gawd!' Sonnie giggled. 'The old girl's been at the cooking sherry.'

After the first initial shock, the unanimous thought that flashed through all our minds was how the devil were we to get up in the morning for the eight o'clock train call. There wasn't a natural early riser among us and we always relied implicitly on the landlady to wake us. We all tried to think of different methods guaranteed to arouse us at the crack of dawn, but we had our doubts, and meanwhile our carousing landlady had exhausted her repertoire and was crawling up the stairs on her hands and knees.

Early the next morning while we were still out for the count sleeping the sleep of the just, there came a knock on the door, and before we had a chance to stir, the landlady barged in uncompromisingly po-faced as before.

We gaped at her open-mouthed as she banged the breakfast on the table and swept out again without uttering. There wasn't a vestige or trace to show for the previous night's revelry and her icy manner defied us to open our mouths. None of us had the effrontery to speak, not until we'd paid the bill and were just about to leave. Then Sonnie turned to me and said, 'I don't know about you, Mary, but I've always favoured pink celanese next to the skin.'

I didn't dare look, but I think she flinched, and I'd give a lot to know how she came out of such a colossal bender in so short a time.

It turned out that Sonnie had broken the golden rule by paying his share of the rent on the Saturday morning.

I don't think I ever met another one like her, but on the other hand there were hundreds of landladies who never stopped talking. The name we gave this type was 'yacker' and every mealtime was the ideal excuse for a yacker to reveal each and every boring detail of her own and all her family's private lives. Nothing was sacred to her, she'd divulge the most intimate revelations without a twinge of conscience. It was always happening to me. While trapped at the dining table, I was forced to listen to the story of numerous miscarriages, the difficulty of her confinements and the medical history of each and every one

83

of her children. On and on she'd go, pouring out confidences like an incessant babbling brook until my eyes glazed over with the never-ending flow of words.

Once I was in digs with an old and seasoned pro who had been touring for donkey's years and was thoroughly experienced in coping with all the trials and tribulations. He could 'suss out' this sort of landlady as soon as he set foot in the house and he had his own method of dealing with the situation.

Directly he walked in and spotted that she was a yacker, 'Sit down, Mrs Boothroyd,' he'd say. 'Sit down and tell me everything. Tell me about your lazy slob of a husband who's never done a day's work and of his ghastly mother who's always made you feel unwelcome. Tell me about your lovely daughter who married a man in a million and never has to do a hand's turn by cooking a meal or washing a dish, and of the no-good girl who got her claws into your poor son and won't make him a meal or wash a shirt for him. Describe to me symptom by symptom the illness which finally snuffed out your angel of a mother and don't spare me any gruesome detail of how you gave birth. Tell me everything you know about the neighbours and the tarty girl who lives next door, give me the whole bloody lot and then don't open your mouth again until the end of the week.'

It shut them up like clams, but that's the way he liked it.

Theatrical landladies often bridged the generations and the most popular digs in Newcastle were run by a mother and daughter. They had two houses a few doors apart in Leazes Terrace and between the two of them they accommodated a good proportion of the pros who came to the town each week. We four girls stayed with the daughter, and our landlady liked to be included in the conversation when we were chatting about the latest scandal backstage. She loved to hear all the dirt first-hand, and indeed she would have felt slighted if she wasn't taken into our confidence.

One day we were having lunch at the table in the bay window overlooking the road and we noticed one of the small-part actresses walking back to the other digs with a comic from the company.

'Hello!' said our landlady, clocking us out of the corner of her

84

eye so that she didn't miss our immediate reaction. 'Here comes Mr and Mrs Farnsbarns!'

Before we could get ourselves together we blurted out in surprise, 'Mr and Mrs?'

'Ee! I thought so,' she smirked, satisfied that her suspicions were correct and that she knew something that we didn't. She wasn't morally offended by this permissive state of affairs, she just wanted to know!

It was a pleasure to play all the number one dates and we travelled to every large city like Leeds, Nottingham and Manchester before we went to Blackpool, then from Blackpool we had the long journey across country to Bristol, which was to be the last week of the tour.

The wartime train service was always dicey and the train finally steamed into Bristol hours late – and Babs and I had no digs fixed. By the time we arrived it was already dark, with the rain coming down in sheets, and to make matters worse I had a heavy feverish cold and would have given half a week's wages to crawl into a nice warm bed.

After trying every address we knew and having no luck, Babs and I finally gave up and went to the theatre to see if anyone could help. We staggered through the stage door, weighed down with umbrellas and carrier bags like two orphans of the storm.

It was always my ambition when travelling to make at least one journey without a carrier bag; catering for ourselves as we did, there were invariably a few bits and pieces of food left to take on to the next town and with rationing allowing us such meagre diets, they were much too precious to leave behind.

That particular Sunday Babs and I had two lamb chops in the carrier bag which we hoped a landlady would cook for us but when we arrived at the theatre that night we had very little expectation of eating them.

Although it was Sunday, everything was bustling and busy at the Hippodrome as the stage crew had their first technical run to get to know the sets and lighting plots. The stage manager was a Mr Goodman, known to one and all as 'Goodie', and it was Goodie who came to our rescue that cold miserable night. He made the two of us comfortable in a warm dressing room and sent across to the pub for a couple of brandies, and after we'd thawed out and he'd finished the rehearsal, he scooped up all our carrier bags, pushed us into a waiting taxi and took us back to his flat.

He lived alone and was very capable of looking after himself. He dosed me up with medicine, tucked me into bed with a hot-water bottle and, best of all, Babs and I ate our meal of lamb chops.

The following day he helped to find us some digs and the week which had started so disastrously had a happy ending for me – and an even better one for Babs.

The theatre digs in Bristol were all near one another in the St Michael's Hill district. It was a long hard climb from the town square but once in our upstairs room it was possible to see the broad estuary of the River Avon in the distance over the rooftops. Each morning that week I looked forward to pulling back the blackout curtains to enjoy the faraway view of spark-ling sea and sky. I stayed indoors most of the week nursing my cold and only went out for the performance in the evening.

On Tuesday night as we came out of the stage door a handsome American officer was hanging about. He'd seen Babs in the line and been knocked off his feet. It was love at first sight! From that moment I hardly saw Babs again that week. She rushed out in the morning and I didn't catch sight of her again unless she tore in to change clothes or borrow a pair of stockings and then ran out once more to be with her 'beau'.

Well, I couldn't expect her to be idle while I was laid up with my cold and there wasn't much else going on in Bristol at the time.

At the end of the week the show folded, we all went back to London and I said goodbye to Babs. The next time I saw her was in a foreign country and in rather unusual circumstances.

8

I'd made it! Could life hold any further joys? I was in the West End at last and going to work every day at the London Coliseum.

Of course the unique electric globe wasn't functioning because of the blackout, and there were no names in twinkling lights outside the front of the theatre, but as mine wouldn't have been there anyway, nothing detracted from my sense of achievement.

Not only that, but I'd been elevated to the position of head girl. The carrot dangled before me was an extra pound a week, and it was only because I needed the money that I took on this unenviable chore. I was 20 years old and in charge of 30 girls, most of whom were older and more experienced in the West End. It was the heyday of the large chorus and the programme included many lavish production numbers. Nervo and Knox, two of the original Crazy Gang, were the stars of this musical, Betty Driver was a feature singer and there was a large cast of speciality acts, comedians and even a ballerina.

We had everything in that show, and it wasn't an easy programme for the dancers. One scene was an authentic replica of Maxim's restaurant, set in the Paris of 1890, and the high spot was an energetic can-can. The costumes were beautiful but the sort a chorus girl dreads with bonnets, feather boas, black stockings, suspender belts and flashy garters. It was only too easy to mislay an item in the frantic panic of a quick change.

The first half of the programme closed with a ballroom scene and for this we wore spectacular crinolines that were so wide they had to be stored in the props room at the side of the stage.

Every night when we made our change, the room would be full of stagehands who just happened to be in there having a quick drag on their fags. The ballet was one of the highlights and I thanked God I wasn't in this because it was my one and only chance to put my feet up during the show.

Experienced ballet dancers had been specially engaged for this presentation. One of them was a very talented girl called Pauline, who never stopped rehearsing and exercising at the barre – it was her whole life. I congratulated her on her dedication and she told me, 'When I go to sleep at night, my last conscious thought is to turn my feet out and try to keep them that way through the night.'

To be a ballet dancer is not just a job, it's a way of life. You could always pick out the ballet girls as they walked through the stage door. After years of training, their feet pointed permanently to a quarter past nine.

For the finale of the show, Nervo and Knox, together with the whole chorus, were dressed as WAAFs, and thanks to the enthusiasm of an overambitious dress designer, we wore authentic air force uniforms. Every day we cursed those uniforms as we struggled with shirts, lisle stockings, collars and ties. We even had to roll up our hair to the standard service length, which ruined it for the next performance because we performed this show twice daily, and it was a long, hard day.

Apart from dancing in all the numbers and supervising the work, I had to collect and pay out the girls' salaries and I was in charge of the insurance cards. Each day I arrived early at the theatre to check that everyone was present. If a girl was ill, it was my job to rearrange the routine. Sometimes, after seeing to all this and working the two performances, I staggered out of the stage door to find an air raid in progress, and then it was a case of getting home the best way I could.

My mother was away touring on ENSA and I was living on my own in Kentish Town and having to shop and cook for myself before getting to the Coliseum by midday. The worries snowballed and it all got too much for me. I lost weight, spots popped out all over my face and I grew jumpy and nervy and teetered on the verge of a breakdown.

Now in my whole life I've never had a major stroke of luck. Whenever I understudied, the leading lady never lost her voice so that I could go on at a moment's notice to tumultuous acclaim. I always miss out on the Lottery and my Premium Bonds are never picked by Ernie, but whenever I've been really down on my luck someone has come along to befriend me, and that's exactly what happened then, just when I needed it most.

My good Samaritans were a family who kept a fish shop in the Brecknock Road not far away in Camden Town. Eva and Olive were sisters, both their husbands were in the army and with the help of their mother they were struggling to keep the business going in the absence of the menfolk.

When she heard that I was ill, their mother rallied round and rushed me off to the doctor, who diagnosed a bad case of overworking and said that I really shouldn't be living alone.

Without a moment's hesitation, Mrs Glackner took me under her wing and brought me back to live with her and her daughters. It was a generous gesture that was typical of the family, who became and remained my friends. My life took a turn for the better. I had company in the home and a well-cooked dinner each day with no housekeeping worries.

Life was certainly easier and so was the food situation – four ration books gave much more scope than one. Eva was a splendid cook and we had the advantage of fish from the shop.

Eva and Olive's mother was a woman of strong character. Before the war her husband had run the fish shop and when he died, Eva's husband Jim had taken over. But Jim was serving with the Eighth Army in Egypt, fighting his way across the Sahara, and at a time of life when most people are happy to sit back and take it easy, she had to start getting up at five o'clock to travel to Billingsgate to buy the fish for the shop. It wasn't easy because she had to compete with hardened businessmen bidding against her for the meagre amount that came into the market.

When I moved into the house I was stuck for a way to address her. 'Mrs Glackner' sounded too formal, and because of the age difference I didn't like to use her first name, but the problem was solved one day when she'd dressed herself up to go out with a friend. She looked so smart and elegant that I told her she looked like a duchess, and 'the Duchess' she became from that day on.

It was Eva and Olive's job to serve in the shop, and although fish wasn't rationed, it was so scarce that long queues of women formed outside, hours before it was due to open. Sometimes when the Duchess returned from market, she only had a couple of boxes of fish to show for all her efforts and then it was a case of 'first come, first served', and many had to go away empty-handed after all the hours of waiting.

Frustration would cause angry words to fly and one day the Duchess, who was also tired, retaliated with, 'For God's sake, I can't feed you all with five fishes. Who do you think I am ... Jesus Christ?'

To combat the food shortage, many weird and hitherto unknown species appeared on the fishmongers' slabs, including whale, which looked like meat but tasted of exceedingly strong fish and once eaten you couldn't get rid of the taste. The aftermath of a whale steak stayed with you for days. A mystery fish called snoek, which everyone pronounced as snook, made a brief and unwelcome appearance. It was grey and soggy-looking, and the first time I saw it I thought that the fishmonger had left his cleaning rag on the counter. It was viewed with the greatest suspicion and only eaten under protest when things got really bad.

Going back to my new home each night, I took the Under-ground train to Camden Town and although it was only about half past nine when I arrived, the station platform was already jam-packed full of people who spent the night there sheltering from the air raids and I had to pick a way carefully over the piles of bedding covering the entire platform. Small babies, children and even the family pets were already tucked down to sleep and were so used to their surroundings that they were oblivious to the noise of the trains rattling in and out, although the adults didn't attempt to get their heads down until the last train had gone through for the night.

Families reserved their positions and I recognised the same

faces when I stepped on to the platform each night. The shelterers got to know me and some of them tried to persuade me to stay there where it was nice and safe. But it wasn't for me, I'm a home bird and I was only too glad to be going back to some friendly company and a welcoming fire.

Even when I left the station I wasn't home and dry. There was a bus to take up the hill and many times I was the only passenger. If there was a bad raid, there'd be no transport and I had to step it out and trudge all the way home. Some nights when the anti-aircraft guns were belting out, I raced round the corner of the road with shrapnel spattering noisily all about. At times like this I kept my eyes firmly fixed on the front door, which I knew Eva would be holding open for me. She knew it was me as soon as she heard the footsteps because there was no one else about even at that early hour, and it was with a sigh of relief that I ran in and shut the door behind me.

The kitchen got hot and steamy as we huddled around the old coke boiler drinking mugs of tea. Eva pulled down the flap so we could get the warmth, and while the noise of the planes, guns and bombs went merry-hell outside, we talked of our hopes and ambitions.

I've always been an optimist and never for an instant did it cross my mind that one of those German planes could put an end to my dreams of the future for once and all. When the doorknob rattled, we knew that Duddles, the family's ginger tom-cat, was signalling his return from the garden. One night there was an urgent note to his rattling. Eva turned off the light before she opened the door and when she switched it on again we saw that Duddles' fur was black and scorched and he had a burn on his back. We all fussed and cosseted our pussy cat hero and after Eva had treated his war wound, she bandaged him and sewed it securely so he couldn't tear it off. It made him look like a mummified cat in the British Museum and I couldn't help laughing, whereupon a hurt expression came over his face. After that, instead of being the terror of the neighbourhood, Duddles refused to go out until it was dark in case he lost face with all the other moggies.

There were nights when the searchlights wheeling around in

the dark night sky picked up an enemy plane in the beams, then curiosity overcame our fear and Eva and I would make for the best vantage point, which was to stand on the lavatory seat with our heads close together as we watched the action from the small window. The planes whirled around trying to escape the probing lights and were like moths caught in a flame.

I was living in a totally feminine world, but so was nearly every other household in wartime Britain. However, I spent so many hours in the theatre that the dressing room became like a second home.

Dressing rooms are allocated according to one's salary or star status. The number of entrances one has to make during a performance is given no consideration whatever, consequently the chorus dressing room was always at the top of the building up several flights of stone steps. While the performance was under way there was a continual panic as the clitter-clatter of the metal taps on shoes beat a frantic tattoo up and down the steps. Girls would scurry down, fumbling to do up their costumes, always dreading the nightmare possibility that they'd be 'off'. Going back they'd have to start undoing the costumes in preparation for the next change, and although panting from their exertions in the last routine, they still found the breath to have the usual moan about the tempo of the band.

The room itself presented a somewhat macabre scene. Girls with heavily made-up faces and exaggerated false eyelashes sprawled about in different stages of nudity, but however chaotic it appeared to be at first glance, it was an organised confusion. It had to be, with 30 girls and their many changes of costume sharing one room.

A long dressing table ran the whole length of the room, backed by a mirror which was lit by the harsh glare of unshaded light bulbs. The table was divided up by the girls themselves into individual places, and once ownership was established each girl kept to her allotted space. If a girl started to spread or encroach, her neighbour could be very caustic. 'Oh, we do need a lot of room, don't we? I suppose it all comes from being brought up in a bloody stately home.'

Each girl would lay her place with a cloth, make-up box, and a large tin of powder and Cremine removing cream, but that was only the beginning. Next came the mascots, pictures of the current boyfriend and good luck telegrams stuck on her portion of the mirror. Gradually the mirror itself became practically obliterated as the girls scrawled phone numbers and messages all over it with sticks of carmine. We got so used to this *Alice Through the Looking Glass* existence that we always spoke to each other through the mirror, it was much easier than turning round and we could see the whole line from there. Any breaks we got during the show would be spent with our legs up on the dressing table to rest them and chatting to each other through the glass.

Strangely enough, in spite of this necessary preoccupation with the mirror, I don't think I ever met a vain girl. Most of them moaned about their looks and only saw their imperfections.

Screams of horror broke out constantly. We were all 'drama queens' and never had common or garden mishaps, they were blown up into calamities and disasters.

'My God! Have you seen my nose! It's just like a prize fighter's,' one girl would shriek, totally ignoring the fact that her beautiful eyes were a constant source of admiration and envy, while another girl I knew spent every available minute banging her hips against the wall in an effort to reduce them because she found they were half an inch broader than the others'.

Although most of the girls at the Coliseum shared a communal dressing room exactly like this at the top of umpteen flights of punishing steps, seven of us had the good fortune to be given a smaller room at stage level. It represented an unusual luxury and this privilege was granted because some of the girls were understudies, others had a couple of lines and I was included as head girl. Living and working together in the narrow confines of that room, we became as close as sisters and knew everything about each other and indeed it was very difficult to keep a secret from one another.

The dressing room was divided into two parts and at one end of the room were Phyllis, Eileen and Lorna.

93

Phyllis was a tall, serene girl with a flawless complexion. She looked more like a society debutante than a chorus girl. She was one who'd been especially engaged to take part in the ballet, in fact she understudied the ballerina. She spent every spare minute with a needle and thread darning the toes of her pink satin ballet shoes and painting them with straw hat lacquer to harden them and give them a longer life, and if she wasn't doing that she was limbering up clutching the back of her chair to do her barre exercise.

Eileen was another girl who you would never have taken for a stage dancer. She was a mousy type who lived in the wilds of some outer London suburb and it must have taken her hours to travel back and forth each day in her little hand-knitted twinset and pearls number. During the run of the show she met and became engaged to a Canadian pilot, and her story had a happy ending because they married and she started a new life in Canada after the war. But that was a long time away in the future and she didn't have that comforting knowledge when he was on 'ops' (operational flights). We all suffered agonies with her, and when he made a welcome return safe and sound we all fell on his neck with relief.

Lorna was something else. She was the perfect example of a self-made lady who knew exactly where she was going. Nothing about her rang true, from the top of her peroxided head to her rather blasé accent. She was a very sophisticated lady indeed and it was hard to tell that she came from the north of England because she had skillfully disguised her accent. It was only now and again that she slipped up and we could detect the northern vowel sounds. At the beginning of the war she'd married into a wealthy Manchester family and because her husband was an officer and away with the army, she'd gone to live in his parents' home, which I imagine was a cut above her own, but when her old man was sent overseas with his regiment Lorna had spread her wings and flown to London.

No picture in khaki decorated Lorna's place on the dressing table. Her husband had served his purpose and now he was well and truly out of sight and out of mind. In fact I don't think he ever saw her again because, like Eileen, she also met a Canadian pilot and this affair became serious. She was eventually divorced and married him.

But before meeting this Canadian we heard the stories of a hundred affairs. I really don't know where she found the time and energy. She was quite frank about her love life and you couldn't dislike her; just the same, she wasn't playing fair. She received the wife's allowance from the army, and her in-laws sent her money each week to help with her living expenses. I'm sure they had no idea what she was doing. They probably imagined that she was on vital war work, and it's true she was doing her level best to keep up the morale of as many Americans and Canadians as she could manage single-handed.

I shared a dressing table at the other end of the room with Vivienne, Betty and Joan.

Betty had made a disastrous wartime marriage and although separated from her husband she'd been left with a small baby to support. Her whole life was dedicated to this purpose, and where the rest of us were always scouring the shops for make-up and clothes, she was buying baby linen and toys. Sometimes she brought the baby to the dressing room and then this poor kid, who spent most of his life in some sort of children's home, was spoiled and fussed over by his honorary aunties. He was fed and clucked over, bathed and held out to pee in the basin and then just when he was having the time of his young life the poor little devil had to go back to the children's home.

Vivienne was also married with a husband overseas in the army, and her marriage was destined to fail as well, but for a very different reason from Lorna's. He came back from the war shell-shocked and a shadow of his former self and their marriage couldn't stand the strain.

Joan was the youngest in the room. She was promptly christened Babe by the rest of us and, like Phyllis and me, was unattached and fancy-free, but ever hopeful that a Prince Charming would come riding along in a white Cadillac to whisk her off to a life of luxury.

There was one other person in our room, our dresser Emmie. Emmie looked as if she'd strayed from the pages of a Charles Dickens' novel. It wasn't hard to imagine her reeling home to

95

some rat-infested hovel with two penn'orth of gin in her. Everything about her was grey, her hair, face, clothes and even her teeth, which were either broken or missing. To quote one of my grandmother's favourite sayings, 'She only wanted one white one to have a full snooker set.'

Emmie was short and squat and I'd bet a pound to a penny that her hips were the same measurement as her height. She had artful squinty eyes which gave her face a furtive expression as if she was permanently up to a bit of no good. Her sparse, frizzy hair was clamped down on either side of her face with heavy metal hairgrips, and when on special occasions it was further tortured by fearsome curlers it was an indication that there was going to be a knees-up back at the 'buildings' after the show.

She was without a doubt the world's most incompetent dresser. There were seven girls in that room having to make nine complicated changes of costume twice daily, and through both performances the room was in total chaos and confusion.

Our current words at the time were 'gala' for the good things in life and 'septic' for anything we viewed with a more jaundiced eye. In times of stress, everything was 'septic'.

All through the two shows we screamed, 'Emmie, where are my septic stockings?' and 'In God's name where have you put my feather boa?' To make matters worse, the other girls, who knew where their own things were, always answered in a bored voice, 'Who knows, darling, but not to worry I've got mine.'

Through all this pandemonium, Emmie remained callously calm and blissfully ignorant of where any article of clothing might be found, and not only was she totally incapable of finding anything, but she couldn't see well enough out of her shifty little boot-button eyes to do up our costumes or thread a needle for any running repairs.

While we were in a state bordering on hysteria, she wandered about the room ineffectually picking up and putting down, serenely oblivious to the curses we hurled at her head. She never took offence at any of 'her girls', and on one occasion when we were all falling over one another in a worse mess than usual, I turned on her. 'My God, Emmie,' I screamed, 'how can we be expected to find anything in this hell hole, if whenever there's an inch of space, you go and put your bloody great hips in it!'

'Now, now, it's lucky I know you don't mean it,' she answered, smiling happily. 'It takes more than that to worry me. It's just like water on a duck's back, it goes in one ear and out the other.'

But with all her failings, we would have fought to keep her because we were 'her girls' and she defended us through thick and thin. Emmie had confidence in us, she thought we were all beautiful as well as talented and was quite convinced that we were the best thing in the show – and that included the stars – and what's more, she didn't hesitate to tell everyone. She also willingly told the most bare-faced lies if she thought it would help any of us, and she was a confidante to our love affairs and a shoulder to cry on in our troubles.

One Sunday a celebrity concert was organised to honour and thank the Battle of Britain pilots at the RAF station at Tangmere. Nervo and Knox were among the many stars who volunteered for this special occasion and they planned to perform the WAAF sketch and take the girls along, not only to appear in the sketch but also to partner the boys at the party after the concert.

We were all thrilled to meet these wartime heroes and it was a very successful evening. It was Tangmere that altered the lives of Eileen and Lorna, because it was here that they both met their respective 'fates'. There was another romance that was started that night too, between a pilot called Johnnie and Jane, one of the dancers from the other dressing room.

The Battle of Britain pilots had captured the imagination and gratitude of the whole country. It was the David and Goliath story brought up to date when a handful of inexperienced young men succeeded against all odds in halting the might of the German Luftwaffe and put an end to Hitler's hopes of invading Britain.

Johnnie and Jane were deeply in love and she went around with stars in her eyes, never knowing when he would turn up at the stage door. There was a popular song at the time, 'He Wears a Pair of Silver Wings', which could have been written for them and Johnnie gave her a brooch of silver wings which she wore with pride.

When friends called backstage, a message was relayed through the Tannoy system connected to the dressing rooms, and Johnnie had successfully charmed the normally dour stage doorkeeper to allow him into the jealously guarded privacy of his cubby hole. Many a night we'd hear Johnnie's voice singing a few bars of 'Silver Wings' through the intercom to let Jane know he'd arrived.

Then one day she came to the theatre with red swollen eyes; Johnnie had been posted missing. Another pilot had seen his Spitfire falling out of control over enemy territory and so, as usual in these circumstances, when nothing was heard he was presumed dead.

Life went on at the theatre and although Jane looked pale and withdrawn she never missed a performance and the rest of us took it for granted that it was yet another wartime tragedy.

Then one day when we were making up for the matinée, the Tannoy was switched on and a familiar voice floated out. The entire cast sat stunned as we heard Johnnie singing 'He Wears a Pair of Silver Wings'. There was a piercing scream from the upper dressing room and I'll never know how Jane didn't break an ankle as she rushed down the steps.

Johnnie's story was that he'd been shot down over France. By incredibly good fortune he had found himself in Maquis country and some of these brave men had taken him to a remote farmhouse where the family had hidden him for several weeks. The French Resistance made arrangements for his escape, and during the hours of darkness he was passed from house to house until he eventually crossed the Spanish border and from there he had to make the long trek to Gibraltar, where he marked time until he was put on a ship to England.

After Tangmere, when the pilots had some free time, they came to the theatre to make up a party to go to the Coconut Grove, a fashionable nightclub in Regent Street.

Emmie was delighted. She'd been sorely disappointed that 'her girls' were 'living the life of old maids', as she put it instead of indulging in a life of wild abandonment. She fondly imagined that we were still in the era of the stage door Johnnies and couldn't understand why we weren't the toast of the town like the legendary Gaiety Girls. If we'd all been kept women dripping in diamonds and furs she would have revelled in it. As far as she was concerned, that was all part and parcel of being on the stage.

When any of the pilots came to the theatre to take out his date Emmie was overjoyed and the favoured girl became her pet. She showed her approval by bringing the privileged one offerings of home-made rice puddings, and that's how we found out that she couldn't cook either. Those puddings were as heavy as lead. They damned near stopped the girl from dancing by anchoring her feet to the floor.

It was a difficult time to find presentable young men for the London stage. The few men we had in our production sported toupees and were well corseted to try and disguise their age, but there was one exception and he was an Australian called George.

None of us knew why George was exempt from conscription because he was only about 30. He was tall dark and handsome and a talented singer and dancer – in fact, all that is required of a juvenile lead – and he was a tremendous asset to the company.

The first impact George made amongst the girls was to cause a few hearts to flutter, but he hadn't been with us long before we became aware that although his admirers were legion, they were all masculine. In his own way, George was one of the most popular boys in town. Night after night the intercom worked overtime requesting George to come to the stage door for phone messages. Interesting parcels were delivered containing delight-ful gifts which he flashed around for all the girls to admire, and the aggravating thing was that his admirers were always generous whereas I always got lumbered with penny-pinching Scrooges.

One night some exotic orchids came by special messenger and another time he showed off some emerald cuff links that he'd just received. It was enough to make a saint green with envy because with boyfriends in the services, most of the girls had little prospect of a date. As we dashed out of the theatre after the last show, the gorgeous American officer waiting at the stage door barely glanced at us; he was there to squire George around the nightspots. There was no doubt that with most of the young men called up, George was in an enviable position in theatreland and he made the most of it.

When the show closed at the Coliseum, he went from one musical to another and was fêted wherever he went. He was the golden boy of show business at the time, but the years went by and after the war when I returned from abroad he had disappeared from the scene and I never heard another word about him. Thirty years elapsed and I was in Australia with my husband. One day I glanced through the theatre news in the Sydney paper and his name jumped out at me from the page. George was appearing in a Sydney theatre production and the report referred to him as 'our own veteran Australian actor'. The lovely George, a veteran? Ah me! Whatever happened to that golden boy? I couldn't bring myself to go and see.

When I least expected it, romance entered my life, and it happened at the theatre.

Just like the rest of us, Nervo and Knox were incarcerated for most of the day in the theatre and it was very much a case of all work and no play. They solved this anti-social problem by having their friends visit them in the 'fun factory'.

As the show settled down into a long run, life was never allowed to get boring because we never knew who we'd meet next. Famous faces came and went, and they didn't confine themselves to Nervo and Knox's dressing room. The Coliseum has a very large stage area and stars from all walks of life could crowd into the wings without interfering with the performance.

Other members of the Crazy Gang, like Bud Flanagan and Charlie Naughton, were regular visitors and were pushed on stage to appear in some of the sketches, much to the delight of the audience. Freddie Mills, the light heavyweight champion, was a frequent visitor, as were all the leading sportsmen of the day. It was like a select club because Nervo and Knox's dresser, Percy, would serve drinks from a salver during the evening performance.

One evening Jimmy Nervo introduced some of the girls to a

group of young men who took us on to a party after the show. A fair young man attached himself to me and introduced himself as Donald Campbell, son of Sir Malcolm Campbell the land speed record holder. From that moment on we were inseparable.

Sunday was my only free day and we always spent it together. After a day out we dined at a Soho restaurant gazing into each other's eyes and afterwards walked hand in hand through the blacked-out streets of London to finish off the evening at a favourite pub. It was the stuff that dreams are made of.

Donald was fascinated by the theatre. Most evenings he stood watching from the wings, waiting to take me on to Murray's Club. Sometimes we visited his father, who had a town flat off Oxford Street. I think Donald went to touch him for some 'readies' because he was always broke and sometimes he was refused entry to Murray's because he hadn't paid his last bill.

He told me he had no plans to follow in his father's footsteps, so I was very surprised in later years when he took up the challenge.

After a few weeks he suggested that we should spend the weekend with some friends of his who had a house near Clacton. 'Come down on Sunday morning,' he said, 'and stay over until Monday.'

Aha, I thought, this is it! Because, quaint and old-fashioned as it must seem today, I was 20 years old and a virgin. In those pill-less days to lose one's virginity wasn't a step to be taken lightly and the consequences if things went wrong, with abortion being illegal, was a much stronger argument against promiscuity than one's conscience or the morals of the day.

However, I decided to take the plunge. I arrived for this romantic weekend to find that Donald's friends' house was the only one occupied for miles around. The place was a ghost town. The residents had left, fearing the anticipated German invasion. The emptiness gave a bleak aspect, and although Donald's friends were charming, the house was cold and draughty, not the background one would have chosen for a seduction.

It was lunchtime when I arrived. A keen east wind blew in from the sea and I was starving hungry. This was a time when

101

food was very scarce. We were all issued with coupons to cover our basic needs, but if you went away for a weekend you had to rely on your hosts to rustle up something. With everybody away and most of the shops closed, all this couple had managed to buy were some faggots, one of the few items sold without coupons. Faggots are quite a delicacy up north but I've always felt that you have to be weaned on them to appreciate their hidden mysteries. As it is, I look on them with the gravest suspicion and if forced to eat them think it's wiser not to enquire about the ingredients.

A depression settled on me. I was wondering if I could make some sort of excuse to leave, and indeed if there would be a train out of this God-forsaken place at that time of day, when Donald suggested that he and I should spend the evening at a country pub a few miles away. The family car had long ago been jacked up for the duration as no petrol was allowed for private motoring, but there were two old bikes in the garage and Donald wheeled them out.

I hadn't ridden for years but it's true what they say, you don't forget, and although we were both a bit out of practice we wobbled our way through the deserted streets and into the peaceful lanes until we came to the pub.

It was a typical 'olde worlde' English country pub, all oak beams and 'mind your head as you go in'. Inside, a blazing log fire extended a warm welcome and for the first time that day I began to thaw out and relax.

'You can always get gin here,' Donald said, bringing me a healthy-looking double. 'The regulars are beer drinkers.'

Spirits were yet another commodity in short supply and landlords were given a monthly ration, so it was a lucky day if you found a pub where the locals' favourite tipple was beer.

I downed the first one pretty smartly and he dashed to get me another. He was eager and I was nervous, and by the end of the evening I'd made quite a dent in the landlord's gin quota.

When 'time' was called, we happily fumbled our way through the blackout curtains draped around the door and immediately found ourselves in the deathly quiet and inky blackness of the country lane. The fresh air, which had been so invigorating on

102

the outward journey, hit me like a bucket of cold water, turning my legs to jelly.

I'd completely forgotten that we had to get back on those blasted bikes and, to make matters worse, at that time it was compulsory for bicycle lamps to be fitted with slatted visors to dim the light, because in the blackout even a small light shone out like a beacon.

A faint glimmer filtered out, casting a pale flickering shadow on the road ahead, and with considerable difficulty I hoisted myself on to the saddle and promptly rode straight into the hedge. Donald roared with laughter as he tried to disentangle me and at last he heaved me back on the bicycle. This time I went all of five yards before I fell off. He still thought it hilariously funny but after I'd managed to fall off another half a dozen times and we'd only gone 50 yards, he began to lose his sense of humour.

As it dawned on him that the romantic weekend was going to turn into a total fiasco, I'm sure the thought of abandoning me to the terrors of the night must have crossed his mind more than once, and we finished up pushing those bikes every inch of the way back, and even that took for ever because I couldn't steer the blasted thing straight either.

The romance was never the same after that, and although I still liked the odd glass of gin, it was a long time before I could be persuaded to get on another bicycle.

Back in London, the air raids began to get severe again and the Civil Defence got busy urging everyone to be on the alert once more.

Most people did a turn at fire-watching in business premises at night for the very good reason that if they were left unchecked, a lot of damage could be done by incendiary bombs and the fires lit the way for the heavy bombers which followed.

One day the London Fire Brigade had the bright idea to organise all the cast at the Coliseum for fire-watching duties and so we dutifully assembled on the roof of the theatre. The instructor warned us that these incendiary bombs were tricky things, you couldn't just chuck a pail of water over them as they were made of phosphorus and would promptly explode, spreading the fire over a wider area.

They were awfully trusting to let Nervo and Knox loose with buckets of water and hoses, and before long all of us, including the firemen, were helpless with laughter as the water sprinkled down on the passers-by walking below in St Martin's Lane. But although we got some fun out of the firemen's lesson, it was very much for real. Not only did we learn how to extinguish these bombs with a thing called a stirrup pump but our enthusiastic instructors had us crawling about on our stomachs rescuing 'bodies' from a smoke-filled hut, and before we finished we were all as black as the ace of spades. With this one elementary lesson the London Fire Brigade entrusted the safety of the Coliseum to us, and it showed a lot more confidence in our firefighting ability than I felt myself.

I had a good look round that roof while I was up there. It was no ordinary one, it was a veritable warren of nooks and crannies all on different levels and I didn't fancy the idea of careering over it in the middle of the night one little bit.

At first the notion of being a national heroine struck me as being very appealing. I have a lively imagination coupled with a tendency to foresee events in the form of newspaper headlines CHORUS GIRL SAVES LONDON COLISEUM. FILM CONTRACT TO FOLLOW ... It was just what I needed to get myself in the public eye. But good sense prevailed and I realised that it was one thing to put out a dummy bomb in broad daylight surrounded by experts, quite another to cope with the real thing in the black of night during an air raid. I made up my mind there and then that nothing was going to entice me up on to that death trap of a roof to grope blindly about for incendiary bombs, and I would have to seek fame and fortune another way.

I never did go up there again, even though small parties of us did have to spend the night guarding the theatre. I tucked myself down in a dressing room, cocked a deaf ear to all the mayhem going on around and hoped for the best. So it's no thanks to me that the London Coliseum still stands where it does today!

We are told that everything we learn in life comes in useful and a couple of years later I was given the opportunity of putting my knowledge of extinguishing fire bombs to the test.

With the hotting up of the air raids, the Fire Service had also got busy in the Brecknock Road. They went round examining all the shops and houses to tighten up safety precautions. Now the Duchess and the two girls didn't live over the fish shop, their home was a few doors away over a hardware store, and during the course of their searchings the firemen came up with the unpleasant discovery that this shop kept a store of paraffin in a large tank under our kitchen. It gave us all a nasty turn when we thought of the nights we had sat in that kitchen during the raids – we might as well have been sitting over a land mine!

The long and short of it was that the premises were declared unsafe for habitation and the Duchess, Eva and Olive were evacuated to Gerrards Cross, where they had relatives.

So there was nothing else for me but to pack my bags and go back to the flat in Kentish Town, which is where I was when the postman called that fateful morning to deliver my call-up papers.

I had a vague feeling that my life was at a crossroad, but I had no idea what I was letting myself in for as I went down the road to get on a bus for Drury Lane to see if they would accept me for ENSA.

9

The Theatre Royal, Drury Lane, had been requisitioned early in the war as the ENSA headquarters for administering and producing all the entertainments required by the giant organisation.

The dressing rooms were the first to go; they were transformed into offices and rehearsal rooms, and then the seats were ripped out of the auditorium and temporary offices sprang up.

As in all government departments, the paperwork had got heavier and heavier until it threatened to take over the whole operation, and by the time I went there the offices had encroached so much that they were spreading over the vast depth of the stage. I suspect it was only the need for some space for auditions and dress rehearsals that stopped the administration from taking over the lot.

What ever can the ghosts of long-dead actors who played there in the days of Charles II have thought of it? Through one door belted the swinging music of a band show, from another drifted the softer strains of a chamber music ensemble, and a straight play would be rehearsing in the next room to a concert party. Performers from every branch of show business met and rubbed shoulders with artistes that they'd never have encountered normally in the course of their careers. Not only were these shows sent out to every area of the British Isles and later to all the war zones, but mini-units played in the air raid shelters and Underground stations which had been taken over by Londoners at the outset of the bombing raids.

Other shows entertained workers in the munition factories during their lunch and tea breaks. These performers had to compete with the constant background noise of chattering, the clatter of knives and forks and the dropping of trays, and to cap it all the factory hooter would often sound in the middle of someone's act. It wasn't the most ideal of conditions, but these modest presentations were the forerunners of the *Workers' Playtime* broadcasts which were a regular feature on the radio and survived long after the war had ended.

Many stars did a stint on ENSA as part of their war effort, but I knew that once accepted I would be in the same position as a conscripted soldier and would have to stay put until the end of the war or when the ENSA authorities saw fit to release me.

I think it was that aspect that depressed me so much as I walked through the cabbages and cauliflowers in Covent Garden market towards the historic old theatre. I carried a small suitcase that held my audition outfit and tap shoes and I sauntered along moodily kicking out at the rotting fruit and vegetables on the pavement.

'Cheer up, darling. It might never happen!' said one of the market porters, and he presented me with a rather battered orange.

I had to smile as he gave me a mock bow. I hadn't seen an orange for months ... perhaps it was a good omen. I'm always on the lookout for good omens. I like to think I'm not superstitious but I always turn my money over and bow to the new moon, a black cat crossing my path has to forecast something good and so does a white horse alone in a field. On the other hand, all the bad luck signs I dismiss as a load of old rubbish. It all comes from being one of the world's optimists but good omen or not, I felt a whole lot better as I came to the theatre and walked along the cloistered pavement that leads to the stage door.

Just as I was about to go in, I came face to face with three musicians from the orchestra at the Coliseum. 'Come and have a beer with us,' one of them invited me.

'I'd love to,' I said. 'A drink would do me a power of good and slip down a treat, but I can't spare the time.'

I told them I'd been called up, and instead of the sympathy which I expected the whole thing struck them as being hilariously

107

funny. The idea that they were free men while I was conscripted set them off into gales of laughter. They fell on each other's necks, and one of them blurted out, 'What sort of a war is this when they're calling up the showgirls?'

'Belt up!' I said, getting more and more irritated at their callous indifference. But they were still laughing as I went through the stage door to get away from them and start a new chapter in my life.

I was directed to a labyrinth of offices under the stage and after I'd checked in and out of half a dozen where my name, age and address and every particular of my past life was duly filed, I began to think I was really under military orders.

At last I was sent to a rehearsal room where an older lady with a dancer's body and an erect posture was waiting to interview me. Her grey hair was classically styled with a centre parting and a knot on the nape of her neck, and it was she who took the dancer's auditions at the 'Lane'. A seedy-looking pianist shuffled into the room with about as much enthusiasm as if he was going to his death, he took the dog-end out of his mouth and balanced it carefully on the open lid of the piano.

'Right,' he said. 'Where are your dots?'

I gave him my tattered and torn copy of 'Bye Bye Blues', the tap dancer's best friend. I knew that any pianist could play it with his eyes shut and it was much safer than taking the chance of him messing up a new and unrehearsed accompaniment.

'Two bars intro and two straight choruses,' I said. He didn't even answer as he took the music and launched into the familiar melody without giving the copy a single glance.

The audition was a piece of cake. ENSA really needed the dancers so it was just a necessary formality. I was sent to join the other dancers rehearsing in the 'pool' from which groups of three or four girls were produced as a sort of pre-packaged mini-chorus line ready to join any show. But before I left the Lane I chucked my copy of 'Bye Bye Blues' in the waste-paper basket. I figured I wouldn't need it again for quite some time.

The address I'd been given was in Covent Garden. I was surprised to discover that the rehearsal room was over a fruit and vegetable wholesaler's in the actual market, I presumed that the constant pounding of the dancers' tap shoes had proved too much for the nerves of the office staff at Drury Lane.

Before I'd climbed halfway up the rickety steps of the warehouse I knew it was the right place because I could hear the rhythmic tattoo as the dancers punished the floor. I even recognised some of the steps. Those who have never tap danced are always surprised to hear that we didn't learn the steps so much by the 'heel, toe, shuffle and hop' method but more by the rhythm of the step. I'd remember a step as 'de dum de dum de da de da, de dum de da de da.'

When I opened the door, the dancers in the large bare room were busy limbering up and practising routines and I saw that some of them had already been formed into small groups. It's always an unsure feeling being the new girl, and I looked round the room to see if there were any faces I recognised, but there wasn't one that I knew. However, my heart lifted when the door opened and a lady I knew very well came in. She was a dance producer – they weren't called choreographers then. It was still the day of a dustman answering to that title, before being elevated to a refuse collector, and no traveller had even heard the word 'commuter'.

Cherry had no idea I was one of the 'fish' in her pool, and after we'd exchanged greetings and had a chat she promised to see what she could do for me. She was as good as her word. After a little while she made her way over to me again.

'Take a look at that girl,' she said, pointing to a strikingly attractive dancer. 'Have a workout together and see how you get on.'

I was a blonde and she a brunette but we were both the same height and build. She told me her name was Margaret Martin but everyone called her Maggie, and by coincidence it was her first day in the pool of dancers. Cherry thought we made a good pair, and instead of putting us with other girls she decided to produce us as a double song-and-dance act.

That was how I first met Maggie. Our dancing lives had followed a similar pattern, we'd both travelled in touring revues and pantomimes and she'd considered herself fortunate when she got into a West End production and was still in a state of shock at being conscripted. Now our paths had crossed and, like it or not, from then on we'd be stuck together as firmly as Siamese twins, working travelling and living together until the end of the war.

So every day we met in the fruit and veg warehouse in Covent Garden to rehearse and work on the two numbers that were required of us and to wait until we were called upon to join a show.

I got so used to the day's routine that it took me by surprise when one morning we were told to report to Geraldo's office in the Lane to join a band show. There was no sign of the famous bandleader, but the lady in charge, a Mrs Simons, told us we were to join a company that had been touring around the service camps for over a year. The show already had a dancing trio consisting of two girls and a man, but Mrs Simons said that although they were good 'wallopers', they lacked a certain style, and the chief purpose of Maggie and I being included was to inject a bit of glamour.

You can imagine that the news and the reason for our arrival didn't go down a bomb with the original act. We were subjected to the sort of looks you could have sprinkled on your fish and chips and had to contend with undercover mutterings of 'West End glamour girls, they won't be able to stand up to the life,' and we even heard 'They've been put in the show because they're girlfriends of Geraldo.' This amused us because we hadn't met the celebrated orchestra leader – and we never did either.

It was the era of the big band shows, which were at the height of their popularity on the variety circuits. The ENSA band shows emulated their style but of necessity on a smaller scale. The whole show was centred on a stage band and the format was for the individual acts to appear in front of it, cabaret style.

The company we joined had eight musicians in the band who were either over-age or unfit for military service, a comedian, a couple of singers, the other dancing act and Maggie and me.

We felt a bit strange joining this well-established company. Most of the others had long ago sorted themselves out into companionable twos and threes like any other group of people

110

who work together for any length of time. We soon cottoned on to the fact that the comedian, who was also the manager of the show, was having an affair with one of the girls in the original dancing act. This particular lady had viewed us both with the evil eye ever since she knew of our inclusion in the company, and from past experience I'd learned that it can be a tricky situation when someone who's not over-keen on you has the confidence of the manager, so Maggie and I prepared to watch our step.

Both Maggie and I had had our fill of touring and had fondly imagined that we'd never have to do it again, but now we were on the road once more and had to get used to the strange new world of the one-night stand. In the theatre it was the wardrobe mistress's job to unpack, iron and give out the costumes and collect and repack them to take on to the next town at the end of the week. But on ENSA it was a daily job and we were on our own. Our first task when we arrived at the camp was to unroll the tap mat and, if the stage was a makeshift affair, we jumped up and down to see if it would take the combined weight of a band and piano as well as dancers.

The pianist's big worry was the state of the piano, sometimes it had to be heard to be believed. On many occasions it had been dragged from the mess especially for the show, where it had been subjected to enthusiastic thumpers belting out choruses and sloshing pints of beer down its strings in an attempt to get the piano as well lubricated as the singers.

The custom was for us all to be invited to the officers' mess for a drink and chat after the performance. Although Maggie and I were a couple of attractive girls, the kind of chorus girl who is popularly portrayed as being 'long in the leg and weak in the head', we had suffered from a shortage of escorts since the outbreak of war. From this scarcity we were thrown into the deep end of the mess and surrounded by a positive surfeit of eager beavers every night. But where I was a success, Maggie was the star attraction. Night after night she had a bevy of ardent young men buzzing around her with foolish expressions on their faces. I'd look across the room and see a three-deep circle of excited enthusiastic officers and know with certainty that

Maggie was in there somewhere as they rushed to and fro to get drinks for her and vied with each other to light her cigarettes.

The show played to camp after camp until it seemed we'd been to every single military establishment in the country. Wherever we went, Maggie's conquests followed her around like a faithful retinue but she took it all in her stride.

The loot just rolled in. It was like Christmas every day of the week as cigarettes, stockings and chocolates mounted up, and she collected enough military badges to stock a government surplus store. It was a pleasure to see it all in action.

This hidden talent didn't exactly endear her to the other ladies in the company, and the crowning blow as far as they were concerned came when we played to an American camp. The commanding officer was completely bowled over and from that day on he turned up wherever we travelled, and he didn't come empty-handed.

With the miserable food rations, Maggie and I were always hungry and, like Oliver Twist, ever on the lookout for something more. This American colonel arrived like Santa Claus each week with a jeep laden with food. There were freshly roasted chickens, whole hams and cartons of tea and sugar. We hadn't seen anything like it in years.

Not only did we eat better than before, but we shared with the company, which improved our image, and sent the surplus home to our grateful relatives.

With the persuasion of a bottle of rye and some cigars, he bribed Arthur, our manager, to allow Maggie and me to travel from date to date in his chauffeured staff car. After years of being packed like sardines in third-class railway compartments, it was no trouble at all getting used to lolling in the back of a well-upholstered limousine. As we rolled through the countryside, stopping for a delicious picnic en route, Maggie and I felt it was the only way to travel.

The rest of the company went by train and crowded coach, and when they saw us bowling up in the staff car with a chauffeur to carry our luggage it almost shattered the uneasy truce we maintained with them.

I don't know what excuse the colonel made to explain his

frequent absences from his camp, but whatever he said it must have worked because he became almost like another member of the company and wherever we went, he came too.

But it all finished with the Allied invasion of Europe. He and his regiment were among the first to go and we never saw or heard of him again.

10

The touring was what I'd dreaded most of all, but I cheered up a little when we learned that our digs, or billets, as ENSA called them, would be found for us. Many of these landladies would never have let rooms to anyone normally, much less to 'theatricals'.

Sometimes we were billeted with women who'd been forced to take in lodgers as part of the war effort. They had no natural inclination or liking for the task and they had no hesitation in letting us know either. But others were fascinated with our jobs; they found show business intriguing and were convinced 'it was a wicked, wicked life upon the stage'.

Maggie and I stayed with a woman just like this on the very first date that we played with the band show on ENSA. We were sent to Margate in Kent. This is the life, I thought. If we're going to places like Margate all the time, this ENSA lark will be a doddle.

The seaside towns on the south coast had been out of bounds since the outbreak of war because the coastline was the first line of defence. Consequently, strict security was enforced and only residents and servicemen were allowed in the area. Patrols were always on the alert for signs of the expected invasion, concrete pillboxes were built at vantage points as permanent lookouts and most of the shore was mined and barricaded with ugly obstructions entwined with masses of barbed wire. So it was an unexpected pleasure to discover that some of the sandy beaches in Margate were free of all this paraphernalia and we could actually walk on the sand and wiggle our toes in the sea.

Maggie and I were billeted in a pleasant semi-detached house with a policeman and his wife. We hardly ever saw Reg because he was always asleep or on duty, but Molly, his young wife, couldn't keep out of our room. She made any excuse to come in and talk. We were bombarded with questions. She was dying to know all about our life ... What did we do in the show? What were the others like in the company? And the thing that appealed to her most was the idea of us meeting 'all those lovely young officers'. She was enthralled by every facet of the whole set-up, but we couldn't satisfy her curiosity about all these eligible young men because it was our first week and we didn't know the strength of it either.

Molly wasn't deterred one little bit. 'If you do meet some young officers this week,' she said, 'why don't you bring them back here? Reg is on nights. We can have a party.'

Now that was a turn-up for the book! We may not have known much about the lifestyle on ENSA yet, but if there was one thing we were both experts on it was landladies. From all our past experiences, Maggie and I knew full well that far from inviting boyfriends in for a jolly party, most of them would have had a conniption if a boy put so much as his big toe through the front door.

When Molly went out of the room Maggie and I had a little chat about her and we came to the conclusion that she must be missing out somewhere along the line. Here she was, married to a fellow who was lucky enough to be living safe and sound in his own home instead of being called up for the forces, she had her own house in an attractive seaside town and yet with all that going for her, she was obviously straining at the leash and raring to go.

There was no travelling involved that week in Margate. We worked locally on the stage of the Dreamland cinema. The conditions were pleasantly deceptive and lulled us into a sense of false security before launching us into the hurly-burly of grim reality. In our innocence we thought that ENSA was always going to be like this; little did we know of the long tiring journeys and tough working schedules that life had in store for us.

On the last night of the week, after Maggie and I had packed the skips, we were invited to have a drink with two lieutenants in the bar on the promenade. When it came to going back to the digs, they tried to persuade us to get in the car and make a night of it. Neither of us had the inclination to go, and although we kept telling them we had to pack and be up early the next morning, they wouldn't take no for an answer. They went so far as to follow us home in the car. 'Come on, girls,' they'd call. 'You don't know what you're missing.'

We ran the last few yards and thankfully closed the door. Molly was waiting and Maggie told her about the eager lieutenants who were still outside the house hooting and making a noise.

We were both upstairs packing our cases when the front door opened and closed, there was a lot of whispering and giggling and we knew Molly had let the men in the house.

'You know, this is ridiculous,' said Maggie, 'but I feel worried and responsible about her.'

However, we decided not to interfere. 'She's a big girl now,' was how we eased our consciences. 'Let's hope they'll be gone by the time her old man gets home.'

We had to get up at the crack of dawn the next morning but Molly had beaten us to it. Even before we left the bedroom we could hear her singing merrily in the kitchen while she prepared the breakfast. She was positively radiant and full of the joys of spring as she went about the household chores. Maggie and I asked no questions but we couldn't help noticing that she looked a whole lot brighter than when we first met her at the beginning of the week.

For some landladies the war shortages were a godsend as a ready excuse to refuse the smallest comfort. It was the reason given for the lack of a fire or why the water was always cold; it was trotted out again and again to explain why we were denied food, light, blankets and indeed anything at all.

Apart from these irritating miseries, we had some very real dangers to contend with, and at one time we always seemed to arrive at a new place in time for a bout of air raids.

In Portsmouth Maggie and I were billeted in digs where there was a permanent lodger who the landlady favoured. He was a middle-aged man with a roving eye and she was plainly quite terrified that it would rove over us. At mealtimes she simpered around him as she piled up his plate with delicacies and it was sickening to see the devoted gaze she gave him.

'She looks as if she's waiting for a pat on the head,' Maggie said, as she served us with a miserable portion.

We were convinced she was giving him our rations to keep up his strength. We hated them both, especially when she refused us our butter and cheese, saying there was a shortage in the town and none was available.

To make matters worse, Portsmouth was being systematically bombed every night of the week. The coach drove us back from the naval barracks into a town raging with fires and we were dropped off at the corner of the street.

'See you tomorrow night, if you make it,' Arthur, the manager, called out as we prepared to go into the dark and cheerless house.

'A fat lot he cares if we're both spattered all over Portsmouth,' Maggie commented.

One night it was extra bad. Searchlights and tracer bullets lit up the sky and bombs were whistling all about us. There wasn't a sound from the rest of the house and we were sure that the landlady and the lodger were having a much better time than us in the Anderson shelter at the bottom of the garden.

'A girl could get killed here,' said Maggie. 'Like it or not, I'm going to join them in the shelter.'

In our panic we got ourselves jammed in the bedroom doorway before sliding and slithering down the stairs and ineffectually protecting our heads with our hands. As terrified as she was, Maggie stopped halfway down the stairs to say, 'You know who we look like? Old Mother Riley!'

Old Mother Riley was a frenzied Irish mother o'mine character made famous on the Music Hall by Arthur Lucan, a dame comic. He dressed in bonnet and shawl and had long skinny arms which appeared to be all angles and elbows as he brandished them in fury at his wayward 'daughter' Kitty, who partnered him in the act.

117

It was true, we were running around in circles as if we both had St Vitus's dance. We rushed to the kitchen door and wrenched at the handle but it wouldn't budge. The landlady had locked it from the outside while she was safely closeted in the shelter with the lodger. For all she cared, we could perish!

Our fear rapidly turned to fury. We made a quick decision that if we were going to die, we weren't going to go with empty stomachs, and as we were alone in the house we'd take advantage of the situation and see what we could find. The first thing we found when we opened the larder door was some butter and cheese ... *our* butter and cheese ration that the landlady had refused us. It made a really tasty snack spread on some biscuits, and the bottle of port we found in the sideboard washed it down a treat.

I think I enjoyed the next morning best of all. The landlady was in no position to make a fuss over the missing butter and cheese, and she looked as if she was going to break a blood vessel with the effort of keeping her mouth shut. Maggie and I figured that it would be Christmas time before she found out about the bottle of port!

One morning that week we met Arthur and his girlfriend walking dispiritedly along the front at nearby Southsea. We were all red-eyed through lack of sleep and Arthur raised a wry smile from the equally tired passers-by when he saw a pleasure boat on the shore. 'Anyone for the *Skylark*?' he cried. 'Who's for a nice trip around the bay and guaranteed to get you back in time for the Blitz?'

In sharp contrast was the week Maggie and I spent in Blandford. We'd had a long journey and didn't arrive until late. The coach bypassed the better part of the town and drove into the old section through mean and miserable areas lined with decaying houses and derelict shops.

My heart sank when we stopped and Arthur said, 'Right, out you get, Maggie and Mary. You're staying at number ten.' It didn't look at all promising. Number 10 was an empty, neglected shop on the corner of a narrow passage and the door to the house was in a dark alcove. We knocked on the grimy door and waited resignedly while bolts were shot and keys turned noisily on the other side. It opened about three inches and a thin white face with a sharp nose peered through the crack.

'We are the girls from ENSA,' Maggie volunteered. It sounded like the opening chorus in a rollicking seaside concert party, but it satisfied the custodian because the door opened to disclose a minute lady of indeterminate age who looked as if she'd drifted out of the last century. Miss Luckett wasn't an inch over five feet tall, she wore her grey hair scraped back in a 'no nonsense' bun and she had something that looked like a lace doily on her head. Her severe black dress and starched white apron were ankle-length and a long chain hung down from her waist, loaded with an assortment of jangling keys. Apart from the 'doily' on her head, the only other frivolity she allowed herself was a white lace collar fastened with a cameo brooch at the throat.

She was so diminutive that Maggie and I looked like Amazon women towering over her and she had to peer up at us through the gold-rimmed spectacles perched on her sharp, beaky nose. She looked so frail and bird-like that I half expected her to twitter, but her voice was soft and hushed as she led us upstairs to show us the rooms.

The first door opened on to a tiny room almost filled by a massive double bed, and we both recoiled at the frightening sight of the amount of glass cases which were stacked on the furniture. Each glass dome covered a stuffed bird and every one was a bird of prey. On the chest of drawers a goggle-eyed owl clutched a mouse in its talons and, further along, a couple of sparrowhawks fought convincingly over a vole. The mantelpiece was chock-a-block with kestrels and harriers, and to crown it all a golden eagle with outstretched wings was balanced precariously on top of the wardrobe.

I wondered if Miss Luckett had gone to an auction sale to buy a stepladder, coughed at the wrong moment and found herself lumbered with this macabre collection. A verse from the 'Pro's Lament' flashed through my mind. The poem describes a performer going on tour for the first time...

> At last he would find a cosy combined that's furnished
> with old fashioned grace,

119

A picture of Randell, a po with no handle and two ruptured ducks in a case.

'Well, that's it,' Maggie whispered. 'I'll never get a wink of sleep with all those glassy eyes staring down at me.'

Miss Luckett opened another door and we reeled back again. The sitting room was filled to bursting point with the most ugly heavy furniture seen outside a museum. It was the sort that was only suitable for the lofty rooms of conservative men's clubs and it must have been built inside the tiny house because there was just no way that anyone could have got it up the stairs. But it wasn't just the furniture, the busy floral wallpaper was almost obscured by the number of pictures in ornate frames. Thick velvet curtains hung over the windows, cutting out the light, and even the mantelpiece was swathed in red plush edged with bobbles.

There wasn't an empty surface in the room. Every shelf and piece of furniture was cluttered up with vases, ornaments, framed photos and souvenirs. The effect was stifling. It was like an overstocked junk shop and I didn't know how I was going to bear it for seven days.

Who could have guessed that this unpromising setting would provide us with the most memorable week of the tour? In the morning when Maggie and I woke up in that taxidermist's dream of a bedroom (we both slept like logs, birds or no birds), we found Miss Luckett standing at the end of the bed with a tray. The tray had an embroidered cloth, fine bone china and a whole pot of tea.

'Breakfast will be served in the parlour in a quarter of an hour,' she said quietly in the manner of a subservient house-maid.

Now Maggie and I were two healthy girls doing an energetic job and we never got our hands on enough to eat. Looking back on that time, the quest for food filled a major part of our lives. I don't mean to suggest we were starving, it was just that we never seemed to get our teeth into a really substantial meal. So that morning when we rolled into the 'parlour', we thought we must be dreaming.

With fondest love
to Marie
from—
Aunt Marie

A party after the show in the Mess

The Brussels portrait
that gave me airs

Matinée at a bomber station

The white tuxedoes were a great success

THE VARSITY THREE

Not only was there a blazing fire in the grate but the large mahogany table locked like an illustration from Mrs Beeton's cookery book. It was a sight to gladden the eyes. We hadn't seen a breakfast like it in years. There were bowls of cereal with cream and sugar. 'Cream,' Maggie sighed contentedly. And when I lifted the cover off the silver chafing dish 'Bacon and eggs,' I triumphed.

It could only be compared to stumbling into Harrods food hall because all these foods were strictly rationed. We hardly ever saw an egg, and a bacon rasher had to be the basis of a main meal.

Although I shall always keep a warm place in my heart for Miss Luckett, she wasn't the sort of lady we could chat to. She had a faraway manner, like an old family retainer who knows her place and keeps to it, so we just thanked her with full mouths and added that it was all very satisfactory.

'The midday meal will be served at one o'clock,' she told us as she quietly left the room.

We had both had our fill of mean landladies who had the perfect excuse with the food shortages to serve us miserable scanty meals. 'Don't you know there's a war on?' became one of the least favourite expressions bandied about and we got sick to death of hearing it.

But now, full of optimism, no one could have been more punctual than Maggie and me as on the dot of one o'clock we came back for the main meal of the day, and we weren't disappointed.

Miss Luckett didn't fail us. It was as though she'd waved a magic wand to fill the table with goodies of every kind. Tureens of steaming soup, meat pies with three or four vegetables, all followed by fruit puddings. It was out of this world. The two of us would have willingly sold our souls for the pleasure of eating like this every week. We literally fell on the meal. Neither of us spoke a word as we put all our energy to the task of serious eating.

It was all too good to be true. We couldn't bear to leave a single crumb, until at last with aching sides, feeling light-headed and almost drunk with food, we heaved ourselves up from the table and collapsed spread-eagled in the velvet chairs in front of the fire.

Miss Luckett slipped into the room. 'Will you take coffee?' she asked. Maggie and I nodded dumbly. We were too full to speak but staunchly determined not to refuse a single mouthful.

The rest of the company suspected that something unusual was afoot, but we didn't let on, and kept this miraculous secret to ourselves.

When we were out shopping in the town with the others or having a beer in the pub, we kept one eye on the clock, and as the hands passed midday, we got more and more preoccupied. We found it hard to concentrate and tended not to listen to the conversation or answer questions put to us. Just before one o'clock, no matter what the circumstances, Maggie would look at me, I'd nod and then we'd jump up and shoot off like greyhounds so that we wouldn't be late for Miss Luckett and her amazing cornucopia of food. I think the others imagined that we'd met two millionaires and were keeping them under wraps, or that we'd realised some other secret fantasy, because in times of adversity and stress we all daydreamed of being rescued from our workaday life of toil and care and whisked away to a world of champagne and caviare.

We didn't tell a solitary soul about our amazing good fortune but we did share it with one other. At every mealtime the smallest mouse I'd ever seen in my life crept out of a hole in the skirting board. While Maggie and I tried to do justice to Miss Luckett's cooking, he sat with nose and whiskers twitching as the appetising smells wafted down from the dining table, and as he was a permanent resident and we were only passing through, we felt it only right to share our bounty with him.

We never found out how she did it; we didn't even try. We just blessed Miss Luckett, received what she provided and were truly thankful.

11

One day Arthur called us together and told us that we were being recalled to London to be specially briefed before going to Scapa Flow, the Royal Navy base in the Orkney Islands.

In London we had to fill in forms and state the nationality of not only our parents but our grandparents as well. I think they took the view that if we had British antecedents we couldn't be all bad and could be trusted not to be spies. The thought crossed my mind that if they went back as far as Dick Turpin, I could be in trouble. After a medical examination, a dentist came to look at our teeth (could they be searching for concealed microfilm?) and he was followed by a hearty 'man from the ministry' who gave us a pep talk stressing the importance of the occasion. It was all rather alarming. I began to wonder what we were getting ourselves into. You would have thought we were trying to join some exclusive club and had to prove our pedigree, instead of going to entertain the navy.

When they judged we were kosher, we caught the train for the extensive journey through England and Scotland. It was autumn and Scotland was at its spectacular best. The bracken was gold and copper-coloured and the mountains in the background were shadowed in a purple haze. Shaggy Highland cattle with horns like the handlebars on an errand boy's bike stood chewing ruminatively as they watched the train rattling through the valleys. The lochs sparkled in the late sunshine while the drifts of heather covered the slopes in a soft mauve carpet. It put me in mind of a calendar that someone had sent me the previous Christmas.

We changed trains at Inverness to go on to Thurso in the far north, from where we should get the boat to the Orkneys.

I forget how long it took to reach the islands but it was definitely too long for me. The sea didn't look particularly rough, but as soon as the boat left the protection of the harbour it got a peculiar motion, rolling continuously from side to side like a drunken sailor. The only way I could keep from throwing up was to find a quiet corner of the boat and sit concentrating like mad, praying that no one would come and talk to me. When we arrived at the quay, I felt rather smug that I hadn't disgraced myself on the bad crossing, until a sailor said jauntily, 'We were lucky today to have a decent trip. Sometimes that stretch of water can get very nasty indeed.'

Kirkwall is the capital of the main island of the Orkneys. It's a small town built of grey stone and it was to be the hub of our universe for the next few months. There was one hotel and a row of shops and in the course of those months I came to know every item in their stock.

The islands were famous for their knitwear, and the local women knitted casually as they walked along chatting to a friend. Without appearing to concentrate, they turned out the most intricately patterned garments, working the traditional designs in multi-coloured wools.

The pride of Kirkwall was its tree. It was just an ordinary tree but it was unique in that it was the only one on the island. It grew in the paved centre of the town, sheltered from the violent winds by the surrounding buildings which enabled it to survive. It was the most famous landmark in Kirkwall. 'Meet you by the tree' was the local equivalent of meeting under the clock at Victoria Station. The only things that grew on the rest of the islands were scrubby bushes and they were gnarled and distorted from being constantly battered by the wind.

Scapa Flow was a natural harbour enclosed by the islands; it was a perfect place for the Royal Navy to use as its base. After the First World War, the German fleet was ordered to surrender at Scapa Flow, but as they steamed into the harbour their admirals directed the men to open the seacocks and scuttle the entire fleet. It was still there, rusting under the waves, while history repeated itself and the two nations were at war with each other again.

The mouth of the harbour was protected against enemy infiltration by a network of booms hidden under the water, which was confidently thought to make it impregnable. But at the beginning of the war, as this boom was opened to let a warship out, a solitary U-boat slipped in and sank the *Royal Oak*. After this shock all security was checked and double-checked, which accounted for the inquisition we were subjected to, I suppose.

The Orkneys had the dubious distinction of having the first enemy bomb of the war dropped on the British Isles. A lone raider jettisoned a bomb and the sole casualty was a rabbit, which occasioned some derisory news coverage and a popular song was written to immortalise this non-event.

The harbour at Scapa Flow always looked dramatically theatrical. Although the great ships were camouflaged with splotches of drab colour, they still made an awesome sight. Destroyers, battleships, cruisers and even an aircraft carrier floated deceptively at peace in a magnificent and impressive display.

Sometimes we gave shows on land in aircraft hangars and NAAFI canteens and at other times we were taken out to the larger vessels. In the rough seas it was a nerve-racking experience to transfer from the small boat that ferried us out to the platform at the base of the ship's ladder. Two sailors would be waiting there and watching as our boat bobbed up and down, swinging towards the ship and then veering away. One minute the boat was alongside the platform, the next it was 20 feet up on the crest of a wave, and then just as quickly it plummeted down until the platform was towering over us. A brawny sailor steadied us as one by one we poised precariously on the side of the heaving boat. He waited until he thought the time was right, and then 'Jump!' he cried, practically hurling us towards the platform, and we had to trust to luck that the other two sailors grabbed us.

The ship's ladder was tall, slippery and continually being pounded by the waves, and when we reached the deck, mussed and bedraggled, we were embarrassed to be piped on board as if it was the Admiral of the Fleet or Royalty who had paid a visit. After this we tried to arrive at the top with some degree of dignity and decorum but it wasn't easy.

An even more hair-raising experience was in store when we went to entertain on an aircraft carrier. The little launch came alongside the colossal vessel, and I should never have looked up because it soared above our heads like a towering skyscraper.

There was no ship's ladder here; instead they lowered a basket type of thing down the side to hoist us all up to the top. As the fragile contraption was winched jerkily up to the deck of the carrier, I had to close my eyes. It was just like being dragged up Beachy Head in a shopping basket. I've never had a head for heights. The spirit is willing, and I tend to forget this minor disability and gaily start to climb a ladder, only to come all over peculiar at the third rung and have to be assisted back to ground level.

The scene in the harbour was always changing. There was a constant coming and going as one ship sailed in and another raised anchor and slowly steamed away. The one resident ship was the *Dunluce Castle*. She was a sort of floating administration office and she was fitted out with a proper theatre with full lighting equipment, curtains and scenery. If one of the ships didn't have the facilities to stage a show, the men were brought over to the *Dunluce Castle*. We did so many performances on that ship, it became like any other touring date.

One day when we went out to give a show, a midget submarine was berthed alongside her. We met the skipper and he invited Maggie and me to go on board.

'How lovely,' I enthused. 'I've always wanted to see over a submarine.'

We climbed down the ladder in the conning tower and looked around. The vessel was absolutely crammed with equipment, machinery and Lord knows what else, and two live torpedoes ran the entire length of the hull. I never have liked or got on well with machinery, and I speak with the authority of one who nearly lost a toe to a rampaging lawnmower, and to preserve my full quota of fingers, the last thing I want for Christmas is a waste-disposal unit.

All the machinery and equipment, to say nothing of the close proximity of the two torpedoes, seemed to close in and I had difficulty in breathing. Panic seized me, my tongue clamped to the roof of my mouth so that I couldn't even cry for help, and it wasn't until Maggie put her hand out to touch some knob on the engine and said 'What's this?' that my voice returned in an agonised high-pitched squeak.

'Don't touch anything!' I shrieked, terrified in case she set the fiendish machine in motion. Once the thought crossed my mind, I became struck with the abject fear that this charming young officer might want to give Maggie and me a real treat and suggest submerging with us inside.

A tremendous pounding began. I fully imagined that my worst fears had been realised and that the engine had started and we were about to dive, until I recognised that it was my own heart hammering away, threatening to choke me.

Oh, the pleasure and relief of climbing out and gulping in great lungsful of fresh air! I'd happily got on board that submarine, eager and enthusiastic to see something new and interesting, only to crawl out a miserable craven coward.

We lived on the outskirts of Kirkwall in three corrugated-iron Nissen huts. One was the girls' dormitory, one was for the fellows and the third was the living and dining quarters.

These huts were pegged down with heavy metal cables against the force of the wind. Sometimes the wind was so fierce that it could support you if you lay back on it, and one night a small hut that was used as a linen store was completely blown away. When we looked out in the morning, only the concrete foundation was left to show where it stood.

The wind never stopped for an instant the whole time we were there. Sometimes it blew gale force and other times a fraction less, but it always raged and at night it howled round the little Nissen huts like a banshee. As Maggie and I walked out of the hostel, we automatically leaned forward at an angle to battle against it. I think if it had dropped suddenly we'd have fallen flat on our faces.

The domestic staff provided by the NAAFI were a bunch of gay boys who had all either been in show business or were dying to get into it and they loved looking after the ENSA parties. The latest catchphrase they had going between them was calling each other 'La Belle'. 'Has anyone seen La Belle Colin?' one of them would ask, and 'Here she comes and every inch a queen. La Belle Sonny.' 'Enter La Belle Barry with the shepherds pie,' another trilled as he bounded out of the kitchen. 'And you couldn't get better at the Savoy. If I tell a lie may I never live to see another sailor.'

I think they were the only ones on Orkney who never wanted to go on leave.

The Royal Navy spoiled Maggie and me something rotten and we loved it. Not for us the usual quick drink and a stale sandwich in the mess, now it was pink gins in the wardroom before sitting down to a beautifully served three-course dinner. We poured pale sherry into our soup navy-style, and after the meal when the decanter of port was ceremoniously passed to the left, we drank the loyal toast seated, according to tradition.

Sometimes Maggie and I were invited to a wardroom on shore and then an escort of naval ratings would arrive at the appointed hour to escort us to the mess. The sailors thought it was all a giggle and vied with each other for the job, and as our little procession left the hostel, all 'Les Belles' NAAFI boys ran after us shouting, 'When you've delivered those two, you can come back for us, sailor!'

We had some marvellous times on Orkney but it wasn't all a bed of roses. We travelled from island to island by drifter. These small craft were similar to tugboats and they served all the islands like a water-borne bus service. When we first arrived I thought it was a pleasant, novel way to travel but then the winter set in and the seas were murder.

One situation recurred so many times that it got to be a running joke in the company. When the seas became too rough, all servicemen would be forbidden to travel by drifter and no boats would go out at all, except for the one used by the ENSA party, and the reason for this was because we didn't come under military orders. We had some frightening experiences. On several occasions we had to climb down to the drifter by an ordinary wooden ladder propped up against the jetty. As the boat tossed about like a cork on the waves beneath, the ladder would slide up and down the wall of the jetty. It took all my courage to set foot on the first rung. One musician fell and broke his arm and he was sent back to London, but the rest of us soldiered on.

The cabin in these boats held about six people comfortably or seven at a squeeze, and as our show had 16 performers it was given to the youngest members to cling to the outside rail, getting soaked to the skin as the waves broke over the deck.

We had a terrible crossing like this to South Ronaldsay and long after we'd arrived my teeth were still chattering. One of the girls contracted jaundice as a result of this pleasure outing and she was sent home as well.

One stormy night we had to drive along a narrow causeway to give a show at an isolated camp. A sentry stopped us as we approached, with the news that in the gale a mine had broken loose in the open sea on the outer side of the road, putting it in imminent danger. 'No vehicles allowed on the causeway tonight,' he said. 'ENSA? All right, I suppose you can go through.'

But on the return journey even we weren't allowed on the road and a launch was sent for us to go back on the inner harbour route.

Down in the tiny cabin the kettle on the hob slid from side to side as the boat tossed about in the wild seas. 'I think a little Nelson's blood is called for here,' said the skipper, pouring out generous tots of rum for us all, and although we had been frozen in the bitter cold we thawed out nicely and then perspired freely in the friendly confines of that little cabin.

Destroyers and battleships cruised into the harbour. We gave shows and made friends and then they sailed away, some not to be heard of again until months later, when listening to the nine o'clock news bulletin, we heard that one of them had sunk with all hands. It was one of my bitterest memories of the war.

At the end of our stint on the islands, as the steamer chugged out to sea, it was dwarfed by the magnificent spectacle of the aircraft carrier HMS *Victorious* steaming majestically into the safety of Scapa Flow.

Like most of the servicemen on Orkney, I was dying to get back to the mainland, especially when we learned that our next assignment was to be in Edinburgh. After the limitations of the village stores in Kirkwall, the splendours of the Prince's Street shops beckoned like a vision of the Promised Land.

All through the long, trying train journey from Thurso, Maggie and I discussed how we were going to spend the money we'd saved, and we planned a campaign for our time in Edinburgh. It was all going to be wonderful, life was on the up and up.

At last the train puffed into the station but no sooner had we set foot on the platform than the area manager ran to meet us. 'Everyone back on the train,' he shouted. 'The orders have been changed. You're all going to Oban and from there you catch a boat to the Isle of Tiree in the outer Hebrides.'

Maggie and I stood on the platform and positively wailed.

'Not to worry,' this cheerful imbecile said, smiling gaily, 'it's only for a week. You'll be back in Edinburgh in time for Christmas.'

Luckily we didn't know at the time that the weather would take a turn for the worse and we'd be marooned on Tiree for the best part of a month with food supplies running out, and to cap it all I was forced to spend my birthday there as well as Christmas.

In Britain during the war the worst form of travel had to be on the trains. They were always packed to suffocation point with servicemen either joining their units or going home on leave. No matter where or when you travelled, the carriages were always crammed with uniformed figures huddled asleep on their kit-bags. It seemed that men were always stationed as far away from their homes as it was possible to get them, and if you were lucky enough to find a seat it was a gala day indeed.

No one, least of all the railway porters, could hazard a guess what time a train would arrive at its destination. We all considered ourselves lucky to be catching one that was at least pointing in the right direction.

The public weren't encouraged to travel. The stations were

plastered with posters bluntly demanding 'Is your journey really necessary?' Just as if anyone in their right mind would endure this particular form of torture if they didn't have to.

But when we joined ENSA we had the benefit of having reserved carriages and we were issued with special luggage labels overprinted with a diagonal red cross to make it easier to identify our baggage. The same labels were used to reserve compartments on the train. Frustrated passengers frantically searching for a seat turned puzzled faces to one another as they read the labels. 'It says here,' we'd hear them say, 'that these carriages are reserved for the ENSAs. Who the devil are they?'

There were so many foreign troops over here at the time I think they imagined we were some strange tribe. Come to think of it, they weren't so far wrong.

As soon as we got in the compartment, a suitcase was upturned to use as a card table and a school of pontoon got under way. Arthur was a fiend at this game but he'd only play if he was banker. He chortled with delight as he scooped in our money but if the bank began to lose he packed in the game. I allowed myself ten shillings, and if I lost that I left the game. It was the only way to stay solvent with Arthur.

Sometimes we travelled by coach and then we always prayed that we'd land a driver who knew the area. Every signpost was taken down in Britain during the national emergency, based on the theory that if spies or parachutists landed or if the enemy invaded they wouldn't be able to find their way around. Sounds more like *Dad's Army* all the time, doesn't it? I don't know if this dastardly plan would have succeeded in confusing the Germans but it worked bloody marvellously for us. We got lost in more places than you can think of if there was the remotest chance of doing so.

One Sunday we were driving from one small town to another in Wales, the driver had no idea of the way and as soon as we left the main road he was completely lost. Round and round we went in ever decreasing circles until eventually we landed up in a village, and as no one had an inkling of where we were, the driver tried to find someone to help him.

That village was deserted. It was like the *Marie Celeste* all

131

over again, there was not a living soul about. It was positively eerie, just as if a giant hand had reached down and plucked every single creature from the land.

Arthur suggested asking for help at the village pub and we all voted that a splendid idea and well worth the trying, but the pub's doors were firmly closed. The driver reminded us that the pubs were not allowed to open in Wales on Sunday. Nevertheless, as we were on the spot we thought it was worth a try to go round to the back door and knock up the landlord to see if he could help.

No sooner had he opened the door than the mystery of the deserted village was solved. Every man jack of them was packed into the back parlour chucking back the beer as if there was no tomorrow.

They were a friendly lot. They invited us into the smoky room to join them in their strictly illegal Sunday tippling, but we had no worries on that score ... the village policeman was there as well.

132

12

You would imagine that having the opportunity to meet all these eligible young men in places where there was a scarcity of female talent, Maggie and I would have the men falling about our feet like ninepins.

It's true that we did cause a pleasant ripple of interest each evening when we walked into the mess; we were well aware of all the eyes flickering over us and taking stock of the two young fillies being let loose amongst them. But most of them looked upon us as a little light relief and some even thought we had been brought in to provide home comforts for officers. If we did meet some really nice boys, it was almost impossible for any romance to flourish because before we got to know each other properly we were off again on our travels.

Whatever the reason, strange as it might seem, neither Maggie nor I met any steadies, let alone got engaged or married.

Maggie kept her faithful retinue who would, transport permitting, follow her from town to town hoping to continue where they had left off the previous week, but if she hadn't given them any encouragement Maggie could be very frigid.

One young officer borrowed a motor bike and drove a hundred miles to see her without an invitation. She came to the door looking frosty and withdrawn and made no attempt to invite him over the doorstep. He stood there squirming with embarrassment as he realised that he'd overplayed his cards, and after hopping about on one leg and then the other he got the message and backed apologetically down the path, never to be seen again.

My most serious beau was a French Canadian doctor named

Paul. He was one of those quiet, intense young men with dark soulful eyes that rested adoringly on me. I suppose my confidence was in need of a boost at the time because I found it very comforting and reassuring. Paul was very serious about me but I was young and flippant and wanted to see a bit more of life before taking the plunge.

When I teased him, his beautiful dark eyes clouded over and looked hurt just like a faithful spaniel's. Sometimes, especially when I was tired and if the digs were awful, I daydreamed and thought, Just supposing I did marry him, after the war I'd be a doctor's wife in Canada and more than likely live in a fine house and own a car. Not many people had their own cars in Britain before the war, so the idea wasn't wholly displeasing.

After years of travelling and living in grotty conditions, it was pleasant to imagine myself being cosseted and having someone to love me and give me the good things in life. But there came a time when we were billeted near his camp in Camberley in Surrey. Paul came to see me every night, he was always there waiting for me after I'd travelled to a service station, done a show, been entertained in the mess and then come back again.

One particular night it suddenly occurred to me that what I really wanted was not to go out with this perfectly nice young man, however much the light of love shone from his eyes. All I longed for was to get my head down for a good night's sleep. It brought it home to me that, feeling like that, I wasn't enthusiastic enough to tear up my roots and go and live on the other side of the world. And car or no car, I wasn't ready to settle down with my knitting as a doctor's wife.

It had been pleasant enough to be put on a pedestal for a short period, but as the dancer said when she painted herself all over with gold paint for a novelty, 'The novelty soon wears off!'

On another occasion we were playing a full week at the garrison theatre in Aldershot when I met up with a boy I already knew. He was the son of performers and they'd rented a country cottage nearby to get away from the air raids, and that week he was on leave from the navy. Now I'd never paid much attention to this boy before, he'd always struck me as being a very

134

ordinary young man with not much going for him. But here he was in naval lieutenant's uniform and everything about him was excitingly different. He was a changed man, full of confidence and personality. All the other girls' eyes lit up when they saw him, but he was only interested in me and I saw him in a whole new light.

David made a big play for me. I met him in the morning and we went for long dreamy walks in the park, we held hands under the table at lunch and at the end of the day when I went to work, he came to the garrison theatre to see the show.

I was completely swept off my feet. This is it, I thought. This is going to be the big romance, the one the women's magazines are always telling us is lying in wait just around the corner.

I walked about in a daze all that week. I was impossible to live with, I got up at the crack of dawn and clattered about, driving all the other girls crazy as I washed and set my hair and got my clothes together before I set out on wings to meet my love. When I got to the theatre in the evening I kept rushing to the peephole in the tabs to make sure he'd arrived, and then I showed off by working myself into the ground.

It was a very exhausting time but love seemed to give me extra energy.

Then, towards the end of the week, David took his uniform to be dry-cleaned and came to see me in his 'civvies'. I'd never seen such a difference! Instead of the dashing hero, an insignificant nobody arrived at the door. It wasn't just that the uniform had made him look handsome and debonair but that without it he'd lost every bit of his sex appeal. Gone was the captivating personality and the winning ways, gone was the romantic air and fascinating manner. Gone ... all gone with the uniform to the cleaners!

We'd been looking forward to the week at Folkestone. The weather was getting warm and if we could muster enough clothing coupons, Maggie and I planned to buy new outfits and show them off by parading up and down on The Leas.

But, to paraphrase Robert Burns, 'How oft the well-laid plans

135

of mice and men go up the spout', because no sooner had we arrived in Folkestone than Maggie caught a really bad bronchial cough and had to be sent home to recuperate. While she was away, I worked on my own, and I don't think the company had been in the town ten minutes before the air raid siren went and the sky filled with enemy bombers. However, Folkestone wasn't their target, the planes were on their way to attack London. Several times a day and during the night the same thing occurred, enemy planes would be sighted, off would go the siren and then we'd hear the sound of the familiar chugging engines as they droned overhead, crossing the coast on their way to bomb London.

I was quite worried about Maggie going back with all this activity starting up again, but she'd been in a bad way and it's at times like that a girl needs her home and a mum to fuss over her.

We all got blasé about the sirens after a few days, and apart from looking up to try and count the number of planes going over, just continued on our way, never bothering to take cover.

I was delighted when Arthur told us that we should be going to Canterbury the following week. Apart from not having to spend all the day travelling, I had another reason for looking forward to going there. A great-aunt of mine was living on the outskirts of the town and, with Maggie in London, I planned to visit her as soon as I'd checked into the digs and put down my suitcases.

My aunt was a Londoner but her son had bought a cottage in a village outside Canterbury shortly before the war, and when the heavy air raids started in London, he evacuated his mother and two unmarried sisters there for the duration.

The village was picturesquely called Thanington Without, and when I asked 'Without what?' I was told it was an old English term for 'outskirts' or 'outside', hence Thanington on the outskirts of Canterbury.

I hadn't known what to expect but when I set eyes on this temporary country home it took my breath away. The cottage was the ideal that most city folk dream of at some time in their lives when they feel like jacking it in and getting away from it all. It huddled close to the ground, protected by a thatched roof,

136

and looked as if it had been there for ever, mellowing over the centuries. The garden was massed with roses and hollyhocks, and the River Stour, which meandered through the village, flowed along the grassy banks at the rear of the cottage. There were ducks resting on the banks and large grey geese honked noisily as they paddled along in the water.

The last time I'd seen my great-aunt Hettie she'd been running a large busy household in London and it was hard to imagine her in these rural surroundings, but as soon as she came to the door I saw that she'd got herself well and truly into her new role. Her face was glowing a healthy pink and she wore a cotton sun bonnet and a gingham frock. It was difficult to believe she'd ever set foot in a town.

She'd taken to the rustic ways whole-heartedly and couldn't wait to conduct me on a tour of the garden, stopping every now and again to tell me the names of the flowers. She showed off her vegetable patch and boasted that her ducks and geese were easily the best in the village.

I could hear chickens scratching and clucking somewhere at the bottom of the garden and Aunt Hettie told me that the original reason for keeping them was to supplement the meat ration, but, she added, unfortunately it hadn't worked out that way.

'Come and help me feed them,' she said, and I followed her down the path to the chicken run, clutching a bowl of some revolting glop that she'd made up for them in the kitchen. As soon as we got to the chicken run, I understood what had gone wrong with the plan to eat them.

'Where are you, Matilda?' Aunt Hettie cooed, and 'How are my little darlings today then?' Next, she introduced me to 'sweet little Emily', but how she recognised it I couldn't begin to understand because they all looked exactly alike to me.

'What do you think of my lovely girls?' she asked me, glowing with pride, for all the world like a mother hen herself. 'Now come and meet my geese.'

Every goose, gander and duck had a name. 'Here come Bess and William,' she said as two geese waddled up the bank. 'Such a happy couple, they adore each other.' I knew then that she was still a Londoner under the gingham frock, and unlike a true countrywoman she'd never be able to kill one of the birds in a month of Sundays.

'It would choke me,' she told me when I asked her. 'It would be just like eating one of my own babies.'

I left this idyllic scene in the late afternoon, promising to return towards the end of the week, then I caught the bus back to Canterbury.

The war seemed a million miles away as I walked up the peaceful streets with the imposing cathedral making a perfect backcloth for the old timbered houses. Strolling along in the mellow evening sunset, I met Jack, a musician in the company, just going out for his usual pint.

'Isn't this a wonderful old town?' he greeted me. 'I suppose you know that it's listed high on the *Baedeker Guide* threat?' I didn't know what he was talking about, so he explained to me.

The *Baedeker Guide* was a German publication which listed all the historic and cultural places in the British Isles for the benefit of tourists, and it was these towns which figured on a German blacklist.

The enemy had an efficient propaganda broadcasting machine which was beamed to Britain from Hamburg, and their most eloquent advocate was an English defector who the listeners in this country christened 'Lord Haw-Haw'. Somehow he captured the public's ear and became compulsive listening. He had an infuriating sardonic 'upper crust' English voice with which he sarcastically lamented our losses and casualties. As no one knew the whereabouts of regiments abroad because of the security risk, he succeeded in causing anxiety among relatives by reporting disasters and hinting that a particular regiment had suffered massive losses.

Lord Haw-Haw's job was to spread gloom and despair, and although the British public tried to turn him into a joke, he couldn't be ignored.

Jack told me that on several of these propaganda broadcasts he'd threatened that all the cities listed in the *Baedeker Guide* would be systematically annihilated by the might of the German Luftwaffe and they would start with Canterbury.

'But it seems very unlikely,' said Jack. 'They're concentrating all their strength on London at the moment.'

What mesmerised people into listening to Lord Haw-Haw's programmes was that you could never be quite sure if he was speaking the truth. Sometimes he came out with some news that hit the papers over here a week or so later, and other times he talked a lot of codswallop. 'What has happened to the *Ark Royal*?' he'd ask in a bored tone of voice, which effectively sowed the seeds of doubt and made his audience wonder if the ship had been sunk or not, and perhaps he knew something that they didn't.

Lord Haw-Haw always finished his broadcasts with a cliff-hanger. 'Tomorrow night I'll tell you all which town will be the next to be bombed into the ground by the superior German Air Force,' he'd boast, and it was this uncertainty which assured him of a regular following and kept the families of men in the forces glued to their sets each night.

But many others who had no relatives in the forces were equally addicted and I had an uncle just like this. He and my aunt lived in Gloucester and soon after the outbreak of war when all the theatres had closed, I went to stay with them.

Uncle Harry and Aunt Ethel were a prosperous couple. They had no children and they lived in a charming house in the best part of town. He was a director of a chain of tobacconists and Ethel was a chiropractor and dietician. She ran her business from the house and very successful she was too.

Hardly anyone could afford to go abroad for holidays in this country before the war; most thought they were fortunate to take a week or fortnight's break. However, being well-heeled with no family, Harry and Ethel regularly went on trips to the Continent, and their last pre-war holiday had been spent on the Rhine in Germany. They'd had a marvellous time and when I first arrived they were still glowing with enthusiasm over the places they'd visited and the people they'd met.

Aunt Ethel couldn't wait to bring out the holiday snaps and at a drop of a hat Uncle Harry launched into his favourite folk song that he'd learned in the *Bier Kellers*. 'I can't believe we're at war with all those nice chaps,' he kept repeating.

139

But as the war hotted up he gradually changed his tune. It was just before Dunkirk, when things couldn't have been worse, and Uncle Harry used to rush downstairs every morning to read the current disasters in the morning newspaper. Disappearing from sight behind the paper, he groaned loudly and at great length when he saw the dismal headlines.

Once, when the news incensed him more than usual, he banged his cup down in the saucer, splashing tea everywhere and choked on his toast. Casting around, his eye lit on me. 'What are we doing about it?' he questioned, as if I had the answer which was eluding the combined brains of our military brass hats. 'Where the Hell is our army? That's what I'd like to know.'

Aunt Ethel and I knew better than to let the word 'Germany' pass our lips, the holiday snaps had long since gone up in smoke on the garden bonfire and all 'those nice chaps' were now 'murderous bloody barbarians', while his fond memories of *Gemütlichkeit* were well and truly forgotten.

In spite of all this, he got himself completely hooked on listening to every word from Lord Haw-Haw. As the hour for the nightly broadcast approached, Uncle Harry kept checking and rechecking his watch, just as if he had a vital appointment to keep on which his life depended. When the time was right, he got up from the armchair slowly and calmly and switched on the set. Then he drew up a dining chair and sat hunched over the radio with his nose about two inches from the speaker, and with head lowered and his chin resting on his chest, he gazed at the wireless as if expecting the hated face to materialise in front of him.

No sooner had the familiar sneering voice come over the air with 'Germany calling, Germany calling...' than a terrible transformation occurred. Uncle Harry's face got redder and redder until he was a truly remarkable purple, then without any warning 'You swine,' he shrieked. 'You bloody unmitigated swine!'

The mocking voice continued impassively and relentlessly: 'Why are you fighting?'

'I'll soon show you why!' screamed Harry.

140

'Soldiers of Britain, put down your guns before it's too late, there's no way you can win this war,' purred Lord Haw-Haw.

It was too much for Harry. 'You filthy Nazi beast,' he thundered, striking the wireless a mighty blow with his clenched fist.

Lord Haw-Haw didn't waver, he went on to enumerate the German victories and predict the dire disasters which would befall the British.

'You lying German bugger!' Harry could take no more and he gave the wireless a good right-hander. 'Take that!' he bellowed. 'And how do you like that?', giving it another wallop to be going on with.

The first time I saw all this carry-on, I was a bit alarmed and looked hastily at Ethel to see how she was taking it.

She sat calmly on the sofa, knitting, and never raised so much as an eyebrow, but when he threatened to smash the set she stirred. 'Harry,' she mildly reproved him. 'Harry, take care now or you'll do yourself a mischief.'

Harry wasn't really a relative, he was my father's best friend and I gave him the courtesy title of 'Uncle'. My father had been born in Cheltenham, which was only a few miles from Gloucester and theirs was a boyhood friendship which had withstood the years in spite of many differences in their lifestyles and personal tastes.

Harry was an opera buff; he had a large and varied collection of operatic records that were his pride and joy, and given half a chance he inflicted them on anyone, whether they liked them or not. My father couldn't bear opera, his taste ran to the tuneful melodies of the current musical comedies and it always amused Harry that when my father visited him, he'd previously prepared himself for the challenge and arrived at the door with a staggering weight of his own favourite records tucked under his arm which he fed to the gramophone non-stop so that Harry didn't get a chance to get in with the arias.

Although their temperaments were completely opposite, Harry and Ethel were very happily married. In spite of the fact that Harry had a fiery temper and was always blowing his top, it was Aunt Ethel who ruled the roost. She was an extremely busy

141

lady. All day long a steady stream of patients came to the surgery for all manner of illnesses. Her work was purely manipulative and she was totally against the use of drugs and wouldn't allow any in the house, even the everyday ones that most of us keep in our medicine cabinets.

One day, without thinking, I complained of a headache. No sooner were the words out of my mouth than Ethel positively leapt at me, and taking hold of my head in a vice-like grip, she wrenched it violently from side to side. 'That'll do the trick,' she confidently told me. 'Now doesn't that feel better?'

'Much better,' I murmured, absolutely terrified to say 'No' in case she had another go.

As soon as I could safely leave the house without attracting attention, I sneaked out to the nearest chemist and bought a bottle of aspirin.

Not surprisingly, Harry with his explosive temper was a martyr to indigestion, but he never learned his lesson, he always came clean, owned up and told Ethel. When he complained of the symptoms, she sighed, went to the cupboard and brought him a charcoal biscuit.

'Indigestion?' she queried. 'With my cooking? Eat this, Harry. It will do you more good than a patent medicine.'

Harry scowled and looked with loathing at this strange new remedy. 'It looks like a blasted dog biscuit,' he grumbled. 'I've got dyspepsia, you know, not distemper.' And when she was safely out of earshot, 'Next thing, she'll have me sitting up to beg for my dinner and woof-woofing for a cup of tea.'

One of his weekly duties was to carve the minuscule wartime Sunday roast. He was hopelessly bad at this chore but equally determined that Ethel shouldn't wrest this traditional husbandly ceremony from him. Like all inefficient workmen, he blamed his tools.

'Look at this knife,' he roared, flourishing it in our faces. 'How can anyone be expected to carve with this blunt instrument? I tell you I could ride bare-arsed to Manchester and back on it and never feel a thing.'

When we sat down to a meal, Ethel saw to it that our diet was plain, healthy and nourishing. I've always thought the phrase 'eat it up, it'll do you good!' is the one thing guaranteed to put a dampener on the keenest appetite, and Ethel always came out with it when she brought one of her nutritious but unexciting meals to the table.

She had a thousand and one reasons why all the tasty foods were no good for us. Vinegar was 'poison' and so we weren't allowed any salad dressing; sugar and white flour were 'arsenic'; while to eat fried food was tantamount to 'asking for a slow and lingering death'.

'What the Hell's this?' Harry asked suspiciously, on being confronted with another of her dull and wholesome dishes.

'Eat it up, Harry,' she encouraged him. 'It's full of vitamins.'

'Bugger the vitamins and for God's sake give me something I can get my teeth into!' he pleaded, but it didn't do him any good. Even though no one had heard of women's lib in those days, Ethel had the upper hand and he didn't stand a chance.

I wasn't sorry when it was time for me to leave. I've always believed in the saying that you can have too much of a good thing.

13

I was interested to hear Jack's story about the *Baedeker* raids but wasn't unduly worried because so many of Lord Haw-Haw's predictions hadn't materialised and we'd all learned to live with rumours and threats of disasters.

I parted with Jack when he disappeared into the pub, and carried on strolling along the sleepy Canterbury streets towards the digs, which were situated at the extreme end of the main road.

As I turned the corner, the evening sunlight was bathing the terrace in a warm apricot glow and I stopped for a moment to admire the view.

The terrace consisted of a row of Georgian houses. The windows had the traditional small square panes and the only decoration was a wrought-iron balcony which ran the entire length of the terrace. The rays of the setting sun caught the panes of glass and caused them to flare brightly as if the houses were bathed in flames.

I think it was the perfect symmetry which made the terrace so pleasing to the eye. I liked the look of the digs and Canterbury was a favourite town so I felt reasonably confident it would be a good week.

We were all in bed when the siren went, and remembering the false alarms at Folkestone the previous week I didn't stir. It was only about a minute later that the first large bombs fell and all hell broke loose.

At a moment like that you can never actually recall getting up. I must have sprung out of bed like a Jack-in-the-box. In London I'd always kept a pair of slacks and sweater by the bed for just such an emergency but I'd become casual since being away. When the landlord and his wife called us down to the cellar, all I could lay my hands on was a coat and some flat walking shoes.

From the furious way that the raid had started, there was no doubt that this was going to be a 'biggie' and when I shot down to the cellar Jack and Arthur were already there, together with Arthur's girlfriend Isobel and the landlady. The other members of the company were scattered in various digs around the town so we had no idea how they were faring.

While the noise outside continued unabated, we huddled together, united by adversity as never before. The landlady lit a candle and I expect my face shone as white as the others in its flickering light.

One of the stories going around at the time was that you never hear the bomb that kills you, although it was hard to find anyone to prove it. I didn't have a lot of confidence in the theory and every time a bomb screamed down I found myself holding my breath until the reverberating *crump* sounded, and with it the knowledge that some other poor soul had copped it. Houses split with sharp resounding cracks just like thunder when a storm is directly overhead and this was followed by a deep rumbling and then a roar as buildings crumbled and collapsed.

Our landlord was an air raid warden and he was on duty outside in all the horror. Every now and again he popped into the house to see how we were coping and on one of these visits he warned us that the planes were sending down showers of incendiary bombs as well as high explosives. Jack and Arthur decided to make regular sorties upstairs to check the premises for these fire bombs and I volunteered to join them. I didn't feel heroic but I found it impossible to sit cowering in the cellar waiting to be annihilated. It felt a whole lot better doing something useful.

Of course I only had myself to worry about in those days. Later when I was married and had the responsibilities and emotional ties of a family, I often wondered if given the same circumstances, I would have been more cautious. As it was, my

145

worst dread during an air raid was that I might lose an arm or leg. In London, where the raids covered a much larger area, I got quite nonchalant and stayed in bed but I always curled up in a tight ball so that if I was unlucky enough to 'buy it' (RAF slang) the whole lot would go.

That night in Canterbury the two men and I walked warily up the stairs. Jack had the stirrup pump and Arthur carried a pail of water and we decided we'd start our inspection at the top of the house and work our way down. We didn't have to look far. As we reached the top landing we saw that an incendiary bomb had crashed through the roof and landed in the linen cupboard and it was burning fiercely.

The principle of the stirrup pump was that one man pumped the water from the bucket while a second man directed the jet on the fire, and it was lucky that I went along too because a third person was needed to keep topping up the bucket.

The first sight of the fire absolutely petrified all three of us and poor Jack, who was doing the pumping, had to stop every so often to throw up. Fear attacks people in different ways. It turned me into a streak of lightning – I was up and down the stairs like one possessed.

The water was in the bathroom on the floor below and all went well until, to my dismay, the tap gave a little cough and spat out a last trickle before drying up altogether. The mains had been hit and the town's water had given out. I saw a vase of flowers on a side table and in desperation I chucked out the flowers, grabbed the vase and ran upstairs with it. Afterwards I realised that there could only have been a cupful of water in that vase.

Surprisingly enough, we had won. The unlikely-looking contraption had actually worked and the fire was out, leaving the linen cupboard a black wet steaming mess. We grinned at each other triumphantly. We were soldiers in arms!

But before we went back to the others in the cellar, Arthur suggested that we'd better check all the bedrooms on the same landing.

He opened the first door and a wall of flame gushed out, sending the three of us reeling backwards. All the time we'd

146

been scoring our piddling little victory over the linen cupboard, the bedroom next to us had been blazing furiously. The noise outside was so mind-bending that it was quite impossible to hear the fire raging only inches away, but it did prove a point the firemen are always trying to din into us, that a closed door can contain a fire for some considerable time.

The room was an inferno and the three of us slithered and fell down the stairs in our haste to warn the others in the cellar to clear out and to be pretty quick about it too. We all burst out of the cellar, scrambled up the stairs to the front door, opened it and stepped out into what was left of Canterbury.

The planes were still unloading their bombs, the night sky was a brilliant yellow, as bright as a sunny summer's day, and the whole world appeared to be on fire. From the terrace I had a clear view over the burning city. The silhouettes of ruined buildings stood out stark and black against the glare of the fires and massive chunks of heavy machinery from a nearby factory were being tossed into the air like shuttlecocks as violent explosions tore the building apart.

I looked at the pretty terrace of houses and felt a pang of pure terror, knowing that Jack, Arthur and I had been on the top landing a minute ago. Not only our house but the whole row was burning furiously and flames were leaping out of every window, putting me in mind of the glorious sunset I'd admired earlier in the day. Even the picket fence was ablaze, and neighbours were pouring out of their front doors carrying a few prized possessions. Air raid wardens were helping out the old folk and others were carrying children, but our landlord was nowhere to be seen.

We had no idea where to go. Automatically we turned away from the town and crossed a footbridge that spanned the old city wall and led into some public gardens, where a warden directed us to a surface shelter.

In London the shelters and underground stations had been made comfortable by adding bunks and cooking facilities because they were in constant use. But no bomb had ever dropped on Canterbury before and I don't think anyone expected it because there were no military or industrial bases to target, and the shelter we stumbled into was black and damp with only a wooden bench to sit on. It soon filled with people who were in the same boat as us. One astute man had the presence of mind to salvage a bottle of whisky, which he generously shared with us all. We were all in a state of shock, shaking violently and numb with cold.

The noise outside continued unabated and the night seemed interminable but at last the bombers flew away and at first light we thankfully staggered out to find Canterbury a mass of rubble, smoke and flame.

As we drifted out into the grey morning, a woman came down to her gate with cups of tea for all. Her house had escaped the destruction and she kept a constant supply going to help the less fortunate.

It was the beginning of summer. The dawn broke early and the day came in hot and sunny – and we knew what it was to be like refugees, feeling lost with nothing in the world and not knowing who to turn to. It was no good asking or worrying people, the Civil Defence was having to prove itself under the most testing of conditions with no previous practical experience. There were hundreds like us, with nothing but the clothes they stood up in, and you couldn't expect men who were occupied with the catastrophe to worry overmuch about those who were alive and had come through unscathed. There were many dead and others still buried under the ruins, while thousands had been injured, so we had come off lightly and were the fortunate ones.

In spite of the appalling chaos, the organisation was at work and some time during the day we were sent to a school which had been taken over as an emergency centre and refuge. There were no facilities but it was a haven to keep the homeless together until something better could be arranged.

The part I hated most was being dirty and unwashed. There was no water in Canterbury and I hadn't even got a comb to tidy my hair. To this day if I'm in circumstances where I'm unable to wash, a terrible feeling of unease comes over me and I remember Canterbury.

After being up all night and wandering the streets since dawn, it felt as if it was halfway through the day at eight o'clock in the morning. Jack asked me to go with him and scout around to see if there was anywhere we could get breakfast.

We walked where we could. Many streets were impassable and unrecognisable with piles of rubble blocking the road, the houses were still burning and gas mains were gushing flames like erupting volcanoes. With no water in the town, the fires were left to burn themselves out but fire brigades from nearby towns were starting to pour in, bringing help and much needed equipment.

Surprisingly, there were buildings and even streets left virtually unmarked by the havoc and the cathedral itself was still standing, towering majestically over the shattered town although most of the beautiful stained glass windows were in smithereens.

Jack and I came to a narrow lane that was completely undamaged. It was amazing to see the prim little shops standing there just as they had the day before, and while we looked a woman came out of a morning coffee shop. The shop was typical of the cafés seen in county towns and cathedral cities, with its dark oak furniture, polished floors and profusion of copper and brass. Jack asked this lady if she could provide us with some breakfast and she invited us in.

Now Jack had had the good sense to dress as soon as the raid started, so he was fully clothed but I was still in pyjamas and coat and by now I was filthy. Sitting there at the gate-legged table in these genteel surroundings, it felt as if I was in the middle of a nightmare. It was like the recurring dream that most people have in one form or another where you're at Buckingham Palace on some state occasion and look down at the crucial moment to discover that your sole article of clothing is a brief and much too short vest.

I relaxed for the first time in hours and let it all wash over me as this angel of mercy brought in tea, toast and marmalade and, wonder of wonders, a boiled egg for each of us.

It would have been heaven to have stayed there for ever while all the babble and confusion went on outside, but Jack and I remembered the others in our party still at the rest centre and asked the café owner if we could send them along too. We felt sure that she had a secret supply of eggs from a local farm.

When the others returned from the café they told Jack and me that she'd given them breakfast but no eggs. She said that she was sorry but she and her husband had given their own ration to two people who'd come in earlier. Sometimes today we're accused of exaggerating the spirit among people during the war years but I look back to that lady with gratitude.

It was fortunate for the homeless that the day was hot and sunny but it seemed endless and we abandoned ourselves to the inevitability of waiting for someone to tell us what to do and where we should spend the night.

The burning town had a strange mirage-like quality as the flames shimmered and wavered through the smoke and dust. Fire engines raced about and ambulances tore back and forth with the dead and injured. Gradually some sort of order emerged. The Salvation Army came to help and the Women's Voluntary Service drove into town with a convoy of catering vans and set one up at the rest centre, where they dispensed an endless supply of free tea and snacks to anyone who asked.

All the company had met up and were lying on a patch of grass by this van when I noticed a woman wearing an ENSA badge in her lapel going up for a cup of tea.

'Hello,' I said. 'Are you on ENSA too?'

She looked round at our dirty bedraggled and underdressed group and did a double-take. 'Don't tell me you're the ENSA show,' she cried, 'I've been looking all over town for you.'

We were soon made very aware that we'd met Madam Vernon, the lady in charge of artistes' welfare on ENSA. As soon as the news of the raid reached London and they realised there was a show billeted in Canterbury, she was sent down to find out if we had survived and if we needed help.

We needed help all right. My first thought was, Thank God. I hope this lady has transport so I can get back to London. All the previous night's bravado was fading. I was at breaking point and ready to start wailing.

Madam Vernon was tall and slim, with iron grey hair. Her back was as inflexible as a ramrod and she had an air of authority which commanded respect. When she gave an order, people automatically shot off like greyhounds from the slips and did what she required of them. She was the ideal lady for the job, a round peg in a round hole, one of those strong characters who reach their full potential in times of trouble and disasters of this magnitude. She took over completely when none of us had a spark of initiative left and came in with all guns blazing. She was like a walking machine that clicked into action, giving out orders left, right and centre. I was only too happy to sit back and let her get on with it.

In no time at all an army truck materialised out of thin air and we climbed in, secure in the knowledge that we were with someone who knew what she was doing. As we drove slowly out of town we could see the full extent of the devastation. It affected me more than the terror of the night before; all the adrenalin had leaked away and tears poured down my cheeks.

The truck passed the terrace of houses that I'd entered so optimistically the previous day. I don't think there was one brick standing on another in the entire row; all that was left of those charming houses was a pile of rubble with a plume of smoke filtering from it and rising up until it merged into the dense black cloud that hung suspended over the whole town.

None of us saw or heard from our landlord again and I have no idea if he survived or not.

The truck humped and bumped its way over the firemen's hoses which were drawing the vital water up from the river. Little knots of survivors sat by the ruins of their homes with their families and pets. They were surrounded by the few precious possessions that they'd managed to save and some had incongruous things like a tennis racquet or a carpet sweeper – perhaps they were the first things that came to hand.

As we reached the outskirts of the town, the road leading in to Canterbury was massed with convoys of fire engines, ambulances and canteen vans all converging in from neighbouring towns. It was like the approaching cavalry thundering in to the rescue at the end of a Western film.

Madam Vernon was taking us to Barham Court, about five miles from Canterbury. Barham Court was a house being converted into an ENSA hostel and due to be opened in the near future. All the stops had been pulled out to get it ready for us in the present emergency. The serene country house with its beautiful garden made a remarkable contrast to the scene we'd just left behind.

Madam Vernon had thought of everything and had come with supplies of spare clothing just in case they were needed. '*Quelle* Heaven' to get out of those filthy pyjamas and the utter bliss of wallowing in a hot bath. She was plainly just getting into her stride. 'You're all to eat a good nourishing supper,' she boomed, 'and then I want everyone of you to have an early night.'

The narrow iron beds which were always such a feature of a NAAFI hostel had never looked so inviting but we didn't have an undisturbed night. The bombers came back to Canterbury and, although we were safe at Barham, we could hear the explosions and see the menacing red glow lighting up the night sky in the distance.

The next morning Madam Vernon still hadn't told us when we were going back to London, but we could see that she was girding herself up for the next item on her agenda. She took over a room in the hostel and called us in one by one while she took our measurements for new clothes, then she drove off to Folkestone to buy all the basic necessities.

Before she left she issued her instructions. 'After breakfast,' she ordered, 'I don't want to hear of any slacking. While I'm away I want you all in the garden for plenty of deep breathing in the fresh air. Everyone will be expected to take some form of stimulating exercise.'

In the few minutes before she left for Folkestone she wasn't idle, she commandeered the telephone and got in touch with headquarters in Drury Lane.

Soon after midday an ENSA van drove into the grounds loaded to the hilt with theatrical skips full of costumes, props and the inevitable tap mat. It was only then that it began to dawn on me that far from returning us to London, this competent and energetic lady would have us all working again by the end of the week.

I couldn't have been more wrong. She had us all back to work that very night!

14

The following week when Maggie returned to the fold she had to put up with a lot of old-fashioned looks and knowing winks.

'Who's a clever girl then?' Arthur remarked, and Isobel put her two penn'orth in with 'You certainly knew what *you* were doing when you went back to London.'

Maggie had left us at Folkestone looking pale and peaky and coughing her heart up while I was hale and hearty, and she came back all bright and breezy to find me a total wreck.

She returned to find a fresh set of costumes, thanks to the indefatigable Madam Vernon, and a spanking new tap mat, and once again we were plunged into another whirl on the touring merry-go-round. ENSA had no intention of giving us any time off after Canterbury, and on the premise that a change is as good as a rest, our location was altered and we were sent to the north of England.

While we were in this part of the country, no Sunday journey by rail seemed to be complete unless it included a change of trains at Crewe. It wasn't just our company that changed there; Crewe station was a seething mass of performers touring with revues or variety bills, all tearing from one platform to another. As we rushed up the stairs to cross the bridge to catch another train in a welter of cases, carrier bags and musical instruments we bumped into pros charging the other way similarly weighed down with luggage. If we had the time, we went into the buffet for a quick cupper and to catch up on all the latest news.

Comics would try and impress other comedians with their success in the previous town and swank of the way they had the audiences rolling in the aisles. One comedian was well known for going through his act gag by gag to anybody who would listen, so much so that whenever his name was mentioned, it was greeted by 'Charlie Cleethorpes? I know his act, I saw it last Sunday on Crewe station.'

Isobel's partner in the act was a girl called Enid who came from a theatrical family like me, and we often saw her dad for a fleeting moment at Crewe. He was on tour with *Snow White and the Seven Dwarves*, and when we met him we had to chat over the heads of the midgets milling around on the platform. One Sunday when it was pouring with rain we saw them all coming along the open platform holding umbrellas, and Enid's dad looked as if he was surrounded by mobile mushrooms.

Another act that we saw running round the station was Terry's juveniles, a well-known children's troupe. You could spot them a mile away because the little girls were all dressed in red blazers and berets. The only trouble here was that the children made the mistake of not buying these clothes from the same shop, with the eye-boggling result that they wore every variation of red from near-orange to dark crimson.

Although both my parents and my aunt had started on the stage as children, I hadn't worked professionally until I left school, but Maggie told me that she'd been in a children's troupe and had started her career quite illegally at the age of ten. Child performers have to be 12 before they're allowed on stage and even then they are required to have a licence issued by the local authority.

Maggie had attended a dancing school run by a Madame Bettina in Piccadilly who regularly supplied children's troupes for pantomimes. One Christmas season she'd booked the troupe into the Theatre Royal Exeter and had applied for permits for 12 little girls, when just before the rehearsals were due to start one child fell ill. Maggie was the only other girl who knew the routines and she was under age and not eligible, but Madame Bettina took a chance. She told Maggie to take the other child's place and to work under her name.

Maggie's never forgotten the name – it was Vicky Lester, the same as the heroine in the film *A Star is Born*. When the producer called the roll call on the first day of rehearsals and came to the name Vicky Lester, there was dead silence until one of the other little girls nudged Maggie and she remembered who she was supposed to be and answered 'Here.'

Her family were Scots and every year they returned to Scotland for their annual holiday. On one of these visits Maggie's mother entered her daughter for the local talent competition and, bursting with maternal pride, she gathered the whole family together to give her some support. Maggie thinks she won the second prize but her mother always insists that she came first, and certainly with all her family in front to applaud her I don't see why not. After the contest the manager of the company offered Maggie a job in the show and she worked there for the rest of the summer and continued like this for every school holiday, working in revue in the summer and pantomime in the winter.

While touring with ENSA, we often stayed in the heart of the country and it was a revelation. Previously my sole contact with the wide open spaces was seeing them flash by the train windows as I hurtled from one town to another on a Sunday. For the first time in my life I had the opportunity to see the countryside and I loved it. I still do, but I wouldn't want to live there because I still think there's no place in the world like London.

I remember once seeing Brendan Behan giving an interview on television. On being asked about his religious beliefs, he replied that he was a daytime atheist but confessed to reverting to staunch Catholicism as soon as it got dark.

I know just what he meant because I feel the same way about the country. It's easy to be sentimental about it when the sun's shining and the birds are singing but it's always comforting to get back to the crowded streets of London before nightfall.

Recently my husband Bernard and I took a country holiday in a remote region of France. We rented an old farmhouse in the middle of nowhere and when we first saw it I flipped. The house was a white-washed gem of a place, completely on its own surrounded by fields and vineyards, and the nearest neighbours were over a mile away. *Quelle* bliss, I thought, to be away from it all, away from the traffic, the petrol fumes and the noise and rush of London.

The weather was beautiful, the scenery was a dream and the local food and wine were delicious. But as soon as it got dark I was finished. I lay in bed rigid with primitive fear. It was shame-making for a grown woman to behave in this fashion but I couldn't close my eyes until my poor husband had gone around the house bolting and wiring up the shutters, and even then I didn't feel myself until the daylight filtered through the wooden slats and the sun rose on a new day.

If forced to live there, I'm sure I'd be hanging out the rowan branches and gathering cloves of garlic to placate the demons of darkness and whatever else is out there with nothing better to do than strike terror in the human breast.

ENSA gradually got more organised and took over large country houses like the one at Barham Court to convert into hostels, and an unusual and varied collection of desirable residences they turned out to be.

One of these hostels was in a village called Potterne a few miles from Devizes and as we drove down the long drive the house looked very imposing from the windows of the coach. I never found out the history of the house but I should imagine that it had been empty for years and we were the first to occupy it for ages because the whole place exuded an air of neglect and decay. The kitchen was a vast stone-flagged room with no modern facilities whatsoever and when the door opened it was like stepping back into the Victorian era. All the equipment was so big, built at the time when labour was cheap and below stairs was packed full of minions.

The arrangement was that when we came in late at night after the show, the NAAFI staff would leave the cocoa ready mixed in saucepans for us to heat. The first night there, we went into this medieval kitchen and were immediately confronted with a swarming mass of cockroaches scuttling about in a mad panic as they tried to get away. I never got used to them, and although I did realise that their one object in life was to get out of the way, I was always nervous that in their blind terror they might take the wrong turning and run towards me.

The entrance hall of this house was panelled in dark oak and had an enormous inglenook fireplace which never saw a fire while we were there. There was a minstrels' gallery running along the far wall with an antiquated organ at one end. The whole place had such a spooky atmosphere that when one of the musicians told me that it was haunted I readily believed him. He said the story was that on certain nights the ghost played the organ at midnight.

No sooner had we girls gone to our dormitory after braving the rigours of the infested kitchen than a wheezing grinding sound started up in the gallery. We all froze where we stood as the music quavered and whined in the heavy silence of the old house. When we plucked up courage to open the door and peer apprehensively down the corridor, a tremendous chord rang out and the organ immediately belted out the Glenn Miller version of 'In the Mood'. A plague on those bandboys!

The previous winter after our island adventures in Orkney and Tiree, we had done a tour of Scotland. One of the most unusual places we had stayed in was a castle in Ecclefechan. Maggie and I got quite carried away with the thought of living in a genuine castle; we visualised the full stately-home scene with tapestries on the walls and saw ourselves retiring to four-poster beds each night. The reality was water seeping down the stone walls, and the iron NAAFI beds did nothing to support the illusion. I don't think either of us felt warm the whole week and although it looked very spectacular from the outside, I've never had the urge to live in a castle again ... not that I've had so many offers.

That was a cold hard winter in Scotland, and to make matters worse, instead of staying in the one location for our usual week, we were constantly on the move. We travelled to all sorts of strange places and played to a positive 'league of nations'.

We lived in flimsy pre-fabricated huts on the site of a coal mine when we worked to Belgian miners and at another camp our audience were Irish labourers. Sometimes we played to the Free French forces and another time it was the Polish contingent, and there was one unforgettable occasion when we were sent to a camp in the heart of the Highlands to entertain a crowd of French Canadian lumberjacks. They were massive men and I don't think they'd ever seen a show in their lives before, because when Maggie and I danced on to the stage, they rose as one man and headed purposefully towards us. Luckily their commanding officer was a bit nippy on his feet and managed to beat them to it, whereupon the show was stopped while he read them the riot act and they all slouched back to their seats and we started again.

The trouble with never spending more than one or two days in one place was that Maggie and I were rapidly running out of clean clothes. There was never enough time to get things washed and dried before we were off to the next place on the itinerary. Then we arrived at the seaside town of Arbroath and were billeted for two nights in a small family hotel on the front. The sea was wild and grey and the rain beat down along the deserted promenade so we had a 'reccy' round the hotel to see what it had to offer.

Years of touring had conditioned us both to always keeping our eyes open and to take advantage of anything life threw in our way. On this occasion while scouting around the hotel we came upon the laundry room conveniently unstaffed and equipped with one of the wonders of the modern world ... a washing machine. That particular model would be a museum piece today but at the time we couldn't have been more delighted if we'd discovered gold.

Back in the bedroom, we flung everything out of the cupboards, emptied the suitcases and got so carried away with this stroke of luck that we stripped off and put every single article we owned into the machine. Who knew when a chance like this would drop in our laps again?

The rain beat against the windows, the wind howled and mountainous waves broke over the promenade, but sitting round the fire without a stitch on, Maggie and I were snug and warm. We wanted nothing more from life than to watch this amazing machine gradually getting through the pile of dirty laundry, and all without us having to put our hands in the water!

Most of the houses that ENSA took over for hostels were abandoned or requisitioned country mansions, and although at first sight they looked inviting, the interiors seldom lived up to expectations. The furniture was strictly army issue and looked rather bizarre in the grandiose settings of elegant drawing rooms; the lofty rooms were difficult to heat in the winter, and the supply of hot water was always a hit-and-miss affair. If by some lucky fluke the water was even remotely warm, the word would go round like wildfire. I remember many occasions when four of five girls would stand in about three inches of tepid bath water, washing down before the supply ran out.

One hostel that we visited over and over again was situated in Frimley Green in Surrey. The Canadian forces were stationed in nearby Camberley, but regiments were constantly moving so we had a new audience every time and all of us looked forward to staying there.

The house was old and comfortable but the main attraction at Frimley was the garden. Acres of lawn stretched out on all sides and the flower beds were a mass of colour, but the feature that made it so special was the truly magnificent lake surrounded by shrubs and woodlands. It was a magic place and we were there in the spring when the wisteria cascaded down the front wall of the house, cloaking it in a riot of purple blossom. Bluebells, crocus and daffodils grew in a dense carpet under the trees around the lake and the rhododendrons were so heavy that the blooms trailed in the water.

We were back there again in the summer to laze away the hot sunny days sunbathing and swimming in the lake, and it was at moments like this I forgot all the hard times and decided that this was the life I so richly deserved.

The last occasion we stayed there was in the summer of 1944; it was the week when we heard on the radio of the D-Day landings when the Allied troops at last made the assault on the Normandy beaches to open the second front. As Maggie and I sat by the lake, a great roar of engines filled the air and then we saw the planes as the whole sky darkened with them. The planes were towing large unwieldy gliders; each one bore the distinctive invasion insignia of three stripes on the wings. These were the reinforcements being flown in to support the initial invasion force and help consolidate their newly won positions. Many of the gliders which flew over our heads that day crashed on landing and the men never got out alive. It was yet another wartime tragedy.

Little did we know at the time that in the space of a few short months, Maggie and I would be over there entertaining those same troops right up in the front line.

15

I stepped on to the boat and looked anxiously out across the Channel. This was to be my first trip abroad, and like millions of others I was dressed in khaki.

Since the day that Maggie and I had watched the planes and gliders flying overhead at Frimley Green, our company had been recalled to Drury Lane to be kitted up and briefed to follow the British Liberation Army in Europe. ENSA prided itself on the motto 'Where the front line troops go, can we be far behind?'

Not only were we in uniform, but we'd been made honorary lieutenants into the bargain. A remarkably quick promotion considering we'd only been in khaki a couple of days, but there was a very good reason. We were about to enter a war zone and it was necessary to wear uniform because if any of us were careless enough to get captured wearing civilian clothes, we ran a considerable risk of being shot as a spy.

So this particular evening, Maggie and I stepped on the boat with the other members of the company, all eager if a little apprehensive to be going to 'foreign parts'. Looking round at the men in the party, I could see that they fancied themselves in their new role as officers, since putting on their uniforms they'd assumed a devil-may-care swagger. They were a little on the old side for genuine soldiers and their physical condition left a lot to be desired – truth to tell, their only exercise up to now had amounted to lifting a glass of beer from the bar of the local pub. They climbed the ship's gangway clutching the oddly shaped cases which held their musical instruments and from which nothing would part them.

The bulk of the luggage, with the skips, was still stacked on the quay waiting to be hoisted up and lowered into the hold and on the very top of the pile I could make out something which resembled a giant sized Swiss roll. It was the tap mat that Maggie and I used in our act and we always liked to check it was there; it was an essential piece of equipment and had accompanied us on all of our travels.

I thought of all the adventures we had shared since Maggie and I had met at Drury Lane and wondered what was in store for us now. We decided the uniforms suited us although they felt strange and gave me the odd feeling that I was wearing stage costume out of doors.

Before the war I'd often dreamed about going to France, but what I'd had in mind was being a first-class passenger on the romantic Golden Arrow train bound for Paris or drifting over the Channel to spend a leisurely weekend at Deauville or Le Touquet. I was an avid reader of the society news and gossip columns in the Sunday newspapers and the lack of money on my part didn't deter me from indulging in these fanciful pipe dreams. What I hadn't bargained for was to make the trip dressed in khaki on board a troopship that was liable to be bombed crossing the Channel. It put the wind up me just to think about being confined to a cabin during a raid, or even worse trapped in a sinking ship.

We had hardly pulled out of Tilbury when a voice boomed through the loudspeaker urging us all to go to the ship's lounge to be given a demonstration on how to put on the life jackets. The voice casually continued: 'In the event of the ship being sunk due to an enemy attack, it will be necessary for you to understand how to use the light attached to the life jacket so that you'll be visible bobbing about in the water and so stand a better chance of rescue' ... or words to that effect.

The blood froze in my veins. I'm one of those characters with a fertile and vivid imagination. It takes just the scent of good news to send my optimistic expectations soaring. I conjure up visions of wildly irrational successes, fantasies of owning Continental villas and dreams of riches to rival Croesus. On the other hand, the smallest hint of misfortune has me predicting dire and fearful disasters of a magnitude unparalleled in history.

No sooner had the announcement been broadcast than courage flew out of the porthole and imagination went to work. I could see the whole frightening scenario in technicolour. It would be Canterbury all over again, only this time when the fire was raging there'd be no air raid shelter to turn to for refuge. I visualised sailors shouting and running on the sloping decks and the ship listing at an impossible angle while the whole boatload of troops slithered down the side.

I remembered the height of the ships in Scapa Flow and doubted that I'd have the courage to jump, and then what? Struggling in the oil-polluted water with not enough lifeboats to go round and fighting over a piece of wood to cling to. Whatever had possessed me to see that film about the sinking of the *Titanic*?

I'm no different today when travelling in a plane. My heart always sinks when the stewardess comes into the cabin with a bright smile to show us how to put on the life jackets just in case we plummet into the ocean. One look down to the sea below is enough to convince me it's a seething mass of man-eating sharks, so I try not to listen. I'm quite sure it's all based on a false premise and it's probably a necessary requirement to appease the airline's insurance companies, because if anyone could find the wind to blow that thing up in a time of panic and terror, I take off my hat to them. For this reason I try to avoid the obvious pitfalls, for instance nothing in the world would induce me to see the film *Jaws* – I'd never be able to go in the sea at Brighton again – and just catching a glimpse of the advertising trailer for *Towering Inferno* had me tearing around the thirtieth floor of a hotel in Johannesburg searching for the nearest fire escape ... just in case!

So when I heard the announcement about the life jacket drill on the boat I looked the other way, hummed a little tune and put my mind to better things, like soft summer days, picnics by the river and rosy-faced children dancing in the meadows. I don't know what Maggie's excuse was but she didn't go to the demonstration either.

It didn't help one bit when the ship left the docks, got as far as the Thames estuary and then called it a day. It anchored in mid-stream surrounded by a forest of masts sticking out of the water, the graveyard of the ships who hadn't made it.

The voice on the loudspeaker, which I was rapidly beginning to hate, informed us that we were to lie at anchor overnight before resuming our journey the following day. On looking back, I presume we were safer there than in the docks, which took the brunt of the bombing, but I didn't see it that way at the time. The speaker pressed on remorselessly: 'As we have an ENSA party on board, I have no doubt that they'll be happy to give us a show in the ship's lounge this evening.'

He may have had no doubts but I had plenty. I doubted that I'd be able to put one leg in front of the other, let alone dance, but actually when it came to it, working made me feel better and in true show business tradition the show went on. By the time we settled down for the night, all fears were forgotten.

It only seemed a few minutes later when we were woken by the wail of the air raid siren and the sound of feet trampling overhead as sailors hurried about the deck. I was sure all my worst premonitions of disaster were about to be fulfilled.

Maggie and I shared a cabin about the size of an average broom cupboard, and in the confined space we both tried to shoot out of the bunks at the same time and got into trouble right away. It was a bit like a Mack Sennett comedy film. Neither of us had the faintest idea how to put on the life jackets. Maggie screamed at me that it was my fault we hadn't gone to the drill, and I blamed her for never being around when things got hot.

'This strap goes through this buckle,' Maggie said. 'Any fool can see that.' Her elbow caught me in the face and made me mad, and then my arm got caught in one of her straps and that infuriated her. If we hadn't been stopped we'd both have been black and blue and permanently interlocked like a Chinese puzzle.

The thing that brought us up short was the familiar throbbing sound of enemy bombers. With straps, buckles and belts dangling uselessly round us, we both shut up like clams and stared at each other, straining to listen as the noise of the engines grew

164

louder. The planes gradually drew nearer until they were directly overhead, and then we breathed again as they passed over and flew on to bomb some other luckless souls.

A lovely Cockney voice broke the tension. 'Anyone for cocoa?' we heard. It wasn't the sort of invitation which we normally went a bundle for but we fell out of that cabin as if we were off to a champagne party. The sailors hooted when they saw the state of our life jackets, especially as Maggie had tried to put hers on feet first, and we happily spent the rest of the night with them, drinking cocoa laced with rum, and made no attempt to return to be cooped up in the broom cupboard.

Some time later I found out that most of the sunken ships surrounding us in the estuary had been destroyed by enemy mines. I'm only grateful I didn't know about this added danger at the time.

Dark threatening clouds and a raw wind greeted us when we landed at a small harbour in France. We had no idea where we were. Most of us didn't care; we were only too happy to have our feet on firm ground once more.

It took ages for us to disembark. Tanks and armoured vehicles rolled slowly out of the bowels of the ship and then, to a great deal of shouting from the sergeants, the troops were marched off and lined up on the quay. They were all weighed down with an unbelievable amount of equipment crammed into back-breaking packs. Nevertheless, they looked very smart as they stood to attention, ignoring the biting wind, as they waited for the order to march off.

In contrast, the sight of our undisciplined raggle-taggle group of improbable soldiers would have broken any sergeant major's heart. With hats at every imaginable angle and scarves protecting our chests, we struggled along the harbour wall in ones and twos, bundled up against the cold, flapping our arms and stamping our feet to get some warmth in them.

The ENSA organisation was already at work. Some trucks were waiting to take us and the luggage to a small village which was to be our first base in France.

The rain started to whip down as Maggie and I climbed into the truck with the others and looked expectantly out of the window to get a view of the country. I was anxious to see the places whose names had become so familiar since the newspapers had exploded with the bombshell of the D-Day landings

The whole of Britain had been following on tenterhooks the sometimes unbearably slow advance of the Allied armies as they battled to and fro.Many people kept large-scale maps of the area on their walls and followed the daily progress of the two armies, methodically copying the positions of the lines from the charts in the newspapers with coloured pins.

Now we saw these villages and towns at first-hand. They had suffered some of the worst hand-to-hand fighting in the war. We had all become used to the bombing at home and the sight of a familiar thoroughfare being made unrecognisable when a local landmark was reduced to a heap of rubble, leaving a space which, like a missing tooth, seemed twice as big. But this was the first time that we'd seen countryside, farmland and even villages and towns which had been used as battlefields.

The driving rain was rapidly turning the landscape into a morass of mud with abandoned instruments of war sinking in the mire. Shattered and broken trees stood starkly in the barren fields. The stumps of their dead branches reminded me of the amputated limbs of men in the army hospitals. Bomb craters filled up with rain, and as far as the eye could see, the countryside resembled one enormous scrapyard filled with the debris of armoured vehicles and planes. The long gun barrels on the tanks tilted at impossible angles, some pointing skywards and others drooping in the mud, and many had gaping holes in the bodywork. There was a wing of a plane here and a tail there, while a piece of framework flapped noisily where it was caught in a branch of a tree. I recognised the mark of the black swastika on some, and others bore the ringed emblem of the RAF, and two were locked together in a deadly embrace.

The most chilling sight of all was the newly dug graves of the men killed in action. They were buried where they had fallen; the mounds of earth were still fresh. Some were identified with a German helmet and others with a British tin hat. We were told that later the bodies would be transferred to the war cemeteries.

Our truck drove on, passing endless convoys of tanks and

armoured vehicles all heading for the fighting line. We had to slow down behind the columns of the PBI (the poor bloody infantry) marching with their nailed boots metallically striking the road in unison, and as they marched they whistled and sang bawdy songs to help them along. When they saw the girls in our truck, they shouted rude remarks and some wit called out that we'd taken the wrong bus, we needed the number 59 for Piccadilly.

It was clear that the villages, although badly scarred, were quickly getting back to some sort of normality. Among the ruins the shops were beginning to open and black-dressed women were buying long baguettes. Small children jumped up and down excitedly as the tanks rumbled through towards the front line, which no doubt the local populace was relieved to know was getting further away all the time.

There hardly seemed to be a habitable house standing but suddenly the truck drove off the main road and took a side turning into a narrow lane. At the end of it was a charming house with wooden shutters which was to be our first base.

It could easily have been mistaken for a peaceful retreat if it were not for the surrounding fields, and indeed all of the immediate countryside, which grew a macabre crop. At regular intervals in the ground were hundreds of wooden signs printed with a skull and crossbones all bearing the warning '*Achtung Minen*', and there were more notices which impressed that it was *Verboten* to walk off the road. I believed them, and there was nothing in this world which could have persuaded me to put so much as a big toe on the grass verge.

The Germans had obviously had to leave in a hurry, because the notices hadn't been put there for our benefit. We saw just how quickly they'd left when we went inside the house. The walls were still hung with notices in German script and when we went upstairs to the bedrooms, the lockers beside the beds and the walls were almost covered with pin-ups, the Germans' answer to Betty Grable. They looked a chubby lot to us, and as one chorus boy I knew would have described them, 'all bum and bust with a sudden rush of teeth to the front'.

We learned that the villa had been used as headquarters for

167

senior officers of the Luftwaffe and that Hermann Goering himself had often visited it when he arrived to urge his air force to put more effort into the Blitz on Britain. I liked to think of him gazing longingly across the English Channel, that narrow strip of water which proved to be such an insurmountable barrier to all his plans.

There was a pretty little stream running against the back wall of the house, absolutely covered with what I presumed to be a fine show of water lilies. Imagine my horror to discover that what I'd fondly imagined to be white flowers was in fact a tangled mass of toilet paper. The sewage system at the villa was quite uncomplicated. You pulled the flush in the lavatory and everything shot straight out into the babbling brook. God alone knows what it was like in the warm weather. It just goes to show how much I knew about gardening at the time, to even imagine that water lilies were in full flower at the beginning of winter.

The local idea of sanitation came as a nasty shock. I was prepared for the much publicised *pissoirs* but not for some of the other ancient relics of a bygone age.

The company patronised the *estaminet* of a formidable widowed lady in the nearby village. One day when I had to ask Madame for the *toilette*, she showed me into a smelly old shed which appeared to have nothing in it for what I had in mind. I was absolutely bewildered and came back to tell the fellows from the show about it and to see if anyone could communicate with her better than me.

'Sweeties,' I said, 'there's nothing in that shed but a hole in the ground.'

It was my first experience of what one of our chaps described as the 'Jaffa squat' and which, once seen, I avoided like the plague in future.

The one big mate that Maggie and I had made in the company was the pianist, Ronnie. He was a little older than us but he was classified as unfit because he was lame in one foot. He was a super pianist and we went round together in a threesome, and back in England we tried to arrange it so we shared digs.

Ronnie was a Yorkshire lad and he'd never lost his accent, which tended to grow broader in times of stress or when he'd had a couple. One day we had a beer in a bar and Ronnie trotted off to the lavatory. When he came back to the table he was slightly pink around the ears.

'By 'eck,' he said. 'Some old girl nearly put me off my stroke. While I was in there having a pee she came in with her dusters and started polishing the brasswork.'

It wasn't only the small towns which held surprises like this either. When we got to Brussels and stayed in a large hotel on the Boulevarde Adolph Max, one day I left the dining room to go to the loo and the first thing I saw when I opened the door was a line of men's backs. I shot out like a dog out of trap one, quite sure I'd stumbled into the Gents by mistake, but it was a communal affair and, to make things even more tricky, it was necessary to pass this row of busy men to reach the cabinet for the ladies. Then, if by some unlucky chance it was engaged, you had to go out and run the gauntlet a second time. After all, it was hardly the place to hang around making polite conversation. But it's surprising what you can get used to. In no time at all I thought so little of it that if one of the fellows from the show was in the loo, I found myself chatting quite casually to him before passing on to the Ladies.

When we travelled on the roads we became accustomed to the sight of a whole battalion of men lined up with backs to the road. They had 'fallen out' but were unable to stray because of the minefields.

It was difficult for us girls when coming back from a camp, especially after a good party. The rule was 'boys to the side of the road' and 'girls at the back of the truck', and hope to High Heaven that no oncoming traffic would pick us up in their headlights.

After one particularly hectic night when we stopped the truck on the way home, Isobel lay down in the road and moaned, 'Leave me here to die!' I was quite prepared to do as she asked but the others insisted and we picked her up and shovelled her feet first back in the truck.

The appearance of an ENSA show with girls was an ideal excuse to throw a party, and as soon as they knew we were on the way, the sergeants and officers saved their food and drink ration. We were fêted and coaxed to have 'just one more' wherever we went, and sometimes it was difficult to keep an even keel, especially as in our party there were eleven fellows to five girls.

You can imagine that in the mess we were five very busy ladies. We danced with the officers and listened to all their troubles, we admired the photographs of their girlfriends, wives and children. Sometimes we met a gorgeous piece of work and at other times we fended off unwanted admirers. It was all part of the job.

The blokes in our show had it much easier than us. They could relax with a drink and sit chatting with no pressures on them at all.

Eleven men with five girls may sound like an ideal arrangement as far as the girls were concerned, but most of the men could hardly be classified as love's young dream – the young and able were all in the armed forces. However, one might take it for granted that working in tough conditions, the girls would be cosseted and cherished by the men. Forget it! It was strictly a working arrangement and it was a case of everyone for himself.

The big pitfall a girl had to watch out for in a situation like this was letting the men see she could do anything in the way of sewing or any of the other domestic arts. A time would come in every show when one of the men would sidle up with a 'little boy lost' expression on his face. Woe betide the girl who imagined he was after her body, because the big approach would be, 'Darling, there's a button off my jacket. Could you be an angel and sew it on for me?'

An experienced girl would recognise this at once as the 'try on' or 'throwing his hat in' routine, and if you fell for this you'd have a job for life as unofficial wardrobe mistress and Chinese laundrymaid rolled into one. The best answer to give was, 'Sweetie, nothing would give me greater pleasure, but I can't even thread a needle, let alone sew a button on.' Then, before he could draw breath, it was wise to get in with, 'And don't ask me to do your laundry because I haven't washed my own clothes yet and I can't find a clean rag to put on my back.'

He knew where he was then, but if he was the persistent type,

170

as most of them were, he'd try it on another girl, and if by some lucky chance he was fortunate enough to meet a 'Little Sister Suzy', she'd be saddled with a never ending chore. While he was down at the pub chatting up the local talent, she'd be back at the digs sewing on his buttons and washing out his rotten socks.

16

We nicknamed the house 'Goering's Villa' and from there we started working in the Normandy area, but the Allies surged forward and we soon found ourselves in the Pas de Calais region. It was the beginning of a long cold winter and the weather was appalling. We could never get warm because there wasn't much in the form of heating indoors and we spent hours and hours travelling around the countryside in freezing rain.

We never knew where we'd lay the tap mat next. Sometimes it was the NAAFI canteen, sometimes the army took over a local hall or cinema and at other times it rested precariously on a platform hastily erected on wooden trestles.

As soon as we arrived at the camp there was always a race to snaffle the best make-up place and next we searched the walls to see if we could find some nails to hang the costumes on. Then we unpacked the skips, ironed our costumes if it was possible, and blancoed our tap shoes.

Before we got down to the business of putting on make-up, we had to 'wet-white' our legs. 'Wet-white' was a misnomer for the tan-coloured leg make-up we used; fishnet tights were an unrealised dream at that time. It was a messy job and it had to be washed off at the end of the evening if we could beg some hot water from some kind orderly. Due to a wartime shortage of glycerine the 'wet-white' always chapped our legs, but we persevered with it. We all took a tremendous pride in our performance and tried to work every night as if we were at the Palladium.

A chorus girl is trained rather like a soldier; she's expected to carry on dancing under any conditions, however traumatic.

Once I was in a show when a sandbag being used as a weight fell from the flies on two of the girls dancing in the line on-stage below. It stunned them both and they fell down, completely out for the count. The rest of the girls immediately masked them, respaced the line and without missing a beat continued with the routine until the curtain fell.

On ENSA, stages collapsed, the lights blacked out, guns blazed away and bombs fell, but Maggie and I carried on dancing. Once when we were in Dover working in the open air, the town was shelled from the enemy-occupied coast across the Channel. Maggie and I were on-stage when the warning went out for the men to put on their tin hats because of the danger of flying shrapnel. There was a terrific scuffling under the seats while they found the hats and obeyed the order, but nobody seemed to think it was at all incongruous that Maggie and I continued to dance on the open stage in our flimsies.

When we gave shows at the Battle of Britain airfields, we lost count of the number of times that the alarm bell sounded for the men to 'scramble'. All the wooden benches would clatter to the ground as the fighter pilots and ground crews made a mad rush from the hall, and then we'd hear the planes taking off to intercept the enemy. We always carried on and soon learned to be prepared for anything.

Later in the evening it was always a harrowing time when the planes were counted when they returned and very often there would be some missing. At these times one was very aware of the personal war of the fighter pilots; each man was on his own, sometimes against overwhelming odds.

Just as we'd all got accustomed to the bomb damage at home, so now the sights which had so appalled us when we first arrived quickly became part and parcel of the scenery. As the truck drove us to a different venue each evening, we hardly gave a second glance to the places where some of the most decisive battles of the war had been resolved.

But Calais was a constant source of fascination. As we bypassed the outskirts of the town en route for the evening's performance, we all pressed our noses to the windows to gaze at this defiant pocket of German resistance. This small enclave had been cut off from the retreating divisions of their fellow countrymen and left isolated but pinned down with the British Liberation Army on one side and the sea on the other.

Driving along the coast road, it was difficult to recognise on which side of the Channel we were travelling. The anti-invasion barricades were identical to those at home, the self-same barbed-wire barricades lay coiled on the beaches and the concrete pillboxes facing out to sea could have been the ones we'd seen at Margate.

The cross-Channel guns now stood muted, their enormous barrels thrust out from their camouflaged positions in the cliffs pointing menacingly towards the coast of England. Maggie was sure they were the ones that had shelled us in Dover and I was certainly glad that I hadn't known how big they were at the time.

Further inland we saw the sites of the unmanned rocket planes which were the last secret weapons the enemy had launched against the south of England and they were quite terrifying. These weapons were called the V1 and the V2.

The V2 was a hellish invention which hurtled from a launching pad and when it had exhausted its fuel, it fell and exploded on contact with absolutely no warning, the main intention being to terrorise and kill indiscriminately wherever it landed.

But the V1 was a different kettle of fish altogether. It was a much more fiendish weapon because it relied heavily on the element of suspense. It came over chugging noisily and then suddenly when the engine cut out it dropped and exploded. If one was heard in a crowded street, everyone walking along assumed a wary and apprehensive expression as they cocked their ears and waited for the engine to stop and the bomb to explode.

The safest and best thing to do if you were caught in an emergency like this was to throw yourself flat on the ground to counteract the effect of the blast. But there is something about the British character that impels the ordinary man in the street to safeguard his dignity at all costs, so that sort of evasive action was left to the very last minute. People could be seen walking bravely along with a look of total abstraction on their faces as they tried to judge which would be the right moment, if any, to abandon the stiff-upper-lip attitude and submit themselves to the humiliation of falling flat on their faces on the pavement. There was quite an art in making this vital decision. Imagine the embarrassment if you misjudged the instant and hurled yourself into the gutter, only to hear the V1 chugging on its way while you had to get up and dust yourself down, smiling sheepishly at the supercilious smirks on the clever Dicks who had timed it better and were casually continuing with their shopping.

Although we were in uniform, we weren't military personnel, we were just a band of 'chocolate soldiers', but we were privileged to witness sights that no other civilians saw. We drove past the invasion beaches where the Allied armies had landed on D-Day and it was a grim thought that for so many that landing represented their first and only view of France. The debris of battle was settling down into the sand and even after so short a period it was hard to imagine the violence. It all looked so peaceful with the waves gently lapping the shore and the seagulls wheeling lazily overhead.

Although I had always loathed the idea of wearing a uniform, I was grateful for it now. We'd been issued with a battledress jacket and trousers, a walking-out uniform for 'best', together with an overcoat and hat, and it certainly simplified life. For one thing there was so much less to pack, and it was goodbye to the woman's eternal worry of 'whatever shall I wear today?' Now the only clothes problem was to see we had a clean shirt every day.

When we'd first been issued with the uniforms at Drury Lane, Maggie and I had been instantly overcome with the novelty of them and we couldn't wait to put them on and career round to show off to our friends at the Café Anglais.

The Café Anglais was in Leicester Square (alas, it's no longer with us). It was more like a bar in a hotel than a pub and for some reason it had been appropriated by the pros as their own. Generally at lunchtime the place was bursting at the seams with performers buttonholing anyone they could get hold of, to describe exactly how they'd 'torn 'em up' on their last date. Nobody paid any attention, they were all much too busy waiting for a lull in the conversation so that they could get a word in edge ways to tell of their own triumphs in some piddling little town that no one in their right mind would be seen dead in.

'Meet you in the Café Anglais!' or 'Twelve o'clock in the Anglais, don't be late!' was the way we usually parted from our friends, so Maggie and I knew it was exactly the right place to parade our new image for the most gratifying effect. Mind you, our friends were all terribly casual, and ten to one, after making a positive promise to meet, they wouldn't turn up at all.

We chose the right moment when the place was packed to make a suitably dramatic entrance 'Ta ra! Ta ra!' we announced ringingly to all and sundry, and we were delighted to see we'd achieved the desired effect and caused a stir.

'Oops, duckies,' said one of the gay boys. 'Don't tell me there's an audition for *Soldiers in Skirts*!'

'Cheeky,' Maggie answered him. 'We know we don't look like real ATS girls, but we certainly don't look like fellers.'

Truth to tell, we could have easily been mistaken for showgirls who'd just come off-stage from a military number, because unlike the women in the services who had to keep their hair off their collars, ours still hung down our backs. We were also lucky enough to have a well-cut uniform more like an officer's and a much more flattering hat. I really fancied myself in it, although I wasn't sure that khaki was exactly my colour, but you can't have everything in this cruel world!

Everyone tried on our hats, including the boys, and then they had the jackets off our backs and primped around in them. They cracked all the tired old gags about girls in the front line, and one of them said that if we were caught by the enemy and rape was inevitable, we should lie back and enjoy it.

They all fought to buy us drinks and Maggie and I revelled in being the centre of all this attention. The accepted drink at the Café Anglais was a light ale. None of us had much money and we knew if somebody felt flush enough to push the boat out, he wouldn't get stung too much.

We eventually left in an aura of bonhomie and light ale. 'See you tomorrow, twelve o'clock at the Anglais,' they all shouted. 'Right,' we promised. 'We'll be there!' But something else turned up and we couldn't make it.

Gradually, as the Allied armies moved forward, our territory was extended and we worked in other areas, following up as the forces progressed into Belgium and eventually to Holland. There seemed to be no set pattern to the itinerary; one week we'd be in France, then maybe two in Belgium and then we'd be sent back to France before going on to Holland.

By now we'd progressed to travelling about in a coach and when we were moving to a new location and the props and personal luggage were packed, the last item to take on board was the box which contained our food rations. They were the usual army rations, tins and tins of corned beef, dried eggs and milk and packets of tea.

We were always relieved when the catering staff were NAAFI boys; at least they went out of their way to make some imaginative meals out of these uninspiring ingredients and tried very hard to get some variety into the menus. Other times we weren't so lucky and the catering staff would be into the black market and flogging most of the rations out of the kitchen door and serving up the Bully beef cold and unappetising straight from the tin.

Everyone was involved in the black market in one form or another. We found that being honorary officers entitled us to some 'perks', one of them being that we got a booze allowance which cost us very little. I think we collected a bottle of gin, whisky and brandy as well as bottles of wine each month, and although the gin found a very good home with me, I've never cared for whisky or brandy, and here we were in countries full of people who had money but no goods, There was no shortage of willing and eager customers. We didn't have to look for them, as soon as we arrived in town we were approached in the street by the locals, who were dying to buy anything they could lay their hands on. If I could have packed in drinking the gin I might have been a rich woman today, but you have to have some vices in this sinful life!

Our rations didn't run to fresh vegetables, fruit or eggs, which had to be bought locally wherever we lived, and needless to say it was exactly the same as in Britain and we rarely saw an egg.

Bartering was a way of life which was already in full swing when we arrived in Europe. It was the only way the people could survive, and we soon caught on and entered into the spirit of it. The local civilians had suffered many desperate shortages and one of them was a lack of soap. We had a ready supply from the NAAFI stores and it seemed only sensible to try and exchange some of our bounty for a few eggs.

Ronnie was my partner in these undercover transactions and so together we strolled out into the unfamiliar country lanes with a small stock of soap to try and locate a likely farm. We hadn't the faintest idea where to find one, so we walked slowly along, stopping every now and again to listen for the sounds of chickens clucking. Eventually we found our objective and knocked on the door, and when a young girl answered, Ronnie delved into the case and brought out one bar of soap as a sample. We were invited into the kitchen and the soap was solemnly examined by each member of the family and passed from hand to hand until it finished up in the grasp of the matriarch of the household for the final approval.

She was an old lady with a weather-beaten face sitting in a wooden chair by the log fire and we all looked expectantly at her as she sniffed and peered at the soap, I knew that if she liked the merchandise we were in. At last she came out with the verdict. *'Oui!'* she affirmed, and now we came to the tricky bit and the real business of the day began as we got ready for the mandatory haggling.

'Combien des oeufs pour du savon, Madame?' I began the negotiations in my best schoolgirl French. I was the interpreter in the partnership, thanks to the convent school staffed with French nuns.

'Deux!' said the old girl firmly.

'Deux?' I repeated scornfully. *'Mais non,* absolutely *non!'* and Ronnie put the soap back in the bag as if he'd been insulted.

We generally worked it up to four eggs for one bar of soap, which was the going rate at the time. Even so, Ronnie and I were rank amateurs at the game compared to the other fellows in the company who rapidly became experts and got it off to a fine art. I think they came to some sort of arrangement between themselves because they each covered an individual beat and didn't infringe on one another's territory.

Back in England they'd been a gang of lazy slobs, never taking any exercise and having to be dragged out of bed each morning, but now they were up bright and early as if they'd found a purpose in life. Each man armed himself with a suitcase of samples and took off to work a location, for all the world like a commercial traveller setting out on a day's business. And this was how the over-ambitious ones got into serious trouble.

The circumstances were that although France, Belgium and Holland were neighbouring countries who'd suffered a similar fate, the conditions varied enormously. Northern France had been a battlefield but the people were rapidly recovering and goods were becoming available in the shops, but when we arrived in Belgium we were surprised to see how little it had been affected and Brussels in particular was full of luxuries like perfume and toiletries that we hadn't even seen in England. In appalling contrast, Holland had been ransacked and scoured of anything of value; there was literally nothing in the shops. However, the people still had guilders, which for all the goods they could buy might just as well have been used to light the fire.

We were in a uniquely enviable position; we were an army of people with goods to spare which they would pay any amount of money to get their hands on. Our big advantage was that we had the opportunity of crossing the frontiers quite legally with the added bonus of being able to change these worthless Dutch guilders into lovely, lucrative worthwhile Belgian francs.

The game was up when the army customs caught on to the fact that some of these 'odd bods' exchanging hundreds of pounds' worth of guilders into francs were only earning ten pounds a week. Many found themselves on the boat for home and their careers as high financiers came to an abrupt halt.

But most of us were satisfied with bartering for a few of life's comforts and in Holland the local bars were the places to go to mastermind a business transaction. A similar procedure would take place in every one you visited. One man would enter with a parcel under his arm and go over to the barman, who was always the middleman in the negotiations. He in his turn would approach someone he knew to be an interested party and then the two men would disappear into the Gents, which was the local stock exchange and the centre of all the financial shenanigans.

Since I was prohibited from the 'stock exchange' (they still had Ladies and Gents in Holland), Ronnie came into his own here. Luckily most of them spoke English and some of them could even understand Yorkshire! Up he'd go to the bar with a holdall, which he unzipped just enough to show the corner of a tantalising packet of soapflakes. This was akin to a bar of gold and generally produced a frenzy of excitement from the barman. He would know exactly the right customer and he and Ronnie would make for the Gents to complete the transaction.

Often the most unlikely people became experts at this new skill. One day we had to share the coach with another company going back to the ENSA headquarters in Brussels. One of the party was a little north country lady who had partnered her husband in a double act touring in the smallest variety halls, commonly known as 'the dumps'. Unfortunately her husband Eddie had died a few years previously and without a doubt ENSA had come as a godsend to Gladys. She was earning money regularly, week in and week out, perhaps for the first time in her life. It would have been extremely difficult for her in the commercial theatre without her husband and stage partner.

She looked a quiet little woman sitting in the coach doing her knitting, but we'd all heard of her reputation – she was the acknowledged queen of the black market and she was making a small fortune. On the journey to Brussels she started to tell us quite unselfconsciously about her amazing success in this field.

'You know, luvs,' she said, as she clicked her knitting needles, 'when my husband Eddie was alive, he did all the business for the act. He dealt with all the agents and negotiated the contracts. I never had to raise so much as a finger, and what's more I never thought I could do it. But now that he's passed on I've somehow been given the strength to carry on. I tell you this, darlings,' and she put down the knitting and looked solemnly over her spectacles, 'I've got this strong feeling that

180

Eddie is watching me from the other side. It's his presence that's guiding and helping me to drive these hard bargains on the black market. I don't mind telling you, it's changed my whole life and converted me into a very religious person.'

17

Our front-line troops had advanced into Holland and we had gradually worked our way up to their forward positions. Driving up to the border, we all sat huddled in the coach, muffled up against the cold in sweaters, overcoats and woolly scarves as we looked out of the windows at the bleak and miserable landscape.

Every day, the weather got worse and a bitterly cold wind was whipping across the flat countryside, causing the trees and bushes to bend in its path. Great waves of depression washed over me as I gazed disconsolately at the wretched sight of the flooded fields which were rapidly icing over to become a giant-sized skating rink.

The whole area was devoid of life. You could see for miles, there were no hills or inclines and there wasn't a horse, sheep or cow to break the monotony of the grim scene, the only features were bare winter trees silhouetted against the threatening grey skies. Holland had been stripped of everything, crops, goods and livestock. It was as if a vacuum cleaner had passed across the land, sucking up everything in its path.

Generally, if times were bad, someone in the company could be relied upon to come up with a gag to raise a laugh, but we were all affected by the sight of so much desolation and sat numbed with not a word between us.

We were on our way to Eindhoven and when we arrived the town was as cheerless and bare as the surrounding countryside. The shops were all boarded up – they had nothing to sell – although later on in the week we did find one optimistic survivor who had fashioned some crude money boxes from the army corned beef tins, and goodness knows there was no shortage of them. He gallantly displayed them in his shop window and we all bought some to encourage his enterprise.

Maggie and I walked through the cold, cheerless streets and found a little corner bar open, but there was no convivial atmosphere inside. A few men dressed in worn, tattered clothes were trying to keep warm by huddling around an iron stove in the centre of the room, and no sooner had we walked in than the bartender's wife came in from the back room carrying a pot of thin, watery stew and put it on the stove. Not only was it the only form of heating in the house but it was her only means of cooking.

The company was scattered around the town in different digs and Maggie and I were billeted in a small flat with a Mr and Mrs Van Gelder. They were a charming couple who made us very welcome and did their level best to make our stay as comfortable as possible.

The high spot of our time in Eindhoven was when the air force threw a special party for us. They were very insistent that we should all attend and extended the invitation to Mr and Mrs Van Gelder as well, and kept repeating that on no account were we to miss the occasion as it was going to be a night to remember. They succeeded in arousing our interest. After all, we were no strangers to being entertained by the officers after the show, so what could be so special? We found out when we arrived at the appointed hour and walked into the mess hall.

As we opened the door, leaving behind the misery of Eindhoven, we walked into a different world. The room glowed with candlelight and was furnished with long trestle-tables covered with large white cloths (we discovered afterwards that they were sheets from the quartermaster's store). It looked like a wedding reception, and at every place was a knife and fork!

A knife and fork had to be promising. There weren't many times we got to use them at parties, even though we weren't short of invitations. The hospitality was always as generous as possible but no one could expect miracles. You can't make a banquet out of bully beef and army rations.

We didn't have to wait very long before the boys came in carrying large platters laden with mouth-watering steaks! Fresh, beautifully grilled, appetising steaks, with bottles of vintage claret to complement them.

We drooled over that meal. It was the first time we'd eaten fresh meat for months and I suspect the Van Gelders hadn't enjoyed anything like it for years. Our normal diet was corned beef, soya sausages, tinned bacon and any mish-mush the staff could make with one or all of them.

The RAF boys told us the story of this unexpected treat. One of their planes had been forced to make an emergency landing in enemy-occupied territory. They'd come down in a cattle field, and while landing the plane had accidently killed a bullock, which the crew immediately decided was the spoils of war. They loaded it on to the plane and flew it back to the station.

That party was just what was needed to see Maggie and me through a bad patch. It represented the little light at the end of the tunnel. The drabness was so dispiriting, Eindhoven brought home to us just what the people of Holland had been suffering for the six long years of war.

Mr and Mrs Van Gelder were very kind and, with nothing to help them, even basic supplies, they succeeded in making us very welcome. Before we left, Maggie and I ransacked our cases for soap and any other toiletries to give to the Van Gelders; the things we took so much for granted were luxuries to them.

We finished our stay in Eindhoven in much better spirits and got into the coach full of optimism to travel on to our next assignment.

Arthur told us that we were going to Helmond, which was just behind the front line, and that we should be resident there for a few weeks. But when I laid eyes on Helmond, I wondered what on earth I could have found to grumble about in Eindhoven. In retrospect, it was a land flowing with milk and honey.

Helmond is on a tributary of the River Maas. The Germans had only just been driven from the town and they were still entrenched on the other side of the river. During the day the sound of heavy guns boomed and thundered, reverberating around the little town like a threatening storm, but the noise was so constant we soon became accustomed to it.

184

At night, however, it was altogether another ball game. When it got dark the noise of the bombardment increased in a menacing crescendo. It was the precise situation that fired my imagination and sent it soaring on horrific flights of fancy. Lying in bed with my head tucked firmly under the blankets, I visualised the whole scene: the Germans taking everyone by surprise and making a sudden attack to retake the town. I could almost see them goose-stepping down the high street where we were billeted; there was no way they could miss us. Then I imagined them clumping up the stairs in their jackboots, opening the bedroom door – and then what? Finding a roomful of showgirls laid out in bed and practically waiting to be ravaged, that's what! I remembered with unerring accuracy every atrocity which had been attributed to the enemy and I despised myself for the light-hearted way I'd laughed when the gang in the Café Anglais had joked about us being debauched.

Luckily my bravado returned each morning with daylight and I never gave it another thought ... until the next night.

One day when there was a lull in the fighting, Maggie and I met an officer in the mess who offered to take us to an observation post on the river bank and let us look at the enemy through his field glasses. I'm sure it was against all army rules and regulations but we couldn't wait to go and have a 'look-see'. He took us to a dugout by the river and when it was my turn to look through the binoculars it was a trifle disconcerting to see another pair of field glasses from the other side of the river trained on me.

The weather deteriorated. Sleet, snow and a biting wind greeted us whenever we had the temerity to put our little red noses out of doors, and the town itself took on all the qualities of a Siberian wasteland. The saying goes 'It never rains but it pours', and that's how it was with us, because we were staying in what had once been a small family hotel and it was the worst billet we'd come across so far.

The conditions made some of the difficulties unavoidable. The electricity only came on in fits and starts at uncertain periods of the day and the water wasn't heated at all. It trickled icily and unwillingly from the taps, and to pluck up the courage

185

to wash, I sang at the top of my voice, which helped to deaden the shock of the freezing water.

Maggie said the cold water was the lesser of the two evils!

We were convinced that the kitchen staff were flogging our rations on the black market, because at a time when we needed something substantial to keep our spirits up we were served cold and sparse meals.

The one thing that made life worth living in those miserable weeks was our work. ENSA was often interpreted as 'Every Night Something Awful' and jokes went the rounds of captive audiences being locked in with no chance of escape, and I suspect there was a certain element of truth in the stories ... but not this time.

The camps near Helmond didn't have much advance warning of our arrival and most of the time the men only knew there was something on when they were told to report to the canteen. It was so rewarding to see their amazed faces when they walked though the door to discover a full band set up, and when they caught sight of girls they were bowled over.

The area manager told us all to do the best we could under the difficult circumstances and not to worry overmuch about getting made-up or putting on costumes. But for us it was the one occasion when the whole thing made sense and it became a point of honour to give then the full treatment. Maggie and I even 'wet-whited' our legs, knowing it would be purgatory washing it off again in that icy water.

There was no protocol or invitations to the officers' mess here. After the show we stayed and chatted with as many boys as we could. All they wanted was to talk about home.

All through the bitterly cold day, we looked forward to the show. Apart from the pleasure of feeling that we were doing a worthwhile job, there was also our concern for our own comfort because it was the only time in the entire 24 hours that we were really warm.

The number one priority for Maggie and me when we were chatting to the troops was to try and bring the conversation round to food and find out who was in charge of the catering section. When we found him, we went to work on him and,

186

believe me, whatever he looked like, to us he represented the most attractive man in the world. At that time some extra rations appeared to be the only thing in the world worth having, and to Hell with romance!

One night Maggie had the wit and good fortune to wheedle a small electric cooking ring from one of her admirers, and then, if by some lucky chance the electricity was working in the billet, we plugged it in, tipped it on its side and used it as a fire.

The only way we could keep body and soul together was to huddle under the bedclothes wearing every woolly we owned and with our overcoats and anything else we could lay our hands on covering the bed.

As if life wasn't hard enough in Helmond, Maggie and I started to have trouble in the company. The manager, Arthur, had been more or less a figurehead back home – he had only had to receive the orders for our working itinerary and allocate the digs – but he was much more in command out here. The power went to his head and he started throwing his weight about.

Because there were no shops or NAAFI stores so near the front line, Arthur was given supplies to share out equally amongst the cast – commodities like soap, toothpaste, combs and razor blades, in fact all the things we normally take for granted but which make life a misery if they're missing. As the weeks went by we became dependent on Arthur and he knew it. We'd always had an uneasy truce with him and his girlfriend and tried to keep out of their way as much as we could, but of course in Helmond it was impossible. He saw to it that Isobel and his friends were well supplied with goods and he completely ignored Maggie and me. I think he enjoyed putting us in our place and there was no American commanding officer to help us out this time.

The last straw came when we'd completely run out of some essential toiletries like soap and toothpaste, and when the supplies arrived, Arthur refused us yet again. They say it's the small annoyances that cause the biggest quarrels in a marriage and that's how it was with us. We felt that we'd come to the end of the road and couldn't bear it a moment longer, and so with Ronnie we confronted Arthur and asked for a transfer to another company. Although we put up a bold front, we never for a minute imagined he would take us seriously, but to our amaze-ment and delight Arthur agreed. I think he was quite happy to see us out of the way and it didn't cause Isobel to lose any sleep either.

It was only a week after this confrontation that Arthur told the three of us that our request had been granted and we were all to return to the headquarters in Brussels.

'Are we joining another company?' Maggie asked.

'Oh yes,' and Arthur gave an unpleasant little laugh. 'You just wait. They've got the perfect show for you three.'

A flicker of apprehension ran through me. I wondered what Arthur was finding so amusing, but it was soon put out of my head with the excitement of being sent to Brussels.

We were both glad that Ronnie was coming with us; we'd all been mates for a long time and, like all the other men who met Maggie, Ronnie had a crush on her. Not only were we friends, but we had a more devious reason for wanting him to stay with us – Ronnie was an excellent pianist.

Once when we were still touring in England, he was forced to leave the company through illness and it was then that Maggie and I realised how much we relied on him, especially when his temporary replacement proved to be more than a slight embar-rassment.

After Arthur had put frantic calls to the Lane, we were told to expect a lady pianist with the splendidly exotic name of Selena da Palma. Maggie and I imagined her to be a fiery raven-haired lady something like Carmen Miranda, and so when she arrived to take over Ronnie's room in the digs, we were staggered to see a blowsy, dumpy woman of indeterminate age come through the door with enough luggage to take on a round-the-world cruise.

We took in this disappointing sight without saying a word. I think we were too stunned to speak, and the first thought that came to me was she looked like an elderly procuress who had fallen on hard times. She stood with her beady eyes screwed up, blinking at Maggie and me as she puffed away at a cigarette which jutted from the corner of her bright scarlet mouth. Her lipstick was applied in a hit-and-miss fashion, just as if she'd put it on without looking in a mirror. She never took the cigarette from her mouth and it was trying to avoid the smoke which caused her to twist her face and gave her such a cock-eyed appearance. Her yellow blonde hair with its navy blue parting had been peroxided so often that it stuck up from her head like a field of corn stubble and her face was heavily plastered an unattractive shade of salmon pink, with each and every pore standing out like a full stop.

In spite of our cool reception, Selena immediately latched herself on to Maggie and me. She waited for us every morning when we left the house, and no matter how we tried to avoid her, she was always on hand to link her arms possessively through ours and walk into town.

Selena stood out like a sore thumb among the reserved tweed-suited countrywomen of that quiet English backwater, and as we strolled along she treated us to the story of her life, whether we wanted to hear it or not. According to her, she'd had a romantic and eventful past. There was nothing she liked better than to tell us of her amorous adventures and she had a positive compulsion to reveal the most intimate details of her bedroom. I don't think I've ever been so embarrassed in my life as her voice rang out with the vehemence of a sergeant major, enumerating all her intrigues, love affairs and indiscretions.

'People can hear you!' Maggie warned, trying to hush her up.

'Nonsense!' Selena answered, tightly pinioning our arms with her two hard pianist's hands. 'Now let me tell you how I've sacrificed my life for love.' She didn't attempt to lower her voice but continued, 'And what have I had to show for it? I'll tell you, my dears ... abortions, that's what I've had, abortions.'

We both cringed, feeling sure the whole town could hear this outburst, but Selena was oblivious to the disturbance she was causing.

'I've always been a slave to men and a victim of my desires. It's my passionate nature,' she went on dramatically, her voice rising to a powerful screech. 'And if I hadn't had the gift of music, I can't think of anything I'd have liked better than to be a tart!'

189

Maggie made some wild excuse and we dragged our arms away and fled, but there was no escaping her in the digs, and she proved to be a very odd lady indeed.

She had a grown-up son serving in the navy. They wrote to each other every day in the strangest possible way and she insisted on reading the letters to us. It wasn't a case of 'Dear Mum', but 'My own beloved treasure, how can I live without you?' and 'Light of my life, I long for news of you', and she replied in the same vein.

Maggie and I exchanged knowing looks when she read out these extraordinary letters, because by then we were ready to believe anything about her, however unsavoury.

More than anything else, Selena liked to inveigle us to accompany her to a pub. The pubs in wartime were always crammed with servicemen and her one object was to lure them to our table. Peering through the veil of smoke swirling before her eyes, she picked out a likely group of men at the bar and set out to capture their interest. Her voice took on a shrill, excited tone, punctuated by girlish shrieks and merry laughs as she waved her fat little hands about, jangling the cheap array of bracelets she wore on her wrists.

It generally had the desired effect and the men would come over and invite us to have a drink. Then Selena went into the full act. She explained that she was an *artiste* who was bringing some art and culture to the underprivileged men in the forces, and she'd wink and positively leer as she introduced Maggie and me as 'glamorous showgirls of *vast* experience'. It conjured up a picture of Myra Hess lowering herself to having a drink with two ladies from the fleshpots of Soho.

Smiling coquettishly at the men, she batted her black mascara-ringed eyes at them and lied in her teeth to confess that we were both devoted to her and wouldn't leave her side. Although Maggie and I were fully aware that she was using us as bait to catch some undiscerning or drunken man on her hook, there wasn't much we could do about it because she was so damn persistent.

No one was more relieved than us when, fully recovered and not a moment too soon, Ronnie returned to the company and we waved goodbye to Selena for ever. I think he was quite surprised at the enthusiastic welcome we gave him!

Ronnie had been with us ever since. The three of us had always gone around together, and since we'd had 'trouble at t'mill', we'd tended to keep ourselves to ourselves, but I have to confess that a major reason that we were so delighted that he'd thrown in his lot to come with us to a new show was that he was one pianist who could play for dancers.

Strangely enough, many otherwise competent pianists and even musical directors in the theatre can be the bane of a dancer's life. All a tap dancer wants is someone to bang out a perfectly strict tempo; she or he does not want light and shade, pauses, arpeggios and twiddly bits when all that's needed is a steady four beats to the bar. Maggie and I did a really superb routine to 'Begin the Beguine' and we were especially grateful for Ronnie in this number, because it was just the sort of music that would tempt a lesser pianist to flash up and down the piano keys on an ego trip and try to make it his own solo instead of an accompaniment.

In a troupe of dancers it was the head girl's job to set the tempo for the band to follow, and when I went to see a show it was easy to pick her out by her agonised fixed smile as she glared at the musical director, at the same time practically drilling a hole in the stage in her efforts to bash out the beat.

Maggie had once been a Tiller girl. The Tillers were possibly the best precision dancers in the world and the general public became aware of them when they appeared regularly on television in the Palladium shows. Audiences who'd never seen them before were amazed at their remarkable technique and the way that even their heads turned together. The simultaneous head movements are the secret of the excellent precision, because when a girl turns her head she automatically checks that her shoulders are lined up to the next one in the line.

I've often thought that this could be used to good advantage in the Trooping the Colour ceremony. I've noticed that when the Guards are marching 'eyes front' across Horseguards Parade, they often get a terrible skipping rope effect, but when it comes to parading the colours in front of the Queen and it's 'eyes right

191

for Her Majesty', the line immediately straightens up. What they could do with is an old-fashioned dance producer to make them turn their heads at every fourth step ... and perhaps it would be fun to see them finish with a shuffle and a time step!

Back in Helmond, Maggie, Ronnie and I prepared to make our escape. We extricated our props, costumes and the faithful tap mat from the company's baggage and got ready to make our way back to Brussels to join the new production.

I wondered with some trepidation what life had in store for us now.

As it turned out I needn't have worried. Fortune smiled and made us a present of Brussels ... gift-wrapped!

18

Since the liberation of Belgium, Brussels had become the headquarters of all the Allied armies in northern Europe.

In spite of the fact that Belgium had been occupied by the enemy, the shops were full of extravagances that we hadn't seen in the shops at home for years – exciting luxuries like scent, silk stockings, perfumed soaps and mouth-watering chocolates.

At the outbreak of the war, Maggie and I had both been in our teens, and nearly six years later it was difficult to remember a time when the world had been at peace and when life had been a bowl of cherries.

Ours not to reason why Brussels was bursting with goodies. We cared not a jot. We were free, free of the cold and miseries of Helmond and free of Isobel and Arthur with his petty tyrannies. A heady euphoria enveloped us all. There was a *joie de vivre* atmosphere in the city and Maggie and I were young and ready to let down our hair and join in the spirit of gaiety that surrounded us.

Perhaps it was a feeling that the long war would soon be over which produced this exhilarating climate, but whatever the reason everyone in Brussels was there with the sole purpose of enjoying himself, because it was the leave centre for all the armed forces in the liberated zones of northern Europe.

Ronnie, Maggie and I lived in the thick of it. Our hotel, which had been requisitioned for ENSA, was right in the heart of town on the Boulevarde Adolphe Max. We were given a suite with a private bathroom, a common enough amenity today but neither Maggie nor I had seen anything like it. As soon as the porter put down our cases and closed the door behind him, we rushed to the bathroom and turned on the taps, and miracle of miracles, out gushed boiling hot water! After the rigours of Helmond and having to put up with an icy trickle dribbling from anti-quated taps, the excitement of an unlimited supply of piping hot water went straight to our heads. The taps flowed until we could hardly see across the room for steam. Filling the bath to overflowing, we wallowed contentedly in a sea of bubbles until our toes and fingers turned to crinkly white crepe.

I still think that a plentiful supply of hot water is one of life's luxuries. Custom hasn't blunted the blissful pleasure of soaking in the benison of a comforting bath. When the blackbirds and starlings splash enthusiastically about in the bird bath in my garden, I feel akin to them. You can see that it's not just a necessary chore, they're really enjoying it, and it's the same with me.

I'm a true believer in creature comforts and my idea of Hell would be to go on a camping holiday. There wouldn't be a scrap of joy for me in washing myself in a spoonful of cold river water. Not for me the desire to creep into a flapping tent to sleep in a hard and possibly damp sleeping bag or the ultimate horror to have to use a chemical loo. I think I'm allergic to all that malarkey because I've done it for real, not for an adventurous holiday to try and get a thrill from life, like some protected civil servant whose most exciting excursion from home has been on a package tour. I've known what it's really like to live with no heating, no hot water and precious little bedclothes on a lumpy uncomfortable bed, so there's no novelty in that sort of life for me.

I like hot water to come spurting out of the taps, a lavatory that flushes at a touch and a relaxing warm bed to sleep in, given that, plus a good dinner and a bottle of wine, I can be as nice as pie to anyone!

Every morning our first and only duty was to report to the ENSA headquarters and the rest of the day was ours to do with as we liked. We learned, to our intense satisfaction, that this happy state of affairs would continue until the new company arrived from their wanderings to pick us up at the hotel, and having heard this, it was surprising how quickly Ronnie, Maggie and I adjusted ourselves to the lifestyle of idle lay-abouts.

We discovered the joys of the Maple Leaf canteen, which was run by a Canadian organisation in the *place* by the Gard du Nord. It was here that they served the most delicious ice cream, accompanied by as much free coffee as you could drink, to anyone in uniform. The Maple Leaf became a regular mid-morning rendezvous and not to be missed.

Whenever I see the words 'Gare du Nord', I'm reminded of the time when writing to my current boyfriend and trying to impress him with my savoir faire, I wrote '*C'est la gare*', when what I really had in mind to describe some wartime shortage was '*C'est la guerre*'. He wrote back to say 'What the Hell's it got to do with the station?'

For the first time since crossing the Channel we had the chance to sightsee, and the three of us started to career around town like the dizziest of tourists. The only attraction that we'd heard of in Brussels was the statue of the Manikin Pis, and after a lot of searching we traced him to the corner of a small street leading off the Grand Place. The statue was enchanting and seemed to represent the gaiety and frivolity that was all around us. On one special feast day we were surprised and delighted to find he'd been decked up for the occasion in a miniature uniform specially made so that he could continue to pee away merrily, much to our enjoyment. Patriotic as I am, I've got to admit that it was a lot more fun than the statues of Queen Victoria back in England.

The Grand Place itself was a constant source of pleasure. Every morning the flower sellers arrived to transform the square into a giant kaleidoscope of colour with masses of flowers and gaily striped umbrellas. It was such an extravagant sight it looked more like an elaborate film set than a scene from real life.

The contrast between Holland, where they were struggling to survive, and the people of Brussels being able to enjoy the supreme luxury of buying flowers never ceased to amaze us.

Even the weather started to improve. A weak sun filtered through the clouds, the temperature rose and it felt as if spring might arrive after all.

Gadding about the town, we were always aware of the constant background music of the carillons as they merrily jingled away the hours, and they were a vast improvement on the ponderous tolling of the church bells in this country. The insistent chiming produces a feeling of ominous gloom in the pit of my stomach. I think it's something to do with memory association – I put it down to hearing the funereal clanging of the bells on Sundays when I was wandering round a town looking for digs.

During the war years no church bells had been heard in Britain; the sound of them chiming was to be the signal to indicate that the Germans had invaded us, which we all fully expected, especially in the period soon after Dunkirk. Some nights when I lay in bed and it was still and quiet, I could actually hear those damned bells ringing. Imagination can be a potent bed-fellow.

While I had the time and was in the right place, I decided to do the obvious thing and have my photograph taken wearing my uniform. I chose the best photographer on the boulevard, and a few days later I was flattered to see a truly life-sized enlargement given pride of place in the display window. I kept walking up and down the pavement, preening like a peacock, until Maggie and Ronnie threatened to do me a permanent mischief if I didn't pack it in.

There were forces of every nationality in Brussels, so one morning I wasn't surprised to see a group of American WAACs wandering along window-shopping. One of them looked vaguely familiar and on closer inspection I was amazed to recognise my old friend Babs, who I'd shared digs with and last seen in Bristol. She was as British as me, so what the devil was she doing waltzing around in an American uniform, I wanted to know.

She was just as startled to see me and we tore over to the Maple Leaf canteen to catch up on all the news over a cup of free Canadian coffee, while Babs told me the story of how she

196

came to be masquerading as a WAAC. She asked if I remembered the American major she'd met outside the Bristol Hippodrome and went on to tell me that the major worked at the US Embassy in Grosvenor Square. When Babs returned to London after the tour their romance had blossomed and they'd consummated this grand passion by living cosily together in a love nest near the embassy. Babs packed in the touring and everything was coming up roses until the major discovered that he was to be transferred to the US headquarters in Brussels. At first they were desolate, but the light of her life was a bright and enthusiastic young man whose love spurred him on to untold heights. When he heard that his section was to be accompanied by WAACs working as office personnel on the administration side, he used his influence and with great ingenuity wangled Babs in with the American girls – and the great romance was alive and well in Brussels.

The only flaw I could see in this master plan was, what would happen if she was ever confronted with a typewriter?

Every evening Ronnie, Maggie and I hit the town. Coming from the Stygian darkness of the blacked-out streets of Britain, it was a revelation to see the cafés and shops ablaze with lights. The busy thoroughfares were crowded with servicemen and women all ready to relax and forget the war in the bars and cabarets that lined the boulevards. As we sauntered along the pavements, the haunting voices of the chanteuses drifted from the smoky cafés. It was all so excitingly different from anything at home.

We tried out a different cabaret each night. Some of them had a nondescript line of dancers and Maggie and I thought they were the bitter end. Watching one particular group of girls who were all at sixes and sevens and didn't look as if their hearts were in their work, Maggie leaned across to say, 'Mary, if we're ever out of a job, we know where to come.' It was easy to see why English dancers are considered to be tops and have an enviable reputation all over the world. I don't want to appear to be biased but old loyalties die hard, and my husband Bernard says I'm the only person he knows who goes to a show and applauds the chorus more than the stars.

We discovered that we could see these cabarets for the price of a drink, but the cost of alcohol came as something of a nasty shock and was way beyond our means. Apparently the cafés bought all their hard liquor on the *marché noir* (there goes my damned savoir faire again!), so to get over this stumbling block, we all filled small bottles with gin from our booze ration and strolled into the cabaret of our choice with them. The only non-alcoholic drink on the menu at a reasonable price was apple juice, and although I wouldn't go so far as to recommend gin and apple juice as the flavour of the month, we had many a cheap evening out and saw most of the cabarets in town on it.

I think it was the first time in my life that I'd been paid while not working. The hard-and-fast rule of the theatre used to be 'no play, no pay', and even when the theatres closed on Good Friday, which was obligatory at that time, one day's pay was stopped from our pay packet. It was just the same if we were ill or forced to be 'off' for any other reason; there was no way we could win because our money was always docked. I've always thought that this was the fundamental answer to the oft-repeated saying that 'the show must go on', the motive that induced actors to carry on with broken arms, that gave them the impetus to croak away with laryngitis and why some had even been known to totter on with crutches – because if they didn't put in an appearance they didn't get paid!

Mind you, it's as well not to rely too implicitly on this. Once when I was in pantomime at the Finsbury Park Empire (how could they pull it down?) and in my usual desperate straits for a little extra money, I volunteered for understudy and the management picked me to stand in for the principal boy.

Now the theatre at Finsbury Park was a Moss Empire date. It was under the same banner as the Palladium and the man responsible for production in both theatres was Charles Henry. He had his hands full with these two shows and it took him all his time to rehearse the pantomime, let alone take any under-study calls.

For my part, I was thankful enough to be left alone, to keep shtum and rely on the principal boy's desire to shine in her one big moment of the year, because she was one of those ladies who had gained a reputation as a pantomime 'boy' but didn't appear to do much work in the interim period.

We hadn't been rehearsing long before we found out that she was a difficult and temperamental lady with the bloody-minded habit of being tricky about every line of dialogue and move she was given. She refused to say the lines as written and demanded that all her entrances were made downstage in full spotlight while the rest of the cast could creep around in the dark as far as she was concerned.

Now Charles Henry was a very competent man. I admired him because he was experienced in producing pantomime. He loved all the old traditions and, unlike many directors, he didn't have one way of treating the stars and another standard for the chorus. So after quietly putting up with all her nonsense, he suddenly said, 'Now look, dear, either you do it my way or we can do without you altogether. You've got a perfectly good understudy, you know.' And he looked at me. 'Step forward, Mary.'

I truly don't know how I managed to take the step forward. I hadn't taken a single look at the part and the only thing I knew was what I'd picked up during rehearsals. The thing that saved the day was that from force of habit I put on a big confident smile and the principal boy wasn't to know that I didn't know one line, but it completely took the wind out of her sails and she finished rehearsals like a lamb.

The pantomime was *Jack and the Beanstalk* and the whole experience gave me such a shock that from that moment on I studied the part night and day and got so nervy and jumpy that if anyone so much as touched me on the shoulder, I was liable to blurt out, 'Oh Mother! Don't make me take poor Bessie the cow to market.'

However, I was right in my original judgement. She was never off or indeed had the slightest intention of being so. But just the same, clever old Charles Henry got the best out of both of us, because from that day on the principal boy never spoke a word out of turn and as for me, I was ready to do the part if the fridge light shone on me.

So in Brussels, Maggie, Ron and I revelled in the unusual

situation of 'collecting' for the first time in our lives without having to work, and to cap it all we were lording it in a luxury hotel and not paying a penny. Given a little time we felt we could all get used to this enviable way of life.

We fancied ourselves as wealthy dilettantes having nothing better to do than float from shop to shop, sampling scents and trying on clothes, only pausing for morning coffee and spending the rest of the day sightseeing. After a day like this, our schedule was to return to the hotel 'limp and exhausted' from these arduous activities and relax in the bliss of a hot bath. Dinner over, we tarted ourselves up and sallied forth to enjoy the night life of Brussels on gin and apple juice!

Completely forgotten was the wretchedness and misery of the previous weeks. We blotted out the memory of danger and discomfort as if it had never been and ran riot in the shops, spending money on whatever took our fancy. We didn't forget our families and friends, we loaded up with gifts and souvenirs as if they were going out of style.

Every now and again we spared a thought for Arthur and the show we'd left behind. The three of us relished and positively gloated over the idea that they might be in some frightful place even worse than Helmond, and Maggie went one better, she gleefully hoped that they might fall into enemy hands, preferably without the benefit of their uniforms.

We were perfectly prepared for this way of life to go on for ever and settled back to enjoy the primrose path without giving any heed to the everyday world of toil and trouble. So it came as something of a shock one morning when we checked into the ENSA headquarters to be told that the new company would be arriving at the hotel that very evening and we'd all be on the road again by the following week.

'You'll be joining a company called The Brainwaves,' we were told.

'The Brainwaves?' Ronnie said, lapsing into broad Yorkshire because he was a bit worried. 'What sort of a daft name is that?'

It did sound odd, but we put it down to the fact that hundreds of shows were sent out from the Lane and they couldn't think of clever names for all of them. But even so ... The Brainwaves?

200

Maggie and I tried to be enthusiastic and to gloss over Ronnie's niggling fears.

'I still think it's a funny name for a band,' he kept saying, while Maggie did her best to reassure him.

She did such a good job that I found my interest being aroused and I started to get all eager and hopeful. Off went my imagination to indulge in the wildest of fantasies until in the optimistic eye of my mind, the new company had built up in size and splendour until it assumed the proportions of a West End musical with an orchestra in the style of Glenn Miller. We spent hours daydreaming about every imaginable type and format of show, but we were still unprepared for what we got.

That evening when the message was given to us to go down to the hotel foyer, we were so keyed up we practically fell down the stairs in our eagerness to meet our new companions.

The first thought that flashed through my mind was that there'd been some sort of mistake because there was nothing in the foyer that resembled an ENSA company. Three people looking tired and forlorn stood on the thick carpet surrounded by an untidy selection of worn and battered suitcases.

I turned expectantly to the door, hoping to see a large company about to come in, but there was not a soul there. A hideous suspicion started to creep into my mind, and when I turned to Ronnie and Maggie and saw their faces registering horror and disbelief, I knew that the same thought had struck them. Could these three people looking like lost orphans in a storm constitute the company that we were expecting? I hoped it was some sort of gag and that someone was having us on.

Then when it finally dawned on me that this really was the entire 'extravagant production', I cursed Arthur for his Machiavellian scheme in conniving to land us with this Mickey Mouse outfit. Life hadn't exactly been a bed of roses with the big band show, so whatever could we expect with this crew? Vivid images of all the impossible little dumps we'd be expected to play with this miniature unit raced through my head. It'll be the death of me, I thought pessimistically, and I was certain that was what Arthur had in mind for us all.

It's true that we were to work harder that we'd ever

done before, in the most trying of conditions, but as it turned out we had the time of our lives and enjoyed every minute.

19

The three of us looked on this motley outfit with stunned disbelief. They in their turn didn't say a word either, and then the man gave a wry smile at the astonishment that must have been written all over our faces. He came forward to introduce himself and the two girls who made up the 'company'. He was in his forties, tall, slim with a Clark Gable moustache and he told us his name was Freddie and the pretty girl with curly red hair was Joyce.

But it was the third member of the party who attracted my attention. To start with, in a sea of khaki, she stood out from the crowd, wearing a pale grey trouser suit instead of the regulation ENSA uniform, and somehow she didn't look like a performer. She was a big-boned lady, not fat but heavy and angular, reminding me of pictures I'd seen of the pioneer women who staked their claims in the Wild West of America, the tough sort of ladies who could kill half a dozen marauding Indians before breakfast without turning a hair.

Her name was Farah, and Freddie was her husband and stage partner in a mental telepathy act which was the star spot in the show. Their rather fanciful stage name was Frederico and Farah, and it was their act which inspired the title 'The Brainwaves' which had worried Ronnie so much – and when I stole a glance at him, he didn't look too happy about it then either. We never found out Farah's real name; she always remained Farah to me and everyone else in the company, and a greater character I've yet to meet.

She refused to wear uniform and told me she'd slung it away somewhere or other. When I asked her why, she shook me to the core by saying, 'Fuck the uniform!' Although I'd been connected with the stage all my life, it was the first time I'd heard a woman swear like that. In those days on the Music Halls a performer was severely reprimanded if he so much as used the word 'bloody' in his act, so to hear Farah letting fly with Rabelaisian eloquence came as something of a shock.

We knew this company had just come back from entertaining the front-line troops, so I wondered how she would have fared if she'd been taken prisoner. But when I came to know her better I thought, God help the German who captured Farah!

As well as the telepathy act, Freddie compered the show and linked up the acts with gags. When Maggie and I joined them he got quite ambitious and put in extra sketches. I think he harboured some optimistic ideas of building the minuscule unit up into a big production, and although there were no fears of that happening, we both got a lot of fun working with him.

Joyce sang and played the piano accordion, and until Ronnie arrived on the scene she'd acted as accompanist if one was needed. She was young and pretty and a talented singer and musician, and she always finished her 'spot' with a medley of the pop songs of the day and encouraged the audience to join in.

This trio's chief virtue was that as well as putting on a good, unpretentious entertainment, they could perform anywhere ... and they had. They'd been to the most inaccessible spots, to remote places where a large show couldn't attempt to play, because with no need of a piano or even a platform, they could work if necessary in a few square feet of space. Freddie told us that the three of them had been together for several years and had played as far afield as Burma and Malaya. 'Actually,' he told us, 'we've counted the number of countries we've worked in and it adds up to thirty.'

'Thirty?' Maggie was amazed. 'I didn't even know there *were* thirty different countries.'

She was never too hot on geography. In fact, when we were touring in England and working in a town she knew well, she had no idea where it was situated on the map.

Freddie was rightly proud of this achievement and every

night at the end of the show he came forward to make a curtain speech.

'Thank you, gentlemen,' he always said, 'for being such an enthusiastic audience tonight. And you may be interested to know that this small band of dedicated artistes has travelled the world entertaining the troops in no less than thirty different countries.'

Deafening applause greeted this modest announcement and I used to get quite carried away with the emotion of it. I tried to put an expression on my face that combined humility and pride, but it always brought a lump to my throat. It was only when I was taking my make-up off and preparing to go to the mess that I came down to earth and remembered that I hadn't actually participated in these worldwide adventures and prayed that no one would question me about these heroic exploits.

Knowing that Freddie, Farah and Joyce had been together for such a long time, we wondered if they would take kindly to three strangers joining their little band, but they seemed delighted to have some fresh faces around. After the first initial shock, Maggie and I got into the spirit of working in a small show. We did miss the strength of an eight-piece band behind us and having the musicians to dress the stage, but to compensate we enjoyed the friendly atmosphere working with pros who made us welcome as part of a team, and of course we still had Ronnie to accompany us.

But Ronnie found it more difficult to adapt. He'd always played with a band and liked the company of other musicians on and off the stage, also he didn't take too kindly to being the accompanist for the others. Then one night Freddie asked him to do a solo spot at the piano, and in no time at all he was flashing up and down the keyboard in true virtuoso style, doing the full 'eyes and teeth' bit. Ronnie had come into his own at last!

The nicest thing about being a member of a small group was that it encouraged a 'one for all and all for one' mood and when any of us came up with some extras to help ease the living conditions, we shared and shared alike. Sometimes Freddie managed to wangle a few more bottles of booze and then we'd

205

have a party, and at other times one of us would hand over a pound of butter, eggs or tea to help with the rations.

It became an accepted end-of-the-day ritual for us to gather in Freddie and Farah's room for a nightcap and to have a natter about the performance and who we'd met in the mess. It was a pleasant way to unwind after travelling to the camp, doing a performance, socialising in the mess and then making the return journey, and it was all very different from the previous show.

Maggie and I did two spots in the show. In our first act we sang and danced to a bright little number. It wasn't anything special, just a rhythmic tap dance, but the success of this routine was without a doubt our costumes. At a time when dancers tended to go in for frills and sequins, Maggie and I wore perfectly tailored white tuxedo jackets – just the jackets, with little panties underneath, and wherever we went they were a hit and always commented on.

In the second half of the programme, we danced an intricate routine to a rather swinging version of 'Begin the Beguine'. This was the number we enjoyed most, but it was always the tuxedoes that attracted attention.

With these two acts we had played from the extremes of a barn with soldiers sitting cross-legged surrounding us on the floor to the magnificent opulence of an opera house. At the Opera House Lille, the stage was so immense that Ronnie had to put an extra couple of bars on the introduction music to get us to centre stage.

The high spot of the programme was Freddie and Farah's mental telepathy act, which always caused everyone to sit up and take notice. I think most people must have seen a similar type of act where the woman stands on stage blindfolded while her partner goes down into the audience choosing certain articles for her to identify.

Freddie and Farah were very fast and good at this lark, they speeded along so quickly... 'That's a watch, timed at half past nine.' 'A silver cigarette case with three fags and a picture of the wife ... or somebody else's!' 'A regimental badge of the Royal Artillery', and so on. It was something different from the usual comedian or singer and it created a lot of interest and speculation among the troops. And the curiosity wasn't confined to the lesser ranks, the officers were just as intrigued by the mystery.

Ten to one when we were in the mess after the show, some idiot would come up to Farah and say, 'I say, that's awfully clever. I suppose there's some sort of knack to it. Ha ha! Now tell me, how on earth do you do it?'

I could never make up my mind if he really expected an answer. I've heard the same fatuous question put to illusionists and conjurers over and over again. Do they seriously think that performers are going to divulge the secret of their entire act to the first Charlie who asks them?

Farah had a set reply to this inane remark. She arranged her face into a deceptively sweet expression and whispered confidentially, 'Well, I wouldn't tell just anyone, but I'll let you into the secret. It's all done with mirrors and a very long piece of string.'

It was a very complicated act and it took a lot of concentration on Farah's part. Freddie was not only handed watches, coins and family photographs but foreign banknotes, which she could identify, and she also rattled off long lists of serial numbers from the notes and army pay books. There was a lot she had to remember and retain in her head during the act and Maggie and I always stood on the side of the stage to keep any staff quiet so they wouldn't disturb her concentration.

Of course the very nature of the act caused people to chat and comment, and sometimes if it got too noisy, Farah would pull up the blindfold, glare down at the offender with a baleful eye and bellow furiously for him to belt up; then she yanked it down again and resumed serenely as before.

Sometimes the show was publicised in the camp before we arrived and then the soldiers had a chance to prepare themselves by bringing all kinds of weird and wonderful objects to try and catch her out, but they never managed it. Many of the men brought bizarre curios they'd picked up on their travels. One night someone came in with a pet snake, and who could forget the performance when another man brandished a shrunken head! We knew what to expect when we were playing to a

207

medical unit and got quite used to the sight of pickled appendixes and other unsavoury portions of the human anatomy floating about in bottles.

Soldiers being what they are, hardly a week went by without some joker handing Freddie a French letter. It was done chiefly to get a laugh from his mates and I'm sure he never intended Freddie to ask Farah to identify it, so it always shook him rigid when Freddie showed no surprise and calmly asked Farah what he was holding. She put on her most formidable manner. 'That,' she said, 'is foreign correspondence', which got a roar, then she capped it and turned the laugh on the soldier by adding, 'And I'll tell you something else, that man hasn't been writing to anyone lately.'

If the troops were made to wait for any length of time before the show started, they often got restless, and when the curtain went up at last, the hall would be full of French letters blown up like balloons and floating over the heads of the audience.

Freddie had his own way with dealing with this sort of thing. He walked forward and said in a hurt tone, 'Gentlemen!' and again stressing the word, 'Gentlemen, I want you to know that the girls in this show are ... ladies, and I ask you to respect them as you would your wives (a little sob escaped him here) ... and mothers!'

It always did the trick, and while they were tidying up the hall, he turned upstage and gave us a dirty big wink. We in turn cast down our eyes and looked suitably demure and ladylike.

Our hosts in the mess after the show weren't all 'officers and gentlemen', and for our own protection we had a plan never to separate. If one girl was given an invitation to 'see the room where we keep the maps' or any other excuse, she'd invariably say, 'How lovely! I'm dying to see them. Are you coming too, Mary?' and it was an unwritten law that you went whether you wanted to or not. Many a time we were propositioned quite openly and sometimes Freddie or Ronnie were asked which one of us was 'all right'.

If Farah was in earshot of any of these remarks, she put the fear of death into the randy offender by thundering, 'Now everyone keep nice and quiet while this gentleman repeats what he just said in a voice loud and clear so we can all hear.'

Very occasionally when we went into the mess, we could see that we weren't welcome and the group of officers considered themselves above consorting with a band of strolling players. This always incensed Farah because we'd accepted their invitation and many a time we'd have given the world to have gone straight back and had an early night for a change. We'd sit down at a table on our own and Farah bided her time until there was a temporary lull in the conversation at the bar. Then her penetrating voice could be heard quite clearly confiding, 'And did I tell you what the Duke said to me in bed this morning?'

It was one of those glorious remarks that always succeeded in riveting the attention of everyone in the room, combining as it did a touch of scandal with prestigious overtones.

There was one question we all got heartily sick and tired of hearing. Every night without fail some pinhead would sidle up as soon as we showed our faces and before he opened his mouth we knew what was coming.

'And what did you do before the war?'

It infuriated Farah that she could be taken for anything less than a professional and she always answered, 'Well, if you must know, I used to clean the lavatories in the Charing Cross Road.'

Farah was a character, but she was genuine. She had no time for subterfuge and always spoke her mind (that's got to be the understatement of all time) and I really liked her; while Freddie, unlike our old manager Arthur, took his responsibilities so seriously, always putting our welfare top of the list that he practically clucked over us.

To all appearances they looked an ideal couple, so it came as a considerable shock one day when Farah told me that she planned to divorce Freddie when they returned to England after the war, and what's more she intended to marry some Polish officer that she'd met on her travels who was now stationed in Africa. I found the whole thing unbelievable.

'Well!' Maggie said when we discussed it afterwards. 'I've met some odd people in this crazy business but these two take the jackpot.'

It was Joyce who told us all the ins and outs of their peculiar relationship and it turned out that Freddie and Farah were an extremely eccentric couple indeed. Not only was Farah committed to marry this mystery Polish officer but she was not averse to having 'a bit on the side' with other partners as well. It seems that she and Freddie had a mutual arrangement to indulge in a 'little of what they fancied' if and when they chose.

Maggie and I were really taken aback, the more so because they didn't look the types to conduct their lives in this curious fashion. They were both over 40, they had a child back home in England and never in this world would Farah have struck me as a femme fatale.

However, we hadn't been with them long before we were made well aware of the situation because Farah took advantage of her side of this unconventional arrangement at every available opportunity. A succession of men came and went, but not before they'd stayed the night. Freddie went along with it, and once he actually took them breakfast in bed the following morning. But although he outwardly condoned this behaviour, Maggie and I were privately convinced that really it was knocking the stuffing out of him because whenever he had a few drinks inside him, he became maudlin and found the nearest shoulder to cry on.

It was both sad and funny that when he tried to take advantage of his side of the bargain something always went wrong and it never worked out.

Once we were given a few days' leave, Farah immediately took off with her current lover while the rest of us flew with the unerring accuracy of homing pigeons to Brussels. Once there, we all went our separate ways, and when we met up again Freddie told us of a romantic encounter. The very first day, he'd gone to a bar and met this cracking Belgian girl who had gone overboard for him. He wined her and dined her and couldn't believe his luck when at the end of the evening she'd invited him back to her place. Freddie told us she gave him a great time,

210

and after a delicious breakfast the next morning he was congratulating himself that he'd got it made for the week. The affair made him feel like a new man and he was just thinking how lucky he was, when she turned to him and said, 'But M'sieu, you 'ave not yet given me the five 'undred francs!'

Poor Freddie, you had to feel sorry for him and he wasn't allowed to forget it because it became a standing joke in the company. If one of us did a favour for another, instead of thanks, she got 'But M'sieu, you 'ave not yet given me the five 'undred francs.'

Added to the worry that his wife was intent on leaving him, Freddie had the anxiety of losing his partner in the act. As soon as he realised that Maggie and I were aware of how things were between him and Farah, he tentatively put out feelers to try and find out if one of us would be prepared to learn the act and join him as partner.

He certainly picked a couple of losers in us! Every time I watched the act I thought to myself, Not for a pension or even to see my name up in lights would I batter my brains to a pulp trying to learn all that gobbledegook. And as Maggie found it difficult to remember the name of the town she was staying in, Freddie had the good sense to know when he was licked and decided to call it quits. We told him that he'd have to look elsewhere for 'The Most Baffling Telepathic Wonder of the Age' and he appeared to relax and we all settled down happily as before.

However, it wasn't long before Maggie caught on to the fact that although Freddie had given up all hopes of enticing one of us into the act, Farah herself was no quitter and she'd started her own campaign to promote a romance between Freddie and either one of us. We kept hearing how considerate he was and what a good husband and provider he'd been, and furthermore how lucky any girl would be to land such a paragon of virtue. It made me wonder why, if he was so bloody marvellous, she was so anxious to get shot of him herself.

Maggie and I weren't born yesterday and we were well aware that anyone who partnered him in the act would have to take on Freddie as well, and much as we liked him, we thought there must be easier ways of earning a living. So once more we made it crystal clear that neither one of us had any intention of taking her place, but Farah wasn't the one to give up gracefully.

She was a camera fanatic and I began to notice that whenever I was with her and Freddie, her camera was always at the ready. Freddie and I had a mutual passion for doing crosswords and when we had our heads together over a puzzle, she quietly took out her camera and snapped us, and when we were sunbathing on the lawn and Freddie happened to lean towards me to say something, *click* went the shutter. It struck me one day that she might produce these candid camera shots to help with her divorce and as evidence of some sort of liaison between her old man and me. I wasn't sure if my suspicions were correct, but once the idea was firmly fixed in my mind I grew exceedingly neurotic about that camera. I did my best to keep one eye on Farah all the time and whenever I saw her pick up the camera, I started darting about like a fiddler's elbow. So many of her photographs were spoiled by having a blurred phantom-like smudge next to Freddie, which was me making my getaway, that she became thoroughly discouraged and gave it up as a bad job. However, I think I might have done her a good turn and set her on a new career, because from that day on she began to get really artistic and turned to photographing landscapes and panoramic views of scenic beauty ... and very pretty they were too!

Although Farah obviously had a guilt complex about abandoning Freddie and would have liked to ease her conscience by unloading him on to some other lady before she left him, she was extremely jealous if he paid any attention to Joyce. Usually the two of them behaved like sisters and they shared and shared alike. Joyce often washed Farah's undies and Farah would iron Joyce's frocks, but if she thought that Freddie had so much as glanced at Joyce there was trouble. It was the one thing she wouldn't tolerate.

Before we'd joined the company, Freddie and Joyce had been left to their own devices when Farah had taken off on one of her amorous adventures, and with supreme irrationality on her return she'd been highly suspicious as to what had been going on in her absence. On several occasions this had led to bad feeling between the two girls which threatened to destroy their normally good relationship, but with our arrival the tension had eased and things had got back to their usual happy state.

So we'd done them a good turn and I was pleased, because although I would have never believed it possible, I was beginning to enjoy myself in this tinpot outfit.

20

Compared to the rest of Europe, it was a doddle working in Belgium. The conditions were easier, the food was better and there were no heating or water shortages. It was almost as if we were on holiday.

One of the loveliest towns we visited was Bruges, the Venice of the north. Bruges is God's gift to the picture postcard business with its network of canals lapping against the walls of the old wool merchants' houses and winding back and forth through the city. Gable roofs cover the buildings which cluster round the old market square, and around every corner there's another view crying out to be photographed for the family album. Farah had a field day here. I loved the square especially on market days, when the stalls were crammed tightly together as the people from the surrounding countryside poured in bringing fruit, vegetables and home-made cheeses to stack in colourful piles to tempt the townsfolk.

It was fascinating to stand and watch the lacemakers dressed in their traditional costumes. They wore long skirts and had starched white linen headdresses which made them look like a band of stage nuns. They chatted unconcernedly to each other as their fingers flashed to and fro in a cat's cradle of bobbins, pins and yarn to produce the exquisite patterned lace for which they are famous.

Every time I went to the square I bought something. I could never resist a market.

I had an uncle Alf who was a market trader. He'd started in the Depression of the 1930s when he couldn't find work and did so well that he stayed in the game. I think he must have been a frustrated performer because he'd worked up his sales talk into an act and gained a reputation in the district as a comedian. People came from miles around to listen and laugh at him. He knew this full well and always waited until the market was crowded before making his entrance.

I went to see him one day and found him standing at the stall with a mop on his head like a judge's wig. 'Gather round, ladies,' he began. 'The court is in session. Now I'm not one of your fly-by-night lawyers, here today and gone tomorrow. I'm here today and gone tonight!'

He started by selling some garden tools that he'd bought in a cheap lot and picked up the first item. 'How many of you ignorant people know what these are? They're called secateurs, and I bet most of you thought that's a girl who sits on the boss's knee.'

The crowd loved it when he insulted them and he went on, 'Tell the truth, ladies, did any of you know that secateurs are what the fashionable society ladies use to cut and gather roses?'

I don't suppose that there were too many fashionable society ladies in Romford Market that morning but he sold the whole box just the same, and when he'd got rid of them he started flogging sets of saucepans He laid them all out on the stall and promised the women that they were exactly the same as used by the finest chefs in France. He cracked on about the quality and swore that it was impossible to burn anything in them because they were made of such heavy aluminium. Then I heard him say to his assistant out of the corner of his mouth, 'For God's sake, Shirley, put the screen round the stall before the wind blows the lot away.'

There was a similar character in the market at Bruges. He was selling his goods as fast as his assistants could unpack them and he had his customers laughing their heads off as they reached for their money.

The weather at last started to get warm and sunny and we spent the afternoons rowing in the flat wooden boats along the waterways. It was an idyllic time floating lazily along on the canals as they meandered round the town between charming old houses and under pretty humpbacked bridges.

A British soldier was leaning over one of these bridges as Farah was energetically rowing underneath. She was in her usual 'civvies' and he must have thought she was Belgian because he shouted to his friends, 'Cor! Look at them fuckin' tits, as big as fuckin' footballs!' Farah screamed with laughter and the soldier nearly fell off the bridge when she told him in basic English what he could do with his rifle – and that went for his tin hat as well!

As soon as the temperature went up, the canals, which looked so picturesque, began to smell and they were the perfect breeding ground for mosquitoes. Although the hotel had made some attempt to deter them by fitting wire mesh over the windows, they made our lives a misery. No sooner had we gone to bed and put out the light than the high-pitched buzzing and lethal bombardment would commence.

It was sheer Hell, but it just bears out my theory that everything in life, no matter how perfect it looks at first glance, has a hidden snag, and once you accept this it makes living a whole lot easier. I'm convinced that very rich or powerful people haven't grasped this and believe that money or position can guarantee them perfection, but there's no such animal!

From Bruges, nursing our mosquito bites, we travelled on to Antwerp. We were billeted in an old-fashioned hotel where everything was built on a large scale. All the rooms were spacious and lofty and the furniture in the bedroom looked as if it had been built for a race of giants. The beds were so high that we had to take a flying leap to get into them each night, and the first time that Maggie got into the antique cast-iron bath she disappeared from sight. But there was a lovely restaurant and we were all agreed that was the one thing that counted.

Antwerp is a cosmopolitan port and although there was a lot of bomb damage, the shops were attractive and there was an interesting atmosphere.

One day we were all walking along looking at the sights when Freddie bumped into an old friend who was a sergeant in the Intelligence Corps. I'm not sure where they'd met originally but Harry was pleased to meet up with Freddie and invited us all to dinner with his company in their billet after the show at night.

216

He told us that Bill, his commanding officer, had requisitioned a gorgeous old Flemish house and they could offer us a gourmet dinner, because as luck would have it one of the boys was a magnificent chef.

He didn't have to twist our arms any further and I practically had my knife and fork at the ready when he arrived in a jeep to fetch us that night, then we all piled in trustingly, unaware of what was in store.

He had seemed a normal enough chap when we met him, one that you'd be pleased enough to take home to meet your mum but no sooner had he got behind the wheel than he was transformed into a speed-crazed demon. The door was hardly closed when he was off at full pelt like a man possessed. We hurtled and careered through the traffic, squealing and cutting corners and leaving every other vehicle on the road standing, then without any warning or slowing down, he wrenched the steering wheel violently to the right and the wagon shot through a narrow archway into a cobblestoned courtyard.

For one terrifying moment I imagined that he was about to drive up the steps and straight into the house but he slammed on the brakes so hard at the last minute that it was all we could do to stop ourselves being catapulted through the canvas-topped roof.

But credit where credit was due, those boys from the Intelligence Corps certainly knew how to look after themselves. The house that Bill had requisitioned was stuffed with antique furniture and beautiful pictures, the floors were covered in faded but exquisite Brussels carpets and we ate the eagerly anticipated dinner at an elegant table where the silver and glass glittered and sparkled in the soft light of a crystal chandelier. It added an extra dimension to the occasion when Bill told us that the house had previously been occupied by the head of the local Gestapo.

It was easy to see that the undercover work of this small group of men extended beyond a wider field than matters of Army Intelligence, because they'd done a very professional job in tracking down a source of excellent food supplies. The dinner was superb as promised and the vintage wine was purloined from the Gestapo leader's ill-gotten gains in the cellar.

There were only about six or seven men in this special outfit that Bill commanded. He was a most unassuming man and looked more like a civil servant than someone whose job it was to live dangerously. Harry was the sergeant and there was a corporal and some private soldiers, but unlike any other army unit we'd come across before, there was no rank-pulling or 'bull'. This lot worked, ate and lived together as a team.

Bill told us that Harry always drove like a 'tiger with its tail on fire', and he was still smarting over the fact that but for the grace of God the two of them could have been in a prisoner of war camp. It appeared that quite recently while on a reconnaissance assignment, Harry had driven him in his usual fairground dodgems style into an unknown village. They'd got as far as the central square when Bill realised that all the soldiers in and around the village were wearing German uniforms. The unpleasant truth hit them both simultaneously as they caught on to the fact that Harry's enthusiasm behind the wheel had landed them in enemy territory. He swore that Harry stopped the truck, reversed, turned and drove away all in one continuous movement. 'Now that was one time when he really *did* put his foot down,' Bill said sardonically.

We had one marvellous evening with them and finally got back to the hotel at about four in the morning, with the unpleasant prospect of having to pack and be ready to leave for Ghent the next day at eight o'clock. By then remorse had set in and I bitterly regretted staying so late at Bill and Harry's party, and to make matters worse when we arrived at the hotel, it was to find that the antiquated lift was out of order. The six of us laboriously climbed the stairs, and as we plodded up we met a little man scuttling down in his pyjamas with his pillow tucked underneath his arm. His eyes nearly popped out of his head. You could see the last thing he expected to be confronted with at that time in the morning was six tired, happy and slightly inebriated revellers.

He was even more embarrassed when Farah stopped and asked in her 'grande dame' voice, 'What sort of man is it, who can only think about his own comfort at a time of illicit passion?'

218

'Well, if you don't know,' Freddie answered, 'I can't think of anyone else who would.'

At eight o'clock in the morning we tottered from the hotel, frail and delicate. We all had strained expressions with the effort of trying to keep our heads from falling off our shoulders and we walked slowly and steadily into the truck. Freddie said that our hangovers were the Gestapo chief's revenge for pillaging his wine cellar.

As we drove along he told us that we wouldn't be staying in the town of Ghent, but at a private house in a village on the outskirts of the town. When we were still some way off, the driver pointed out the house to us. It looked stark and bleak and it stood on the horizon like a dark, ominous silhouette, the sort of building they use for a horror movie.

The house was a little way from the village but it was never out of sight, it crouched over the small huddle of shops and dwellings with an air of malevolence and the nearer we got the more sinister it became. As the truck approached the house, the villagers averted their eyes, and when we came to the entrance, a shiver went down my back when I saw that someone – or several people – had taken a brush and defaced the gates, the front door and the walls with graffiti. We couldn't understand it because it was in Flemish but we knew it wasn't complimentary because huge black swastikas had been painted on every available space.

We thought at first that it must have been local defiance against the occupying Germans. We often stayed in houses they'd recently vacated because they were at hand to take over with the minimum of fuss, but we'd never come across anything like this before.

It was no better inside the house. There was a chilling atmosphere even though the day was warm. It had a stifling effect so that we gradually lowered our voices until we were whispering, and even Farah was unusually subdued.

It was the NAAFI staff who told us the history of the house. The owner had been a successful businessman. He'd collaborated with the enemy during the occupation and as a result he'd gained certain advantages over the neighbouring villagers in the way of food and personal liberties. But worse still was the fact that he'd informed on the local Maquis, the patriotic underground movement. You can imagine that this didn't go down too well with the locals, especially when many of them disappeared overnight, never to be heard of again.

The people bided their time and when the area was liberated by the Allies, the entire family from the big house had gone missing and weren't seen again until a young boy fishing in the river had caught sight of them floating serenely downstream. When they were hauled out, every last one of them had been stabbed and their bodies mutilated.

Although suspicion fell on the villagers, the times being what they were, nothing further was done by the authorities, who had more important things on their mind than to worry about the fate of collaborators.

Sometimes I went shopping in the local store and the villagers looked friendly enough as they went about their daily tasks, but I always had an uneasy feeling with them. Looking from one smiling face to another, a hair-prickling sensation crept up the back of my head and made me wonder, Was it you? Or maybe it was you?...

Girls who'd consorted with the German soldiers couldn't expect much mercy either, although the punishment meted out to them was more humiliating than fatal. They were dragged from their homes to the village square and, surrounded by a jeering mob, stripped of all their clothes. Their heads were completely shaved, and none too gently either.

I saw some newsreel films of some such events at the cinema and although I didn't know the circumstances, the girl herself bore all the public disgrace with a quiet dignity while the crowd had all the attraction of a lynch mob.

I hated that house and the village. Every day Maggie and I hitch-hiked a lift to Brussels and spent the day there, only returning in time for the 'pick-up' each evening. We travelled everywhere in the back of a canvas-topped army truck. Regularly each evening it bowled up to take us to the camp and the driver picked up the cases and skips and, of course, our tap mat and packed them all in the back. When they were all safely stowed away, we got in. Sometimes we sat on wooden benches which jumped and rattled about like something in a fairground but most of the time we sat on the skips.

To travel in this manner over the cobblestoned roads of Northern Europe is an experience one doesn't forget in a hurry. The canvas flapped about, letting in the wind and rain, and we often arrived at our destination blue with the cold. Sometimes when I climbed out of the truck with trembling legs and a sore bottom, it felt as if every tooth in my head had been loosened.

Generally a soldier would be sent to ask us if we'd like some tea to restore our shattered nerves and it always arrived, like everything else from an army kitchen, in a bucket. I *can* think of a few things which are more reviving than a large sweet bucket of stewed army tea, but that's what we got. Then two other buckets would be handed to us, one was full of hot water so that we could wash and the other was for a more basic function.

The dressing room was usually one small space divided by an army blanket slung over a line and it was a case of girls on one side and boys on the other. We soon lost all sense of false modesty.

There was one unforgettable night when Farah was using the 'third bucket' while Freddie and Ronnie were dressing on the other side of the blanket and no one could have been under any delusion as to what was happening. We were all quite hysterical at the noise of her peeing into this metal bucket and Ronnie made us collapse when he shouted over the blanket, 'By 'eck! Take it easy, luv. What the devil are you trying to do, get a head on it?'

221

21

We returned to France and learned that our next base was to be Calais.

Things had been improving all the time and not only had the Germans been routed from the town but it had been completely transformed. The harbour was in working order and a large transit camp had been built by the docks to house the troops waiting to go on leave.

ENSA was also getting more organised. They'd taken over a small terrace house in a back street for a hostel and it was staffed by NAAFI ladies instead of the men who'd looked after us up till now.

The house wasn't too strong on all 'mod cons', in fact it was very like the pro digs we'd been used to when touring in Britain, but the three ladies were motherly types and we had confidence that, like the best digs, it was going to be a home-from-home experience.

When the area manager told us that we'd be there for several weeks to entertain locally in the transit camp, we all congratulated ourselves on our luck, confidently expecting that it was going to be a picnic. *Quelle* rapture! I thought, to have no long journeys bouncing and joggling about in the back of that blasted army truck, and settled down to what I optimistically hoped would be a comparatively easy part of the tour. We worked like dogs!

The war was grinding to a halt and the heavy fighting was more or less over, and there were thousands of men streaming into the transit camp to go home. All these men were housed in one vast area down by the docks and hanging around hopefully, never knowing from one day to the next when they would be the lucky ones to get on a ship.

They were all weighed down with souvenirs for their families back home and one enterprising young man wheeled his presents on board in a baby's pram. The army customs men were very lenient; the unwritten law was 'If you can carry it on board single-handed, it's yours!' Meanwhile, they had to put in a lot of tedious waiting and so ENSA pulled out all the stops to provide them with round-the-clock programmes of cinema shows and live entertainment.

Our little group was based not a stone's throw from the docks and we were on the spot ready to be called at a moment's notice whenever we were needed. For weeks we worked harder than we'd ever done before, never knowing what it was to have a day or night free. One show followed another morning, afternoon and evening, and we only saw the ENSA hostel in the little back street when we staggered home exhausted to tumble wearily into bed.

I began to feel punch-drunk and would have been hard put to name the day of the week, but then one bright and beautiful day the impossible happened and the transit camp was temporarily cleared of troops. Our area manager looked upon us with compassion and gave us a couple of days off to recover our strength before the next batch of men arrived and we'd be back on the conveyor belt again.

It was then that Freddie came up with a minor miracle. While in the naval wardroom in the docks, he'd met the skipper of a minesweeper whose job it was to make regular daily searches in the Channel. Over the camaraderie of a few drinks, Freddie did a deal with this chap, who promised as a special favour to take any of us to Dover with him so that we could enjoy a day with the family. Then he'd pick us up the following day when he was due to return to Calais. Of course it was strictly a hush-hush deal and would never have been allowed normally; this was just one instance of Freddie's ability at 'wheeler-dealing'. He was a shrewd and practised operator in the survival stakes.

This caused a tremendous excitement as all the others prepared to spring such an unexpected surprise on their families. I

223

say 'the others' because I was the only one not going on this magical mystery tour. My family were all on tour themselves (what's new?) and even my grandmother had been evacuated from her East Ham home when the constant bombing of the docks had got too much for her.

I didn't mind, because while the rest of them were away, I was glad to relax in Calais. It was the first opportunity to take a look at the town since we'd arrived. One day had rolled into another as we got up in the morning, drove to the transit camp to perform non-stop during the day and then returned at night, sometimes too tired to even make the effort to speak to one another.

But now the sun was shining and here I was with the pleasing prospect of a day of leisure. I strolled through the town and went into a café to have a mid-morning cup of coffee, marvelling at the way life had returned to normal. But everything was not as good as it looked, the coffee was the 'ersatz' variety – I think they made it with acorns – and on tasting it, as far as I was concerned the squirrels could have it back.

When Maggie came back the next day she told me she regretted the impulsive trip home as soon as she stepped on the boat. Like me on the journey out, her sole concern had been fear of an attack from the air; neither one of us had given a thought to the danger of mines laid in the sea. So when she saw all the paraphernalia on the minesweeper and realised that the chief object of crossing the Channel was to search it for mines, she protested that no one had warned her about this hazardous sideline. The skipper assured her there was no need to worry, it was all in a day's work for him and he'd do all the worrying that was necessary. He did his best to alleviate her fears by keeping her well topped up with pink gins during the trip. But although he tried every way he knew to distract her, Maggie swore to me that she was so busy peering at the sea that by the time they reached Dover her eyeballs were aching with the strain.

It's always the same when you try to put something from your mind. Do you remember the story of the man who was told whatever he did, he wasn't to think about bears? From that second on, although he'd never given them a single thought before, he couldn't for the life of him think about anything else. Whenever I go on a diet, I know I mustn't think about food and I immediately become obsessed with it. I daydream of crisp golden roast potatoes, I'm tortured with visions of fruit pies with lashings of Devonshire cream and yearn with all my soul for French bread thickly spread with butter and any other yummy goodies which are all so damned fattening.

It was exactly the same during the stringent food rationing in the war. Maggie and I whiled away hours talking about food and we planned and replanned menus we'd indulge in, if ever food was plentiful again. It was a bitter-sweet form of masochism because Maggie fancied lobster and I thought I'd have sole meunière, and then we'd groan because it all seemed such a fanciful pipe dream and we never thought we'd get the chance to sink our teeth into any decent food again.

It wasn't surprising, the week's food ration was so small that it could all be eaten as the ingredients for one meal today and you still wouldn't be overeating. The butter ration was a pitiful two ounces, so we had the tantalising option of either scraping it on thinly to last the week or blueing it all in one glorious splurge. Sometimes I tried to imagine the sensual pleasure of being able to spread it so thickly on my bread that when I bit into it, I'd leave a perfect cast of my teeth.

Now that we can have as much butter as we want, the experts tell us it's no good for us. Well, I've got news for these miserable Jeremiahs, it's good for me, I love it! I've never forgotten those lean years and there's nobody, but nobody, who's going to swing margarine on me however well they advertise it.

The Ministry of Food was always bombarding us with helpful hints and wartime recipes and constantly assuring us that we were getting an adequate diet. Because potatoes were home-grown and there was a plentiful supply they were unrationed, consequently we were always being urged to eat them, and the way the ministry went on about the food values of potatoes you would have thought we'd all been fools to eat anything else.

One of my most gruesome memories was of eating Woolton

225

pie. Lord Woolton was the Minister of Food, and in the belief that he was being helpful, he kept promoting recipes that could be made from unrationed foods. Woolton pie was one of his more diabolical inspirations. The sole ingredients for this dish were onions, carrots, parsnips and any other root vegetable you could get hold of. I only had the misfortune to eat this horrendous concoction once, with the result that I became doubled up with wind and couldn't sleep a wink all night. The poor long-suffering British public did get some sort of revenge, because I've never met one person of my generation who can remember Lord Woolton for anything else but his bloody pie. What a way to go down in history!

Another atrocity was 'the yellow peril', the dried egg powder that was supposed to make up for the lack of eggs. It was a bright sinister yellow and when made into an omelette wouldn't have fooled anyone, let alone a chicken.

We were also absolutely inundated with advice from the Ministry of Information, so much so that it was called the Ministry of Aggravation. It was forever inserting notices in the paper which we were recommended to keep as helpful reminders and we all got heartily sick of it. I shall never forget one bulletin which was headed 'Cut this out and stick it up'. If I'd known the minister in question, I'd have been only too happy to oblige.

When the Americans came into the war and their troops were sent over to Britain, we started entertaining at their camps. The main attraction as far as Maggie and I were concerned was that we stood a very good chance of being invited to eat in the canteen. When we were first asked, we could hardly believe our luck as we were handed trays with large helpings of chicken and salad, fruit and ice cream. The standard was so much higher than the British NAAFI and it amazed us that they ate like this every day.

The Americans caused a sensation amongst the girls, especially in the smaller towns and villages. Even the private soldiers had smart well-cut uniforms which made them look like officers and they were much better paid. Apart from these advantages, they came over in the wake of the glamorous

Hollywood films that everyone in this country had cut their eye teeth on. There was a widespread belief among the girls that every single person living in the USA lived in a luxury penthouse or a cattle ranch 'just like the movies'. All this didn't make them too popular with the British Tommies whose much publicised complaint was 'They're overpaid, oversexed and over here.'

The first time we played to an American camp came as a considerable eye-opener to Maggie and me. We ran on stage in the white tuxedos and our long bare legs and the audience went wild. We didn't know what had hit us. We were used to wolf whistles and the odd whoop from our own boys but we were totally unprepared for the reaction we got from the GIs. At the first sight of us, caps were thrown in the air, and we couldn't start singing for the loud 'yahoos' and cries of 'Home was never like this' and shouts of 'Guess what I want for Christmas?' It was sheer pandemonium. For one awful moment I really thought I'd forgotten to put my panties on under my tuxedo.

I wondered if they were naturally over-boisterous as a result of all that good food and a surfeit of vitamins or if we'd struck a camp full of hill-billies; after all, they didn't all come from film star apartments, as many a GI bride found out the hard way. But the noise and excitement was the same at every American camp we played and we got so used to it that when we went back to playing the British we missed the uninhibited exuberance of the GI Joes.

So when we returned to Belgium and Freddie told us that we were due to work in the American sector, we knew exactly what to expect in the way of audiences and food.

We drove to a hotel in Ostend and there was another larger unit staying there too who were also playing the same circuit. As soon as I walked through the door I spotted a tall girl with a crop of short curly hair dyed an unnatural and startling red. There was only one head like that and I recognised it immediately. 'Vera!' I shouted and she turned round to greet me.

Maggie and I had originally met Vera in England when she joined our previous ENSA show, but she'd only stayed a few months because Arthur had played her up from the beginning and she wouldn't stand for any of his nonsense and made a quick getaway.

Being called up had disrupted my life but it was much harder for Vera because she'd had her own solo act in variety and conscription had effectively cut short a promising career. Although she was only a couple of years older than Maggie and me, the years of travelling on her own and having to fight battles with managements and agents had toughened her up.

Vera was a really tall girl. She told us that as a child she thought she was never going to stop growing and eventually her height made her feel awkward, inhibited and lanky. One day she made up her mind that she wasn't going to creep around with bent knees apologising for her height for the rest of her life, and if she was going to stand out she'd make a proper job of it, be bold and dye her hair bright red. There was no missing her in a crowd, Vera was about a head taller than the other girls and with her crazy mop of red hair she stood out like a beacon.

She loved playing to the Americans and there was something about her tough, vivacious personality that they responded to and they adored her. She was never short of dates when we were in their sector, but the strange thing was that as tall and striking as she was, it was always the smallest insignificant boys who went overboard for her. Every night in the mess, you'd see Vera's red head towering over an excited group of undersized men. They'd all be running around her, fetching and carrying and gazing up at her with adoring faces.

'I tell you, girls,' she said once, 'it makes me feel like Snow White and the seven dwarves.'

One night we were at an American camp and as usual it was the shortest officer in the mess who made a beeline for her as soon as he set eyes on her. 'From now on you're my little red tomayto,' he said, beaming up at her.

Tomato she may have been, but little she was not! Just the same, this lieutenant thought that she was the answer to all his dreams and if she was out of his sight for a second, he ran around the mess shouting, 'Where's my bubble-headed tomayto gone?'

Vera tried her best to give him the slip but it wasn't easy for a girl like her to melt into the background. At the end of the evening she deliberately left early to try and get away from him. But this little pipsqueak wasn't to be put off so easily and he rushed after her and backed her up against the side of the coach.

'I don't know where he got his strength from,' Vera told us afterwards. Apparently he flung himself on her and began tearing away at her clothes. She screamed at him to control himself but he'd gone too far for that and she really started to panic. She was praying that the rest of us would start coming out and at last to her relief she heard voices.

'Stop it, for goodness sake stop it!' she cried. 'There's somebody coming!'

'Oh my God,' he moaned. 'I only wish it were me!'

Vera was having exactly the same effect on the Americans stationed near Ostend, and one day when a midget-sized officer arrived at the door of the hotel, I knew before he opened his mouth that he was one of Vera's beaus. He hadn't come empty-handed, he'd been on leave in Brussels and had bought her an enormous bottle of perfume. Now apart from looking colourful, Vera had a refreshingly unsophisticated approach to life; she was a marvellous extrovert at a party and when she enjoyed herself she really let herself go. So when she was given this outsized bottle of very expensive scent, she flipped.

'How absolutely gorgeous!' she raved, and while the boy looked on in amazement she took out the heavy glass stopper and poured the lot over her head in an ecstasy of delight. That scent permeated every room in the hotel for a week until even the food tasted of it, and as for Vera, when she drifted by in a cloud of Chanel, passers-by reeled back and fell away respectfully all around her.

Maggie and I met some smashing boys at one camp. We had a great time and when we left they wanted to know where we were working the following night so they could come along. We couldn't tell them because we genuinely had no idea; we never knew where we were going, we just got in the truck each evening and went wherever it took us. But the next night as we danced on-stage, to our surprise the same group of boys were sitting in front. They'd somehow found out our itinerary and smuggled themselves into the audience. From then on it became a challenge for them to find out every camp we were going to and to be grinning up in triumph as we made our entrance. On the very last night in that sector, they'd managed to commandeer the entire front row in the hall and when Maggie and I danced on, they all bent down as one man and reappeared wearing enormous black moustaches. It took all our training to get us through that night without corpsing.

On our last Sunday in Ostend, Maggie and I went into a café and saw Vera surrounded by Americans. They were all playing a game called Colonel Puff. It was one of those army drinking games where you have to recite a verse and perform a ritual of movements while you drink a glass of beer. If you made one mistake you had to start with another glass of beer, so if you wanted to stay sober it was vital to get it right by the first two or three drinks, otherwise you didn't stand a chance.

All we girls were past masters at games like this – we needed to be. In any case, we were so used to picking up dance routines that it came as second nature, as many an officer who tried it on found out to his cost. I don't know who'd started the game that night, but if it was the Americans they'd backed a loser in Vera because she was still as bright as a button while they all looked considerably the worse for wear.

A band in the café struck up the conga. Vera was enjoying herself by now and didn't need any encouragement to jump to her feet to lead the dance. She pulled us all up to join her, and although by this time the American boys were in no fit state to do anything, you could see they were determined to follow her to the ends of the earth if needs be, and they did the best they could under the circumstances by staggering up and hanging on to the more able.

Vera wasn't satisfied until everyone in the café had left the tables and joined her in the conga line, which trailed around the room getting longer all the time. Then, carried away by enthusiasm, she sailed out of the café on to the pavement outside and everyone followed, including the band, who picked up their instruments and merged into the procession. Up and down the street we danced, accumulating people as we went. Half the bystanders had no idea what it was all about but they got drawn in just the same.

We went further and further afield and when the procession reached our hotel, Maggie and I dropped out. The last view we had of them was seeing them jigging along until they disappeared into the distance, just like the end of a Charlie Chaplin movie, and still in the front was the flaming red head of Vera leading her faithful followers to the Lord knows where.

It was four years before I saw her again and even then I forgot to ask if anyone ever went back to that café to pay the bill.

22

It was April and we were on our way to Nijmegen. When the truck crossed the border of Holland, it was clear that things were on the up and up. As if to make amends for the appalling winter, spring had come early; it was unusually warm and the country-side was starting to blossom. A lacy green foliage was begin-ning to appear on the trees and rapidly camouflaging the broken branches and distorted stumps which we'd seen previously. Farmers were working in the fields, ploughing and planting, and it was heartening to see how people can survive and begin to pick up the threads again after six terrible years.

When we arrived in Nijmegen, the shops were open and the townsfolk were bustling about. It was a far cry from the first view we'd had of the stripped and bereft towns in Holland.

Nijmegen was only a few miles from Arnhem, where one of the biggest Allied disasters of the war had occurred. Thousands of our parachutists had been dropped behind the enemy lines in a bold bid to secure the bridge and hold it until reinforce-ments arrived, but it all went tragically wrong. Arnhem takes its place in history as one of the worst blunders of the Second Front invasion, and if you pass the cemetery, you will see at what cost.

Not only did the Germans destroy the bridge at Arnhem, but they blew up every other one across the River Maas in an effort to halt the Allied advance. The only one saved was at Grave, where our troops made a last-minute rescue, and that was one busy bridge at the time. A steady stream of army vehicles, including our little truck, was continually creeping back and forth in a slow-moving traffic jam.

Freddie told us that the plans were for us to play what amounted to a resident season at the winter gardens in Nijmegen.

It was a really cushy time and we all felt thoroughly spoilt, having a proper dressing room and a washbasin with running water, to say nothing of a lavatory down the corridor. It was a luxury to be able to lay out our make-up on the table and hang up our costumes for a few weeks, knowing that we wouldn't have to pack, unpack and iron them every day.

The theatre at Nijmegen was rather like a seaside pavilion and reminded me of the concert party days I'd known as a little girl. I half-expected a shrill soprano voice to boom out, 'Chee-ild! Come here, chee-ild! Help me with my hair, and here's a nice glass of port to put the roses in your cheeks.'

We lived on the outskirts of the town in an imposing residence standing well back from the road. It was another of the houses that had been so hurriedly vacated by high-ranking German officers; they always requisitioned the best properties for themselves, and we thought that what was good enough for them was even better for us. The weather was sunny and warm and during the day we lazed in the lovely garden with its well-kept lawns and ornamental ponds. I would have been more than happy to call it quits and stay there for the rest of the war.

Although we all knew the war would be over in a matter of weeks, we still had to carry on, and before long we were sent to Breda. It was a bit of a come-down after Nijmegen.

We got a slight needle to the people of Breda because, far from falling on our necks as we'd come to expect as part of the great liberation force, the town council had issued a set of rules that the military had to abide by. There was to be no chatting up the local girls, no drinking on the streets and lots of other petty rules and regulations. I think it was something to do with the Dutch Reform Church, which came on a bit strong there. This attitude caused no little resentment and we couldn't help wondering if the town's people had been as assiduous in demanding that the invading Germans toe the line in the same puritanical manner when they marched into town.

One Sunday Farah and I were strolling along the bank of the

canal. Farah was in her usual civvies and I was wearing my uniform, but because it was such a hot day I'd taken off my jacket and tie and opened my shirt at the neck and Farah had unbuttoned her blouse a decorous two buttons' worth. As we passed a group of local women we were aware that they were muttering under their breath and casting malevolent glances in our direction. Suddenly one of these ladies was pushed forward to act as spokeswoman and rather hesitantly and in halting English she piped up that they thought we were dressed in a slovenly manner considering it was the Sabbath.

I could actually feel Farah steaming up but she turned to face the woman with a disarmingly composed expression and said, 'Now you have gone just a teeny weeny bit too far...' It was at this moment that I took the coward's way out and wandered off but I couldn't resist looking back. Farah had braced herself and was standing defiantly with feet apart and chin held high like Queen Boadicea confronting the full might of the Roman legions. She didn't raise her voice but it was easy to see she was letting them have it with both barrels. I knew the local women wouldn't be able to understand every word (after all, she'd taught me a few I hadn't heard before) but it was obvious they'd got the gist of what she was saying and were beginning to back away before the onslaught.

When Farah saw she'd got them on the retreat she let rip with a voice that would awaken the dead, 'You will *not* tell me what I may or may not wear,' she thundered. 'If I want to, I'll undo every single button I have,' and with that she wrenched open her blouse, baring her splendid bosom to the cowering women.

'Take a good look,' she yelled. 'They're British, they're mine, and by God I'm proud of them.'

We were still in Breda when the great day dawned at last and we knew that we'd lived to see the victory.

The whole town forgot its stolid image, slung away the rule book and prepared to celebrate. Church bells rang out from early in the morning, the bands played and children sang and danced in the streets. It was all exhilarating and lovely, but I don't think there was one of us who didn't feel homesick and wish to be back in London.

As if by magic, hundreds of flags appeared, fluttering from every window, and the entire town bubbled in an excited frenzy of rejoicing.

The six of us were invited to celebrate with a champagne party at the British Officers' Club in the square, and when at last we called it a day and tottered out into the sunshine I felt on top of the world.

All at once Maggie clutched my arm. 'Mary!' she said dramatically. 'Mary, can you see anything?'

I was having the greatest difficulty in seeing at all. 'Give me a clue,' I asked her.

She waved her arms expansively. 'There's thousands and thousands of Dutch flags...'

I peered around until I succeeded in focusing my eyes. 'True!' I agreed.

'... but not one single, solitary Union Jack,' she finished triumphantly.

Taking a long, careful look, I had to admit she was right, there wasn't one British flag to be seen.

'You know what this is,' said Maggie slowly and carefully 'This is one hell of a diabolical liberty.'

So, full of bravado and champagne, we set out to remedy this slur to our national pride. First we tried the staff at the hotel to see if they had a Union Jack but we drew a blank there, they were much too busy with their own high jinks to be bothered about us and Maggie said that if we couldn't fly the flag we must improvise and hang something else out of the window.

Overcome with patriotic fervour, we frantically ransacked the hotel until we came up with two brooms which we decided to use as flag staffs, but we were stuck for anything that resembled a pennant. Then Maggie had an inspiration. 'Our pyjama trousers!' In those days Maggie and I had a penchant for wearing men's old-fashioned striped pyjamas. We thought they were chic and different and, being on the large size, they made us look vulnerable and fragile. Fragile we were not!

They were the ideal thing. We pounced on them and threaded one broomstick through a single leg of each pair, suspended them from the bedroom window and stood back to admire the effect. As banners go, they were certainly unusual, and we both thought they had a certain *je ne sais quoi*, an original charm all their own.

Below us, the town square was packed with the entire population of Breda as they marched purposefully round and round waving their flags and singing patriotic songs. It took a little while before anyone noticed the opposition. Then one woman spotted the strange new decorations. The pyjama trousers had caught the wind and were billowing out beautifully, the legs inflated like windsocks on an airfield. The woman pointed out the extraordinary sight to her compatriots, who came to a halt and stood transfixed, all looking upwards in dumb amazement.

Then others following on behind came to a standstill and more and more, until a solid mass of men and women stood open-mouthed with faces upturned, hypnotised by the sight of two pairs of striped pyjama trousers flying valiantly from our bedroom window. There was not a flicker of a smile on one single face.

So far so good. Now Maggie and I judged the time was ripe to go down among the good citizens of Breda to promote the cause of Anglo-Dutch relations. We explained that this was an old English custom and, furthermore, we were about to teach them an old English folk song.

Nobody said a word. They stood around us submissively and watched in complete silence as Maggie and I picked up our skirts, turned to face each other and then launched into 'Knees Up Mother Brown' at the top of our voices.

They loved it! We couldn't believe it but they loved it. One or two of the women nearest to us modestly lifted up their long skirts and tentatively began to give a decorous kick or two, then they looked at us enquiringly and said painstakingly, 'Knees op Mudder Braun?'

'*Ja!*' we said. 'Knees op Mudder Braun!'

They were plainly quite delighted with themselves when

they'd mastered the simple steps, then they turned to those behind them and showed them how to do it and they too began to dance. Gradually others joined in and then the ones behind them. More and more men and women took the plunge, and all the time Maggie and I kept the pot boiling by kicking our legs even higher, flashing our suspenders and stocking tops. It was more like a can-can than a knees-up.

It was smashing! Everybody was at it. The whole square was a bouncing hurley-burley of people dancing, bobbing up and down, skipping, jigging and kicking their heels in the air to a good old Cockney song.

Honour was satisfied.

When the time came to leave, I was astounded at the mountain of luggage I'd accumulated. On the journey out from Tilbury, I couldn't get over the fact that my suitcase was only half full; it was the one and only occasion that I remember achieving this minor miracle, and the reason was that wearing the uniform had cut down all my usual clutter of bits and bobs. But we'd been away nearly a year and it had been my first trip abroad so I'd bought presents for all my friends and relations in a positive orgy of generosity. Of course Brussels had been my undoing, there were so many temptations and I'd succumbed to every one – at least all those I could afford.

I suppose the years of searching out the little extras at home during the shortages had given me a good basic training for finding a bargain. When on tour in a strange town, I'd developed quite a skill in traipsing round the local shops and running my eyes expertly over the shelves to see if they'd taken a new delivery of stock recently. It was a gala day if I came back to the digs with a tin of salmon or sardines – tinned goods were all rationed on a points system but there was such a scarcity that you had to have a nose like a bloodhound to scent them out.

This animal cunning had stood me in good stead because I even managed to buy something in war-torn Eindhoven, in spite of the fact that it had been thoroughly cleaned out by the occupying forces. The Philips factory had some sunlamps left on their hands which were pretty useless to them as there was little or no electricity in the town and they were happy to sell one to me for £2. I can't grumble about the price because it's done me well and is still in good working order today.

But my chief weakness had been the markets. I found them impossible to resist, especially those in Belgium. The combination of them having goods and me having money was just too much. From the trader's point of view I must have come like manna from Heaven.

Travelling by road as we did, there'd been none of the usual hassle of lugging our cases to the railway station, it was all too easy to squeeze one more piece of luggage on the truck. Little by little my belongings had grown out of all proportion without my realising it. I tell you if there's one gift or knack that I possess, it's the ability to fill up any given space without effort. I've a natural talent for the task and I defy anyone to beat me at it.

It's exactly the same today at home. Cupboards mysteriously fill to bursting point and chests of drawers overflow, forcing me to buy extra furniture which I'm always convinced will relieve the congestion, but before I can start to get used to having the new space, that too is bursting at the seams, just like the rest of the house. I put it down to supernatural forces because I never seem to buy anything much and my husband co-operates by trying to arrange that we go out on early closing days. When my son got married and left home I had the supreme luxury of an empty room. I kept opening the door to gloat over this amazing phenomenon and Bernard and I had long discussions as to how we should furnish it. He was of the firm opinion that if we ignored it, the room would fill itself up in no time at all. He said he couldn't see why not, as every other room in the house had managed to do so without any trouble.

When the day came when we all walked up the gangway to board the ship for home, I was very conscious that my suitcase was emitting a loud *glop-glop* sound as the liquor I'd stashed away slopped around in the bottles. I'd been saving up my booze ration until I'd collected a supply of some magnitude so that I could splash out on a party when I got home, and although

I'd carefully wrapped each bottle amongst my clothes, at every step I took, a tremendous slurping noise could be heard quite distinctly.

The customs man raised a quizzical eyebrow.

'Would you believe a bowl of goldfish?' I asked, at which both eyebrows shot up but he passed me through.

Maggie and I had formed no definite plans about how we were going to spend our lives in peacetime. Every now and again we'd spoken vaguely about producing a dancing act to try and get on the variety circuit but we hadn't done anything constructive about it. The one thought uppermost in my mind was to turn in the khaki uniform, have a little holiday and then, like Mr Micawber, wait for something to turn up.

I think the whole British Army, at least those coming back with us on the ship, had the same idea. There was a distinct feeling of achievement for soldier and civilian alike in having the good fortune to come through the war.

This time there were no fears about the Channel crossing. It was an emotional experience for all of us and I felt a catch in the throat when the white cliffs of Dover gradually materialised out of the mist, slowly grew bigger and finally rushed forward to meet us. It was all over, we were home at last.

In the rush of sorting out the baggage and greeting friends at the station, the farewells which I'd been dreading were over before I knew it. Just the same, it was a tearful moment saying goodbye to Joyce, then Farah and Freddie.

'We mustn't lose touch,' I said, knowing in my heart that it was more than likely we'd never set eyes on them again. It was harder still to see Ronnie walk away. Perhaps one day, I thought, I'll look down from the stage to see him playing in the orchestra pit.

But it could never be the same. The people with whom we'd shared our lives so intimately over the last months were scattering to go their individual ways. Even on the station platform you could see them adjusting to the new conditions, and as time passed, if we did meet up again, we'd find the closeness had disappeared and we were now mere acquaintances.

Surely it wouldn't be that way for Maggie and me? Before we

parted, she arranged to meet me in a few days to hand in the uniforms at Drury Lane, and then I returned to my 'Good Samaritan' friends Eva, Olive and the Duchess for a monumental 'Coming home and getting out of uniform' party.

There was so much to tell them and Eva indulged me in idleness by not letting me lift so much as a cup. The days drifted by until it was time for me to keep my appointment with Maggie at the Lane.

This will be the last time I walk along this way to the ENSA headquarters, I thought as I picked my way through the cabbage leaves and squashed fruit that littered the pavements in Covent Garden. I remembered how depressed I'd been the first time I'd made my unwilling way to the historic old theatre. I thought with gratitude of the porter who'd presented me with the orange and how he'd cheered me up, it seemed like a lifetime ago.

Some of the marketmen recognised me and one grinned. 'Nice to have you back' he shouted. 'I knew you'd win the war for us!'

'Nice to be back,' I answered, but it was more than nice, it was Heaven to be home. As shabby, grey and battle-weary as London was, it was where I belonged. I hadn't realised how much I'd missed my home town.

I filled my lungs with great breaths of smoky dirty air; nothing had ever smelled so good. I felt as if I couldn't gulp in enough of the lovely familiar smell. I smiled on the whole world as I struggled along with my khaki uniform in the suitcase, and when I turned the corner I could see Maggie waiting for me at the stage door.

She smiled at me self-consciously. We both felt as strange in our civvies as we had when we first wore the uniform.

'We'll turn them in,' Maggie said, 'and collect our back pay, then let's go along and see who's having a beer at the Café Anglais.'

She had *The Stage* tucked under her arm and she told me that there were several auditions for London musicals. 'Let's go together,' she suggested. 'We can dance "The Beguine" and if we land the job they won't split us up.'

My spirits rose. 'We could share a flat,' I volunteered. I could

240

see it all, the two of us working in a sensational new revue, sharing a smart modern flat where we could entertain our friends and throw gorgeous parties after the show.

'We'll be the toast of London,' Maggie said confidently as we went into the theatre.

'I'll learn to cook,' I promised as we casually sauntered across the stage and into Geraldo's office.

No sooner had the door opened than we were met with an absolute barrage of voices babbling incoherently in a frenzy of agitation. The secretary took one look at us and then leaped from her desk to rush into the inner sanctum shouting, 'They're here, they're here at last. Thank God, they're here!'

Maggie and I looked behind to see if two famous stars were following us in; after all, we weren't used to attracting this sort of attention.

But the familiar voice of Mrs Simons rang out loud and clear. 'Send them in this minute!'

We smiled brightly at her, slightly overwhelmed by the enthusiastic reception. But instead of 'Hello!' and 'How are you both?' All we got was, 'Well, I must say you two have taken your time in getting here. Where the devil have you been?'

'What's the panic?' Maggie asked in all innocence.

'Where's the fire?'

'Panic?' Mrs Simons screamed back at us. 'I'll tell you what the panic is. A dancing act has dropped out of a show at the last minute and we've all been sitting here for days waiting for you two to make up your tiny minds to stroll in. There's not a moment to lose,' she went on, hardly pausing to take a breath, 'it's all been arranged. You're to pop into the medical officer for another dose of injections, then go and collect a tropical uniform and be ready to start with the new company tomorrow, and I don't want you late for rehearsals.'

'But,' Maggie faltered, 'the war's over now. We only came in to sign off and walk out of your life for ever.'

'Nonsense,' Mrs Simons said curtly. 'The war may indeed be over but it's not over for either of you. If all goes according to plan, in three weeks' time you'll both be on the ship sailing for Egypt.'

'Egypt!' we chorused in unison, seeing all our dreams going down the pan. 'You can't send us to Egypt!'

However one look at Mrs Simons' determined expression convinced us that she could.

But that, as they say, is another story.